This Is Our Land

Nature, Society, and Culture

Scott Frickel, Series Editor

A sophisticated and wide-ranging sociological literature analyzing nature-society-culture interactions has blossomed in recent decades. This book series provides a platform for showcasing the best of that scholarship: carefully crafted empirical studies of socio-environmental change and the effects such change has on ecosystems, social institutions, historical processes, and cultural practices.

The series aims for topical and theoretical breadth. Anchored in sociological analyses of the environment, Nature, Society, and Culture is home to studies employing a range of disciplinary and interdisciplinary perspectives and investigating the pressing socio-environmental questions of our time—from environmental inequality and risk, to the science and politics of climate change and serial disaster, to the environmental causes and consequences of urbanization and war making, and beyond.

This Is Our Land

Grassroots Environmentalism in the Late Twentieth Century

CODY FERGUSON

RUTGERS UNIVERSITY PRESS

NEW BRUNSWICK, NEW JERSEY, AND LONDON

LIBRARY OF CONGRESS CATALOGING-IN-PUBLICATION DATA

Ferguson, Cody.
    This is our land : grassroots environmentalism in the late twentieth century / Cody Ferguson.
        pages cm —(Nature, society, and culture)
    Includes bibliographical references and index.
    ISBN 978–0-8135–6563–7 (hardcover : alk. paper)—ISBN 978–0-8135–6562–0 (pbk. : alk. paper)—ISBN 978–0-8135–6564–4 (e-book (web pdf))
        1. Environmentalism—United States—History—20th century. 2. Environmentalism—Montana—History—20th century. 3. Environmentalism—Arizona—History—20th century. 4. Environmentalism—Tennessee—History—20th century. I. Title.
    GE197.F47 2015
    363.70973'09049—dc23   2014040925

A British Cataloging-in-Publication record for this
book is available from the British Library.

Visit our website: http://rutgerspress.rutgers.edu

Manufactured in the United States of America

Dedicated to the thousands of activists around the globe working to make our communities and world more equitable and sustainable.

CONTENTS

ACKNOWLEDGMENTS

In many ways, this is a book I began to write before I had even graduated college. It started as a senior seminar paper and honors thesis under the direction of Robert Swartout at Carroll College in Montana in 2000. My name is the only one that appears on the cover, but dozens of people had a hand in its production. Here, I would like to acknowledge some of the people, organizations, and institutions that encouraged and sustained me over this project's long gestation.

This book would not have been possible without the help of the people involved with the Northern Plains Resource Council, Southwest Environmental Service, and Save Our Cumberland Mountains, who talked with me and generously allowed me to view the private collections of their organizations. Of special note are Teresa Erickson and Steve Paulson at the Northern Plains Resource Council and Pat Sweeney and John Smillie at the Western Organization of Resource Councils. In addition, thank you to veteran citizen activists in Montana: Wally McRae, Ellen Pfister, Nick Golder, Helen and Gordy Waller, Jeanie Alderson, Tom Breitbach, Charlie Yarger, Steve Charter, and his inspiring and powerful wife Jeanne, who was taken from us far too early. In Arizona, I wish to thank Barbara Tellman and the late Priscilla Robinson for sharing their memories of the Southwest Environmental Service and their extensive knowledge of southern Arizona politics and history. In Tennessee, thank you to SOCM stalwarts Maureen O'Connell, Charles "Boomer" Winfrey, Landon Medley, Franz Raetzer, Linda and Larry Smotherman, Mike and Wanda Hodge, and David Hardeman for taking the time to tell me your stories and to Amelia Parker, Ann League, and the whole staff of Statewide Organizing for Community eMpowerment (formerly Save Our Cumberland Mountains) for opening your office to me and showing me around the hills and hollows of eastern Tennessee.

In addition, I am indebted to the librarians and archival staffs at the Montana Historical Society in Helena, the University of Arizona Library Special Collections in Tucson, the Arizona State University Arizona Collection in Tempe, and the Tennessee State Library and Archives in Nashville. Your skilled assistance made my research incredibly productive and this project a success.

Various institutions supported this project including the University of Arizona Special Collections, the Morris K. Udall Scholarship and Excellence in National Environmental Policy Foundation, the Udall Center for Studies in Public Policy, and the Max Millett Family Scholarship. The Arizona State University (ASU) Graduate College and School of Historical, Philosophical, and Religious Studies provided crucial travel and dissertation completion funding. Finally, a two-year postdoctoral fellowship in environmental and public humanities at ASU's School of Historical, Philosophical, and Religious Studies provided me vital time to revise the dissertation, continue research, and finish the book.

The staff and editors at Rutgers University Press deserve special recognition. I am grateful to Peter Mickulas for his faith in the project and for all of his help in guiding it through every step in the process. Michael Egan provided thoughtful and thorough reviews of the manuscript. Michael's keen eye noticed nuances and potential in its arguments that, once brought to the surface, help make it a better book. Likewise, Scott Frickel contributed invaluable critiques and perspectives from sociology. I am honored that Scott chose to include *This Is Our Land* in the Nature, Society, and Culture series.

Throughout the project, many colleagues and friends have influenced my thinking and help to bring the book to fruition. First and foremost, I must recognize the dedication, guidance, and inspiration of my dissertation chair, mentor, and friend Paul Hirt. In Paul, I found an intellectual kindred spirit and scholar comrade. Paul challenged me to expand my conception of environmental activism and produce work that uses history to inform contemporary social and environmental problems. Through formal brainstorming sessions or casual conversations while hiking or over beers, this project emerged and grew. As we worked together, first as adviser and graduate student and then as colleagues, he taught me how to be a teacher, a scholar, a mentor, and a colleague. He and his wonderful wife, Linda Jakse, opened their home to Lauren and me and graciously shared themselves with us, making our years in Arizona a time we will cherish always. I cannot begin to express my gratitude, Paul. I only hope that I might emulate your enthusiasm for life, learning, and justice with my own students and in my career and life. I look forward to our continued collaboration and friendship for years to come.

Thank you to my other dissertation committee members who provided valuable direction for this project. Stephen Pyne contributed his considerable talent and experience to help me craft the narrative structure and tone of the project. Joni Adamson urged me to consider my case studies in relation to environmental justice. Susan Gray's attentive and sometimes exacting critiques of my interpretations and arguments were invaluable in shaping the dissertation. Further, I am grateful for the energy, intellectual stimulation, and encouragement I received from my many fine colleagues at ASU in the School of Historical, Philosophical, and Religious Studies, Global Institute of Sustainability, and Institute for Humanities Research.

Finally, I could not have even begun this project without the loving support of my friends and family. My friends around the country and in Arizona were a constant source of inspiration and sometimes a needed distraction. Fellow graduate students at ASU or in other programs, activists working in other states, adventure partners—you always inspire me to dig deeper, ask tougher questions, appreciate what I have done, and look forward to the future.

To my parents, Roy and Phyllis Ferguson, my sister and brother-in-law, Rebecca and Ryan Brice, and second parents and sisters and brothers in Wisconsin, thank you for your unending optimism and faith in my abilities in this endeavor. Your laughter and almost daily encouragement kept me sane and continue to give me hope.

Lastly, thank you to my beautiful wife, Lauren, for your constant love and patience throughout this project. From beginning to end, you were there. When I struggled, you listened. You read and critiqued the entire manuscript. As I finished a chapter, and then another, and then the revisions, we celebrated together. I could not have done this without you. I love you.

This Is Our Land

1

Introduction

Think Local, Act Local . . . Think Global

I first met Helen Waller in the winter of 2003 when I was working my first session of the Montana legislature for the Northern Plains Resource Council.

It was cold, but not unseasonably cold for Helena, Montana, in February. The wind whipped down Sixth Avenue in the dark before dawn, shaking the naked branches of the trees that lined my short walk to the Capitol. Like every morning that winter, I was thankful when I stepped into the moist heat and yellow lights of the building. I hung up the overcoat I had inherited from a veteran lobbyist on one of the free hangers on the ground floor and made my way to the mezzanine where Helen and I had scheduled to meet. Having talked to her over the phone for the past few weeks, I knew her only by her voice—soft and sometimes gravelly, encouraging and determined. I scanned for the plain dress of a wheat farmer and maybe a man who would be her husband. I heard a familiar voice behind me: "Cody?" I turned around to meet a short, solidly built, white-haired woman in a winter coat, bright eyes shining behind large glasses, and an inviting smile. A tall, balding man in plaid stood slightly hunched over by her side, also smiling. "I'm Helen Waller; this is my husband, Gordy. Let's get to work." It was 6:30 in the morning.

The work Helen referred to was lobbying. Specifically, citizen lobbying. The Wallers had traveled through snow and wind from their wheat farm in the rolling plains near Circle, Montana, 400 miles east of Helena, to talk to state legislators and to testify on behalf of a proposed law that would regulate genetically modified wheat in the state. The multinational chemical corporation Monsanto was preparing to introduce a new strain of wheat that would be resistant to broadleaf herbicides. The maker of the popular weed killer Roundup hoped that it could sell wheat farmers on their new product with the promise of simplified weed management. Because the wheat would be resistant to Roundup, farmers could simply spray their entire field with this one chemical. It would dramatically cut weed-control costs and the amount of fuel required since farmers no longer had to apply multiple applications of herbicides to their fields. To reap these benefits, farmers only had to agree to use Roundup Ready wheat exclusively, buy only Roundup brand herbicide, and promise not to save their seed.

Because Monsanto owned the intellectual property rights associated with this new, patented, genetically modified life-form, Roundup Ready wheat seeds and the offspring of those seeds were the property of the company. If Roundup Ready wheat seed or plants were found on a farmer's property without the farmer having paid to use them, Monsanto could sue the farmer for patent infringement. The Wallers, like thousands of wheat farmers throughout the Great Plains, were concerned about Roundup Ready wheat. They had heard stories of Canadian canola farmers being sued by Monsanto and losing their farms. They worried about what would happen if a neighbor's Roundup Ready crop cross-pollinated with their plants or if the genetically modified seeds or pollen were carried by the ubiquitous Montana winds onto their property. They worried about losing access to critical Asian markets that refused to buy genetically modified wheat. They worried about the long-term impact of spraying so much Roundup on the land, water, and wildlife. Most importantly, they worried about their ability to operate as independent farmers and maintain control over their lives.

This was Helen and Gordy's first trip to Helena this legislative session, but they were no amateurs. Every other year when the Montana legislature was in session, for the better part of the past three decades, they had driven to the capital to lobby on behalf of their farm, their community, the environment, and their way of life. Gordy drove, Helen talked.

"Who are our targets?" Helen asked.

I showed her the possible swing votes in the legislative directory. They were mostly Republicans and a few Democrats from wheat-growing districts—from the towns of Shelby, Havre, Plentywood, Choteau, Fort Benton, Great Falls. Her lips pursed slightly and her eyes narrowed as she studied their photos. She circled names and made notes in the guide.

"Okay," she said, "let's go."

Helen Waller had not always been an activist. At first sight, most people would not assume she was one. In good health at age seventy in 2003, she still carried the markers of age. Her posture was straight, eyes as sharp as her wit, but she had a grandmotherly quality about her. This worked to her advantage in dealing with politicians. Her voice and countenance made her inherently disarming. She could make you feel loved; just as easily, she could make you feel guilty and ashamed.

Helen was made into an activist by the fight to save her farm from strip mining. Before 1974, when coal company men visited the Wallers' sprawling wheat ranch with plans to strip mine the land and promises of high-paying jobs and irrigation for farmers, she was far from a political activist. She served on the board of her local church and sang in the choir. She chaired the local Republican Party in McCone County. The fight to save her farm changed her. "It was real troubling to me," she told me when I visited with her in 2010, "after having farmed for as many years as we had, to think that we would not continue to preserve the land for agricultural use." She joined the Northern Plains Resource Council (NPRC), a grassroots organization formed in 1972 by ranchers and farmers from across eastern Montana who were similarly threatened by strip mining. She helped found a chapter of the group in her county. After repeated trips to Helena and Washington, DC, she stood beside other ranchers, farmers, and environmentalists as President Jimmy Carter signed the landmark Surface Mine Control and Reclamation Act into law in 1977. By the end of the decade, she served as NPRC's chair. In the 1980s, as thousands of farms across the country succumbed to bank foreclosure, she steered NPRC toward working on family agriculture issues. In a comment now famous among NPRC members, she told the group's board, "I didn't fight to save my farm from the coal company just to lose it to the bank." She helped start the National Family Farm Coalition and played a role in the creation of Farm Aid. In 1988, Frank Morrison Jr. tapped Waller as his running mate for his unsuccessful bid for the Democratic nomination for governor of Montana. That same year, she attended the Democratic National Convention as a delegate to cast her vote for Jesse Jackson. Despite the demands of farming, family, and church, she found time to spread her populist message of self-determination, responsibility, and justice across the country as a speaker to countless social change, family agriculture, and environmental organizations.[1]

The degree of Helen's activism is extraordinary, but her transformation was not. The group that Helen joined and came to lead, the Northern Plains Resource Council, was full of people like her: ranchers who, before their land was threatened by the designs of government bureaucrats and energy companies, had only ever served on the board of their local Stockgrowers Association or church or Parent Teacher Association. Within months, they were driving their neighbors in convoys through snowstorms to testify in Forsyth, Miles City, and Helena. Schoolteachers in Billings wrote letters to the editors of local newspapers. Farmers mobbed hearings. As members were transformed, so was NPRC. By the 1980s, it had chapters across the state of Montana and worked on issues ranging from mining to alternative energy to promoting family agriculture. Groups in other states followed a similar trajectory. By the time I came to NPRC in 2002, it had branded itself as a "grassroots conservation and family agriculture organization that worked to protect Montana's land, air, water, and unique quality of life." In 2012, members celebrated its fortieth anniversary.

The Northern Plains Resource Council was a unique hodgepodge of ranchers, farmers, and environmentalists, but it was not so different from other groups that coalesced around the country during the early 1970s whose efforts we might classify as grassroots environmentalism. Individuals, feeling their property or way of life threatened by industrial development, organized to fight back. Sometimes they harbored what might be recognized as environmental values. Usually, their primary concern was their property and a sense of being victims of injustice.[2] The solutions they sought were immediate: take away the right of coal companies to condemn farms and ranches for strip mining and give local residents the ability to participate in decisions regarding the land, water, and air. Over time, many began to link their local issue with the struggles of others fighting similar kinds of industrial development. They began to understand threats to their environment as intertwined with threats to their communities, health, and ways of life. Observers of the environmental movement often quote the maxim "think global, act local." In the case of grassroots environ-mentalism, a more accurate description might be "think local, act local," and then, in many cases, "think global." Giving citizens the ability to par-ticipate in the decisions that affected their communities, livelihoods, envi-ronment, and health became a primary means of achieving their goals—in fact, participation often became a goal in and of itself. Citizen activists—the people who made up and continue to comprise the grassroots of the modern environmental and environmental justice movements—will prob-ably recognize much in Helen's story and the stories that unfold in the pages that follow.

These are stories of common people who, confronting perceived threats to their property, the health and safety of their families and com-munities, or their way of life, bonded together to protect their interests. They include successes and failures as citizens learned how to participate in their democracy and redefined what participation meant. These stories stress how individual activists became reformers and self-trained environ-mental experts. They demonstrate how citizen activists came to connect their local and personal interests and struggles to larger systems of power and injustice and the struggles of others fighting to protect themselves in other parts of the nation and world. They show how grassroots groups evolved with their members. Finally, they reveal how citizen activists understood environmental issues not merely as matters of science but of justice and good governance and saw expanding citizens' abilities to par-ticipate in environmental decision-making as a primary remedy to threats to air, water, land, and public health. This is a familiar story to citizen activists, but for those studying the environmental movement or theoriz-ing a sustainable global future, these pages will hold much that is new.

I came to this project from my personal experience working as a young organizer and lobbyist for the Northern Plains Resource Council in Montana from 2002 to 2005 and confronting the realities of environ-mental activism and decision-making on the ground. I had barely started the job when I realized that the environmental movement in which I now worked looked very different from the one I had read about in books. These "environmentalists"—farmers I met lobbying in Helena and ranch-ers who welcomed me into their homes and gave me tours of their ranches in the coal mining country of southeastern Montana, concerned residents from Billings, Bozeman, and Missoula who organized to promote local agriculture and alternative energy—mixed self-interest and local interest with pragmatism and the ideal that informed citizens were the people most capable of making decisions regarding the public good. They had faith that, if kept accountable to the people, government could work and could right environmental wrongs. As I met more of these citizen activists, I began to notice coherence in how they understood environmental issues, the function of government, and the proper role of citizens in a democracy. I wondered if this was specific to the northern Great Plains and Rocky Mountain regions or if citizen activists in other parts of the country held similar views and organized themselves in a similar fashion. Dozens of interviews, countless hours in archives, and thousands of miles of driving between the northern Plains, the Southwest, and Appalachia over the next five years revealed the answer.

What I found holds important insights for how we understand the history of the environmental movement and the role of citizen activists in American civil society in the late twentieth century. In their victories and defeats, their ability to adapt to changing social and political landscapes, and their perseverance, the histories of the three groups I profile here—the Northern Plains Resource Council in Montana, the Southwest Environmental Service in Arizona, and Save Our Cumberland Mountains in Tennessee—teach us valuable and unexpected lessons about how everyday people understand and work to remedy environmental problems. These stories emphasize the importance of the 1970s as the beginning of the modern environmental regulatory movement and illuminate common connections between the mainstream environmental movement and the environmental justice movement. They also change our perspective on the history of the environmental movement and beg us to consider grassroots environmental activism as an integral component of evolving American political culture. In addition, they force us to recognize how environmental and democratic reforms were intertwined in the late twentieth century. The history of these three groups provides context for understanding grassroots organizing in the twenty-first century to promote environmental and food justice, to stop "fracking" and the Keystone XL pipeline, and to address climate change. The stories of the Northern Plains Resource

Council, the Southwest Environmental Service, and the Save Our Cumberland Mountains offer pathways for affecting change, and they inspire.

A quiet revolution occurred in the United States during the 1970s. Far from Woodstock and the antiwar protests that marked the cultural upheaval of the late 1960s and far even from the hundreds of thousands of people who gathered to celebrate the first Earth Day in April of 1970, change silently coursed its way through the country. General rising economic prosperity and consumption after World War II and increased democratization of American society blossomed by the 1960s into a popular critique of American affluence, the economic and political gap between the rich and privileged and the poor and disenfranchised, America's place in the world, and the human and environmental costs of industrial production and mass consumption. From this critique manifested a series of social movements including the civil rights movement, the women's movement, the New Left, the counterculture, the Black Power movement, the Chicano movement, the gay rights movement, the environmental and consumer rights movements, and, in response, the New Right. This is the story usually told about the 1960s. From within these movements, at the intersection of popular politics and governance, emerged a populist-driven regulatory revolution. Played out not so much in the streets as in government institutions—legislatures, city councils, planning and zoning commissions, and federal and state regulatory agencies—it moved slowly and was not as obvious or sexy as the other revolutions of the 1960s, but it was just as significant.[3]

One of the outgrowths of the 1960s was the popular call for participatory democracy. Couched as a continuation of America's founding democratic ideals, the New Left's demand for participatory democracy was a challenge to government secrecy and a perceived disconnect between "the people" and government during the postwar era. Progressives argued that the solution to this divide—and its resulting injustices—was to allow citizens increased access to the political process by making the workings of government more transparent and allowing citizens to more directly take part in the decisions that affected their lives. As progressives and journalists argued for more transparency in government, participants in the nascent environmental movement argued for more access to information and public involvement in decisions affecting the environment and public health.[4] After more than a decade of political wrangling and congressional hearings, President Lyndon Johnson begrudgingly signed the Freedom of Information Act (FOIA) into law in 1966. The Freedom of Information Act marked the beginning of a subtle but powerful change in the relationship between citizens and their government. Over the several next decades, it would prove a vital tool for citizens fighting environmental threats.[5]

In the decade following the passage of the Freedom of Information Act, Congress and state legislatures passed a series of environmental laws that not only made environmental decision-making more open to public scrutiny but also enshrined citizens' ability to take part in those decisions. The National Environmental Policy Act of 1970 (NEPA) created an unprecedented requirement for environmental review of proposed federal actions that might negatively affect the human and natural environment. The review process included requirements for public notice of proposed activities, public participation in the review process through hearings and comments, and the ability of citizens to appeal agency decisions.[6] The importance of NEPA can easily be overstated, but considered alongside the succession of environmental laws that incorporated similar public participation provisions passed over the course of that environmental decade, it represents a significant transformation of the American environmental regulatory regime and the relationship between Americans and government. Joining NEPA was the Clean Air Act in 1970, the Clean Water Act in 1972, the Endangered Species Act in 1973, the National Forest Management Act in 1976, the Federal Land Policy and Management Act in 1976, the Surface Mine Control and Reclamation Act in 1977, the Comprehensive Environmental Response, Compensation, and Liability Act in 1980, and countless state laws. The inclusion of public notice and participation requirements in all of these laws, including the ability of citizens to appeal agency decisions, enhanced not only environmental regulation and protection but democracy in general. During the 1970s, environmental and democratic reform went hand in hand. Environmental law became a great experiment in participatory democracy.[7]

This experiment coincided with the emergence of hundreds of grassroots environmental organizations across the country.[8] Discerning the causal relationship between the environmental laws passed during the

1970s and these new groups is a little like solving the classic dilemma of the chicken and the egg. The cultural and political milieu of the 1960s and the federal government's aggressive support for expanding energy development further complicate the story. More Americans were environmentally aware during the 1970s than in previous decades, and many interpreted industrial activities as threats to air, water, the land, and public health rather than as markers of progress. At the same time, the nation's growing population and demand for energy and natural resources in the postwar era intensified existing and created new conflicts between different interests. Increased demand for metals and energy minerals pitted rural people against mining companies and the federal government. Residents of American cities worried about air and water pollution and the destruction of their quality of life by urban sprawl. Cities and waste management companies looked to rural and impoverished parts of the country as places to dispose of their ever-growing streams of solid and toxic waste. As sociologists Erik Johnson and Scott Frickel have demonstrated, when confronted by these threats, citizens organized groups to advocate for clean air and water, pristine land, and public health.[9] After 1970, they did so within a new and evolving legal and regulatory framework.[10]

As the new laws of the 1970s increased the ability of Americans to influence environmental decisions, they also provided rallying points around which citizens could organize themselves. Before 1970, formal citizen participation was limited to testifying in local government meetings and legislative hearings and citizen lobbying in state legislatures or in Washington, DC, access to which varied greatly from state to state. Citizens could protest or demonstrate to make their voices heard, but their ability to access the decision-making process was limited. After 1970, at multiple points in the process, they could review a proposed activity, submit written comments and testify at hearings to express their opinions, and make suggestions regarding the proposal. After the agency made its decision on the proposal, citizens could appeal the decision through the courts. Courts handed down decisions and set precedents that shaped the interaction among agencies, industry, and citizens. In effect, citizens played a role in enforcing environmental laws and actively keeping the government and industry accountable, taking part in what Karl Brooks calls the messy business of making environmental law.[11] Each of these points of participation provided an opportunity for citizens to act. Activists built on the experiences of other popular social movements and reasoned that many voices were better than one. Their intuition was correct. Sociologists including Robert Brulle and Erik Johnson have demonstrated that larger group size encouraged a diversity of tactics that enhanced grassroots groups' impact on political agenda setting, a precursor for passing laws and effecting change.[12] Activists recruited their neighbors, friends, family, and other like-minded or similarly threatened individuals to increase their political power. Submitting comments became political action; hearings became events in which united groups of citizens made their voices heard. Organizations could raise money to support a lengthy legal appeal of an agency decision. As citizens participated in the new environmental regulatory regime, their expectations of the government changed. Participation in government decisions regarding the environment and public health became seen as an inalienable right.

Historians have paid a great deal of attention to the emergence of conservation and the environmental movement during the twentieth century, but few have examined closely the emergence of grassroots environmental groups during the regulatory reform revolution of the 1970s and how these groups relate to American civil society as a whole. Their work instead focuses on a small elite group of experts, resource management agencies, and national organizations and their protection of wilderness areas and wildlife.[13] Sociologists and political scientists have paid more attention to environmental and social movement effectiveness, but much of the quantitative work has been confined to national organizations.[14] This emphasis on elites and national organizations has attracted some criticism—both of the literature and the environmental movement itself. By the end of the century, the apparent disconnect between the mainstream environmentalism of national organizations and the experiences of people who made a living working with natural resources prompted Richard White to ask, "Are You an Environmentalist, or Do You Work for a Living?"[15]

In the 1980s and 1990s, environmental justice scholars and activists revealed the uneven distribution of toxic waste and environmental hazards near working-class neighborhoods and communities of color.[16] They identified an "environmental racism" in American society dating back more than a century to attempts by African Americans to improve the living conditions of slaves and opposition by people of color to the "appropriation of land, erosion of treaty rights, and the share-cropping system."[17] Further, they observed a relationship between the growth of the environmental movement and environmental injustice. Historian Andrew Hurley warns that the rise of mainstream environmentalism "coincides with the rise of environmental inequality." Sociologist Dorceta Taylor argues that for most of the history of the environmental movement, activists and scientists focused their attention on the nonhuman components of environmental issues and ignored their human and social dimensions. "In many cases," she writes, "when the people affected were the poor or minorities, they received scant attention from environmental activists." Taylor argues that to fully understand environmental issues, we must recognize how racial and ethnic relations, inequality, and civil rights are intertwined with environmental problems.[18] In their work on what they call "just sustainability," Julian Agyeman, Robert Bullard, and Bob Evans reiterate this point. "From global to local," they insist, "human inequality is bad for environmental quality."[19]

Environmental inequalities extend from racial, social, economic, and gender inequalities.[20] Stymied by legal strictures on political participation or, as theorists of resource mobilization have suggested, a lack of social connections that translate into political power, the poor and people of color are less able to protect themselves and their communities from environmental degradation than the more affluent and socially connected, who tend to be white. In the modern era, economic growth of the developed world—the industrialized North—was made possible by externalizing much of the environmental and human costs of affluence and progress. Initially, industrialization distributed these costs more evenly among the rich and poor living in cities. As transportation and communication technology transformed the American economy and American cities, allowing the more affluent to flee industrial centers, these costs have been increasingly shifted to the poor and nonwhite, who have borne a disproportionate share of the externalized costs of economic development.[21]

The stories presented here add diversity to how we understand the environmental movement. It was not as monolithic and homogenous as has been depicted, and was much more interested in justice issues than acknowledged. While all three of the groups profiled in the pages that follow were comprised predominantly of whites from working- and middle-class backgrounds, their activism illuminates a way between the poles of the mainstream environmental movement and the environmental justice movement to help us imagine possible ways to rectify the inequalities that undermine current and future attempts to achieve sustainability and justice.[22]

Already by the 1980s, scholars observed the emergence of local, volunteer-based grassroots environmental groups as an extension but also an alternative to the national mainstream environmental movement. By 1992, Robert Gottlieb moved our understanding of the environmental movement beyond national groups and a vanguard of elites by arguing for a new conception of environmentalism as "a complex set of movements with diverse roots, with the capacity to help facilitate profound social change."[23] A decade later, Adam Rome illuminated the connections and common roots between the environmental movement and other social change movements during the 1960s.[24] What emerges from their work is a complicated picture of environmental activism based not on a single coherent environmentalism or even general agreed-upon environmental principles but on common calls for fairness, justice, and access to the decisions that affect the land, air, water, and public health. The histories of the groups profiled here similarly demonstrate how citizen activists understood their environmental activism as part of larger projects of increasing citizens' access to and ability to participate in environmental governance but also as part of other goals including achieving gender and racial equality.

In their actions and tactics, the activists who organized and led the Northern Plains Resource Council, Southwest Environmental Service, Save Our Cumberland Mountains, and countless other grassroots groups across the nation in the late twentieth century began to disrupt the social, political, and economic structures upon which environmental inequality is constructed. Simply put, they stood up to industry and government and refused to bear the costs of American progress. In some cases, their initial activities to address local threats to their environment, health, and way of life perpetuated the process of shifting the externalized environmental and human costs of affluence to the poor and people of color. The laws they helped to pass and enforce and the precedents they set for citizen oversight and participation in environmental decision-making coincided with other civil rights advances and opened the way for all Americans to affect the decisions influencing the health of their communities. Over time, many grassroots activists began to recognize the social, economic, and political structures that undergirded environmental problems and connected their issues to others around the country and the world. They began to link social, economic, racial, ethnic, and gender inequality to environmental exploitation. Mirroring a process observed by sociologist Andrew Szasz in his study of the toxics movement, their perspective changed from "NIMBY" ("not in my back yard") to a "radical environmental populism" that explained environmental exploitation as the fault of big business and big government and pitted "the people" against the wealthy and powerful.[25] Activists embraced a revisionist ideology of "NIABY"—"not in anybody's backyard," to borrow a phrase from Save Our Cumberland Mountains (SOCM) activists fighting toxic landfills. By the 1990s, SOCM members united with African American groups fighting toxic waste in Tennessee and actively pursued "antiracism campaigns." Northern Plains members united with farmers in Central America to fight the North American Free Trade Agreement. For members of these groups, like environmental justice activists, their movements became transformative—questioning and seeking to change the foundational social and ideological structures of society.[26]

Examining the activities of grassroots groups reveals another commonality between the grassroots environmental groups and the environmental justice movement: the central role of women. As they did in grassroots efforts to address toxic waste and pollution around the country during the last decades of the twentieth century, women also disproportionately led the efforts of the Northern Plains Resource Council, Southwest Environmental Service, and Save Our Cumberland Mountains. The histories of female activists like Anne Charter in Montana, Priscilla Robinson in Arizona, and Maureen O'Connell in Tennessee extend the observations of environmental justice scholars about the tendency of women to lead local movements to address environmental threats to public health and their communities and reflect how women have understood the environment

and their relationship to it as an extension of gender ideology in the twentieth century. The critical leadership of women unites the environmental
and environmental justice movements at the grassroots.[27]

If the poor and disenfranchised are protected and empowered to
defend themselves from the environmental costs of economic development, then society will have two choices: either accept that costs and risks
will be spread equally across the population or eliminate those costs and
risks. Because the world's wealthier inhabitants are not likely to accept
increased degradation of their environment and risks to their health and
will no longer be able to externalize these costs onto the newly protected
and enfranchised poor, they will have no choice but to eliminate them.
Thus addressing social justice, civic engagement, and community and
local organization connections becomes central to achieving sustainability
in addition to larger humanitarian values and other environmental benefits. By the 1990s, many grassroots environmental activists recognized this
relationship between inequality and environmental protection implicitly,
if not explicitly. This pulling of the social component into the middle of
the sustainability conversation by emphasizing environmental justice led
Agyeman and Evans to proffer a new definition of sustainability as "the
need to ensure a better quality of life for all, now and in the future, in a
just and equitable manner, whilst living within the limits of supporting
ecosystems."[28]

The experiences of citizen activists reveal how common people understood environmental threats in conjunction with and connected to other
concerns. Viewed this way, the lines separating the activism of white
middle-class and working-class environmental activists from those fighting environmental racism and injustice become blurred. As many of the
activists in both movements came to recognize, their strategies, demands,
and goals were more similar than different. They were united by an understanding of the environment as the places "where we live, work, play, and
worship."[29] By the 1990s, many citizen environmental activists and environmental justice activists might have answered White's query with the
same response: "I am an environmentalist, and I do work for a living."

The choice of the particular groups I profile in the pages that follow
is deliberate. Hundreds, if not thousands, of grassroots environmental
groups formed in the United States between 1970 and 2000 to address

countless environmental threats.[30] These three groups represent a diverse cross-section of this segment of the American environmental movement. Much work has focused on environmental movement mobilization among Americans in cities along the East and West Coasts and in the Deep South. Less has been written about the experience of citizen activists in rural areas in the interior and Sunbelt. The struggles of activists in Montana, Arizona, and Tennessee demonstrate how ubiquitous the impulse for environmental and democratic reform was during last decades of the twentieth century and enrich our understanding of grassroots environmental activism. As it provided me with my entrée into understanding grassroots environmental activism, I begin this study with the Northern Plains Resource Council (Northern Plains or NPRC) of Montana. NPRC provides an example of citizen activism in the rural West among traditionally conservative people. Land owning farmers and ranchers were the backbone of its membership. Although they often owned large amounts of land and operated businesses with assets totaling millions of dollars, they primarily experienced and knew their environment through manual labor. They might be defined as middle class, but their life experiences also aligned them culturally with the working class. They were socially well-connected, but they existed between the myth of rugged individualism and the instability of fluctuating global agricultural markets and the harsh climate of the northern Plains.[31]

I chose the second group, the Southwest Environmental Service (SES) of Tucson, Arizona, to provide an example of middle-class environmental activism in the urban Sunbelt. The story of the formation and evolution of SES in the 1970s and 1980s differs markedly from that of Northern Plains and demonstrates an alternative trajectory for citizens' environmental action during this era. Its members fit the usual stereotype of environmentalists— urban, middle-class, educated, white, and socially well-connected.[32] The case study reveals, however, SES's commitment to protecting and improving the environment of Tucson and all of southern Arizona through citizen access to and participation in environmental decision-making at the local, state, and federal levels. Further, it demonstrates how SES's leadership consciously promoted gender equality, enlarging the space for women in politics in Arizona through environmental activism. It helped train citizens, especially women activists, to become environmental experts in order to participate more effectively in government and corporate decision-making about the natural and urban environment.

The final group I profile, Save Our Cumberland Mountains in Appalachian Tennessee (SOCM or "Sock 'em"), moves the study from the West and provides an example of grassroots activism among mostly non-landowning, working-class people who were less socially connected to the seats of power. SOCM formed around the same issue that prompted farmers, ranchers, and environmentalists to band together in Montana during the 1970s: strip mining for coal. However, differences in geography, class, political culture, and land ownership patterns caused the group to evolve in different directions. By the 1990s, it began to consciously articulate its work as environmental justice and challenged the structures of racial, social, and economic inequality that its members associated with the neglect and degradation of their communities and environment. SOCM shared many of the organizing strategies and principles of NPRC and SES, but it demonstrates a tangible link between the mainstream environmental movement and the environmental justice movement.

I have organized *This Is Our Land* into three case studies—one for each of the groups I profile—but the case studies are not symmetrical. I begin each in the 1970s to show the diverse ways in which grassroots environmental groups formed in this first decade of the modern environmental movement. After these origin stories in chapters 2, 4, and 6, the studies diverge to demonstrate how activists, the groups they formed, and their strategies evolved in relation to changing social, political, legal, and economic conditions over the next three decades.

In chapter 3, I examine how the Northern Plains Resource Council sought primarily legislative solutions to the threat of strip mining and successfully advocated for new state and federal laws to regulate the activity in the 1970s. NPRC employed other tactics as well, including direct action and legal appeals to enforce existing environmental laws, but as for other grassroots groups during this era, the legislative strategy was central.

In the 1980s, a changed political climate made it more difficult for environmental groups to pass new laws, and citizens' environmental organizations found themselves working increasingly to hold government and industry accountable to the laws passed in the previous decade.[33] This is the focus of chapter 5. In the 1980s, the Southwest Environmental Service embarked on a nearly decade-long effort to force Arizona's copper smelters to comply with air pollution laws. Its campaign included multiple tactics, but essential to its success was the professionalization of SES's leadership into citizen experts on air quality and environmental law and its pursuit of a remedy through the courts. The story of SES's fight against the smelters is typical of the evolution in tactics and strategy that many grassroots groups underwent during the 1980s.

Finally, chapter 7 examines Save Our Cumberland Mountain's campaign to prevent the locating of toxic landfills in rural and impoverished areas of Tennessee during the 1990s. It reveals how citizens' groups adapted the tactics they had learned over the previous decades to make their voices heard in the environmental decision-making process and how they began to understand their struggles related to those of others working for social, economic, and environmental justice. It also reinforces the vital importance of persistent citizen participation and engagement in environmental decision-making to protect and improve the places "where we live, work, play, and worship."[34]

A note on terms: I use loosely and sometimes interchangeably the terms "grassroots environmental groups," "citizen's groups," and "citizen activists." Beginning with the term "citizen," I employ an expansive idea of citizenship used by the activists themselves in the case studies that does not necessarily require legal citizenship with regard to the state but was based on residency. For activists in groups like the Northern Plains Resource Council, Southwest Environmental Service, and Save Our Cumberland Mountains, "citizen" was an identity tied to living and working in a particular place. It implied authority and a right to participate in the democratic processes of state and federal government and agency decisions affecting the environment and public health based on one's localness and connection to place and community. Over time, as activists began to connect their local issues to larger political, economic, and ecological systems, the term "citizen" expanded to include the entire nation and even the whole global population.

Scholars from political science, sociology, environmental justice, and history have attempted to define what constitutes a "grassroots environmental group." They stress group size, how organizations are funded, group strategy and tactics, whether organizations work primarily on local or national or global issues, and the makeup of their membership. I draw on aspects of all of these and define "grassroots," or as I also call them, "citizen," environmental groups as membership-based organizations in which the members build the organizational structure of the group on philosophies of democratic decision-making. In these groups, organizational funding can come from a combination of memberships or donations and often outside funding sources. These groups incorporate a diversity of tactics but tend to rely more on strategies that employ "people power" than on capital-intensive tactics such as paid lobbying and paid media campaigns. These tactics include grassroots lobbying and direct-action activities, including demonstrations and sit-ins but also litigation.[35]

By the turn of the twenty-first century, in their words, actions, and expectations, grassroots activists echoed the assertion from a SOCM handbill opposing the siting of toxic landfills near small, impoverished towns in rural Tennessee in 1989: "This is our land, we have the right to be heard."[36] On its face, this simple statement asserts the right based on residency of citizens to participate in the decisions that affected their lives and destinies. This was the argument put forward by Helen Waller and fellow activists in Montana, Arizona, and Tennessee and in communities throughout the United States during the 1970s, but over the course of the next three decades, its meaning grew into something bigger. It assumed the right of people to have a say in the decisions that affected the world around them, including the air they breathed, the water they drank, the land on which they made their living and recreated, and the communities they called home. Through their experience over the course of the 1970s, 1980s, and 1990s, citizen activists and the groups they formed came to understand "this is our land" to mean this is our community, this is our country, this is our democracy, and this is our planet. As they did, they redefined political participation and expanded the ability of citizens to shape their world. This is their story.

2

Coal Boom on the Plains

When Boyd and Anne Charter and their alarmed neighbors heard from the Musselshell County attorney that Montana's eminent domain laws allowed the state to condemn their ranches for mining and that they could do nothing to stop Consolidated Coal ("Consol"), a subsidiary of Continental Oil Company (Conoco), from strip mining their land in the rolling Bull Mountains north of Billings, Montana, in 1971, they fought off feelings of helplessness and hopelessness. This group of neighbors loosely tied together over the vast distances between their houses by common work and life experiences had survived droughts, fires, low cattle prices, and hard winters that froze cows to death. This was a new kind of threat.[1]

The Bull Mountain ranchers learned about the proposed mine over a few months. Beginning in December 1970, the landowners spotted smartly dressed men in suits carrying briefcases driving fancy cars over the country's rutted roads. These "land men," hired by Consol, traveled door to door making offers to landowners either to buy their land outright or to lease it for strip mining. In many cases, the land men informed the ranchers that Consol owned or leased the minerals beneath their ranches and had a legal right to mine whether the landowner consented or not. Legally, they were correct. The building of the Northern Pacific Railroad left the state with a checkerboard pattern of land and mineral ownership and a legacy of "split estates" in which land was owned by one party and the minerals beneath it by another. Northern Pacific had originally acquired about 14 million acres of the public domain in Montana in compensation for building the railroad linking the Great Lakes region with the Puget Sound a century before. As Northern Pacific sold off the land to eager settlers, the company retained the mineral rights. To prevent the abuse of the Homestead Act by coal-land speculators, Congress legislated that the federal government keep the mineral rights on the large portions of the land it made available for homesteading after 1911. The surface properties may have changed hands several times by the time a coal company bought or leased the right to mine the old Northern Pacific or federal minerals beneath them. Landowners usually did not know who owned the minerals beneath their property. Montana law, greatly influenced by mining interests in the late nineteenth century, privileged mineral rights over surface ownership.[2]

The land men were aggressive in their tactics. They combined flattery, subtle and sometimes overt intimidation, and occasionally outright lies to convince landowners to lease or sell. They applied such tactics to Boyd and Anne. The lease hounds told the Charters that all of their neighbors had sold or leased, and that if they did not fall in line, they would be "an island of nothing in a sea of plenty."[3] To persuade Louise Pfister to sign a waiver that would allow the company to drill core samples anywhere on her ranch in exchange for one dollar, they provided a list of people including the Charters, their neighbors Bob and Joan Tully, and others who had supposedly signed. Surprised and concerned, Louise Pfister called her neighbors. The phone lines burned hot that winter as ranchers verified if their neighbors had in fact sold out to the coal company. They found that some had signed the land men's papers but that most had not. "We all agreed that they were bastards and not to be trusted and we'd better find out what our rights were," Anne remembered years later.[4] They began to pull together as they usually did to meet a communal threat, though this challenge was different from any range fire or blizzard they had ever encountered. How it would be resolved, no one knew.

Little did these ranchers know, but the coal boom of the 1970s was not confined to the Bull Mountains. Years before the Bull Mountain ranchers learned of Consol's designs for their homes, the Montana Power Company was planning to construct two giant coal-fired electrical generation plants in Colstrip, about one hundred fifty miles east in Rosebud County. Colstrip 1 and 2, as these plants would come to be known, would supply electricity for more than half a million homes as far away as Chicago and Seattle.

Thick black seams beneath the prairie grass and hills—blasted and dug by the Peabody Coal Company, a subsidiary of Kennecott Copper, using machines so large they walked on large platform feet more like robotic dinosaurs than conventional bulldozers—would feed the plants' insatiable appetite for coal. These "draglines" stripped roughly forty cubic yards of coal in a single bucketful—enough to fill a railroad car with 100 tons of coal in four massive scoops. The proposed power plants would devour that train-carload of coal practically as fast as the dragline could fill it.[5] Rosebud County ranchers, many from families that had homesteaded in the region in the 1880s and 1890s and had been on the ranches for three or four generations, faced a threat similar to that of their neighbors to the north.

Unlike the Bull Mountain ranchers, the ranchers near Colstrip were more familiar with coal strip mining. While there had been underground coal mining in the Bull Mountains near the town of Roundup in the twentieth century, it was mostly dormant by the 1970s. However, the Northern Pacific Railroad mined the thick coal seams under the red scoria and bluffs of southeastern Montana for decades before Montana Power set its sights on Colstrip. Third-generation rancher Wally McRae remembered that before anyone ever imagined a power plant, Colstrip was already a coal mining town. The Northern Pacific Railroad (later Burlington Northern) had mined and shipped coal from Colstrip all over the country since the early twentieth century. For decades, McRae and his neighbors interacted with the mine and its employees when they traveled to town, and he remembered a general sense of cooperation and congeniality. "They were very responsible," said McRae, recounting how Northern Pacific paid to remodel the local school that serviced Colstrip and the surrounding area.[6] As a result, McRae and the other Rosebud County ranchers were hardly alarmed when Montana Power first came on the scene. Montana Power had a good reputation and initially gave them little reason to worry. The company, the electricity-producing subsidiary of the powerful Anaconda Mining Company based in the western part of the state, bought the coal mines from Northern Pacific in 1958 when diesel replaced steam-powered locomotives. Montana Power delivered its first shipment of Colstrip coal to its 120-megawatt Billings power plant in 1966. Little did area residents know that Montana Power intended to increase its production capabilities by building a power plant near the mine. As the company's plans developed during the 1960s, it became apparent that the Montana Power Company and the Peabody Coal Company, with which Montana Power contracted to supply coal from the mines to the new plant, were going to do everything in their power to get the coal under these privately owned ranches.[7]

As in the Bull Mountains, Peabody Coal Company's land men soon began showing up at Rosebud County ranch houses telling landowners that their neighbors had already agreed to lease or sell their land and that they should do the same. McRae and fellow rancher Don Bailey began to keep track of Peabody's agents and organize other landowners to protect themselves. "We said, 'Don't believe [what they tell you]' and told them to make sure that what they tell you is true—to write down dates, write down times, write down the guy's name and what he told you," McRae remembered.[8] Bailey and McRae would then meet with their neighbors and check the facts against each other. McRae remembered his parents, who lived through the Great Depression, telling him, "It was tough in the thirties; it was damn tough in the thirties. The only reason we're still here is that *we* were tough in the thirties."[9] Now he faced his own crisis, and this time it was unclear whether resilience and tenacity, learned over generations of dealing with the unpredictability of nature and agricultural markets, would save his and his neighbors' ranches and way of life.

While Consol was focusing its energy on the Bull Mountains north of Billings and Montana Power was working near Colstrip, ranchers along the Tongue River and Hanging Woman Creek, near the tiny hamlet of Birney adjacent to the Northern Cheyenne Reservation, were experiencing similar run-ins with land agents. Ranchers Irving and Carolyn Alderson and Art "Bunny" Hayes Jr. and his wife Marilyn, and Bill and Anne McKinney began to hear rumors about a proposed strip mine and power plant planned for the Decker area just south of their ranches, close to the Wyoming border. In addition to the danger a strip mine posed to land, water, and air quality, the disruption thousands of workers, trucks, and equipment traveling up the Tongue River Road would cause to agriculture concerned landowners. Massive power lines and a railroad were also proposed for the valley. In some cases, this corridor threatened to cut ranches in half. Like their neighbors in Colstrip and the ranchers in the Bull Mountains, landowners along the Tongue River found their land and way of life threatened by landscape-scale industrial development. As the Tongue River ranchers organized a defense, gossip floated across the prairies of another strip mine planned by the Westmoreland Company for Sarpy Creek, just northeast of Colstrip. Cafes and bars across the border in Wyoming were abuzz with reports of proposed giant mines and power plants for the Gillette area.[10] Like a summer storm that builds slowly on the horizon throughout the day and then arrives with a crash, the coal boom of the 1970s arose as rumors and then poured like a deluge upon the region.

Energy Crisis and the Northern Great Plains

The arrival of the coal boom on the prairies, hills, and badlands of the northern Great Plains during the early 1970s was prompted by two developments at the national level: the emerging energy crisis of the 1970s and the ambitious attempt by the federal government and dozens of corporate partners to address it. Over the course of the twentieth century, American economic growth, prosperity, and prestige on the world scene were tightly connected to its ability to produce energy. Fueled by inexpensive and plentiful energy supplies, industrial development bound the

FIGURE 1. Hay and alfalfa fields in Sarpy Basin slated for coal strip mining, June 1973. National Archives photo no. 412-DA-549141.

continent, connecting the resources of the American interior to manu-facturing centers and ports east and west and the world at large. The con-struction of massive federally funded hydroelectric projects in the West during the 1930s provided cheap electricity that attracted industry and emigrants to rural backwaters and played a vital role in powering war-time production during the 1940s. Seemingly overnight, small towns and cities grew to major metropolitan areas. Americans' ideal standard of liv-ing increasingly emphasized life in clean, neat new houses in suburban developments only a short drive from the workplace on new multilane highways. This ideal was encouraged and reinforced by a sticky amalgama-tion of housing developers, household appliance manufacturers, electric utility companies, automobile manufacturers, and pop culture and was underwritten by a booming economy and generous federal loan programs following World War II. As American homes became completely reliant on electricity, including standard electric heat and air conditioning, electric-ity consumption jumped by a factor of seven to ten. As Americans trav-eled farther to work, shop, and recreate, oil consumption increased—by more than 300 percent between 1920 and 1960.[11] By the 1960s, America consumed energy like never before. Some journalists, economists, and politicians maintained the optimism of the previous decades and forecast that the development of new oil reserves in Alaska would surpass increas-ing demand. In the words of a *U.S. News and World Report* journalist in 1969, new oil exploration would "turn the power politics of the world upside down" by undermining the growing power of the Arab countries in the ever-more volatile Middle East.[12] For others, though, threats to the supply of Middle East oil presented a looming danger to the nation. One way to minimize those threats without inflicting the economically and politically painful shortages Americans had experienced during World War II was to increase domestic energy supply within the continental United States.

For most, the energy crisis of the 1970s came suddenly and unexpect-edly, but its underlying causes had built for years before Americans felt its effects. Although it is commonly associated with the 1973 Organization of Petroleum Exporting Countries (OPEC) embargo of American oil imports in retaliation for U.S. support of Israel in the Yom Kippur War, the embargo simply exacerbated already rising foreign oil prices and systemic weak-nesses in America's ability to meet its growing thirst for energy. The energy

crisis developed in stages from the late 1960s through the early 1980s. In
the late 1960s and early 1970s, economists and energy advisors to President Richard Nixon began warning of the potential danger of oil shortages.
Low prices for abundant imported oil during the economic boom of the
1960s, despite government quotas that restricted importation of foreign
oil, encouraged increased consumption and stifled private investment
in domestic production. The number of drilling rigs in the United States
declined from the mid-1950s and hit its lowest level by 1970. The second
stage of the crisis developed after OPEC imposed price increases and oil
restrictions in 1972 and the embargo in October 1973. Fuel shortages,
emblazoned on the collective memory by iconic images of cars backed up
for blocks at gas stations and trucks abandoned on the highways in protest
of the government's inability to deal with fuel prices that doubled over the
course of a few months, prompted Nixon to action.[13]

In November 1973, Nixon announced Project Independence, which
committed $10 billion to research and develop domestic energy supplies.
Modeled after a World War II program to produce synthetic rubber, Project
Independence combined a variety of tactics. It deregulated prices to disci-
pline citizens to use energy more efficiently and adjust their consumption
practices. It promoted more domestic energy development, including more
nuclear power plants, oil and gas leases on the continental shelf, research
on fusion power and technologies to turn coal into gas, as well as accelerated oil drilling on federal lands. Despite its ambitious name, administration officials quickly realized that Project Independence could not achieve
complete energy self-sufficiency for the United States. It did set the course,
however, for the federal government's energy program for the remainder
of the 1970s, a program that tied energy producers to government and
promised healthy corporate profits. President Gerald Ford moved his sights
beyond Nixon's stated goal of energy self-sufficiency toward increasing
domestic production to the point that the United States would dominate
world energy markets as it had earlier in the century. Ford's program called
for the insulation of 18 million homes and manufacturing of more fuel-
efficient automobiles and trucks. Its core, however, was the construction
of hundreds of new major power production facilities—200 new nuclear
power plants, 250 new coal mines, 150 new coal-fired power plants, 30 new
oil refineries, 20 new synthetic fuel plants, and the drilling of thousands of

new oil wells.[14] Although he was less supportive of nuclear power, Democratic president Jimmy Carter steadfastly supported the development of
large, centralized energy-producing facilities and coal gasification plants
that exploited federally owned minerals until he left office in 1981.

The crisis shifted into another stage when Iran cut off its oil to the
United States during the Carter administration. The spike in energy
prices fueled simultaneous economic inflation and stagnation and further embittered and angered the public. Finally, during the first term of
President Ronald Reagan, the crisis eased. Oil prices fell as OPEC proved
unable to keep some of its members from overproducing and selling to
the United States, while new oil fields opened in Alaska, the North Sea,
and Southeast Asia.[15]

Before the energy shortage reached full crisis in the 1970s, Nixon recognized a potential disaster in the making. He instructed his secretary
of the interior, Walter J. Hickel, to get ahead of the coming storm after
entering office in 1969. The Department of the Interior began organizing
meetings of private and public power producers with the aim of creating
comprehensive regional plans for increasing domestic energy production.
It was from these meetings that the *North Central Power Study* was born. The
study sought to implement several of the major supply-side components
of Nixon's eventual Project Independence and became one of the foundational elements in federal energy planning during the 1970s.[16]

In October 1971, after a year and a half of research and meetings with
dozens of energy and mining experts from government agencies and
private industry, the United States Department of the Interior's Bureau
of Reclamation issued the *North Central Power Study*. The study, which
attempted to forecast the energy needs and resources of the central United
States through the year 2000, drew together the expertise of representatives from nineteen investor-owned power plants, six cooperatively owned
plants, two public power districts, one federally owned plant, and eight
municipalities. Their study area was expansive. It included parts or all of
Utah, Colorado, Wyoming, Idaho, Montana, North Dakota, Missouri, South
Dakota, Nebraska, Kansas, Iowa, and Minnesota and small parts of Illinois,
Oregon, and Wisconsin. Their findings: U.S. domestic power demand would
increase to 494,000 megawatts by 1980 and increase annually at a rate of
about 6.5 percent per year through 2000 to about 1.7 million megawatts

by that year. Without massive cooperative effort and investment by public and private entities in new energy production and transmission facilities, the nation was marching headlong into a crisis. "Never before in the history of our Nation," the committee wrote in a news release issued by the Department of the Interior following its first meeting in May 1970, "has there been as much need for broad, imaginative, and sophisticated approaches to the task for providing adequate and reliable electric power for our citizens."[17] This group of energy moguls and bureaucrats had a solution, however, and it lay just a short distance beneath the farms and prairies of the northern Great Plains.

The coal of the Great Plains was an obvious solution to the country's energy needs. With the passage of new federal air quality regulations in the 1960s and the likely passage of the Clean Air Act in 1970, coal companies coveted the cooler but cleaner burning low-sulfur coal of the Fort Union formation beneath northeastern Wyoming, the western Dakotas, and eastern Montana. "In order to provide for the future electric and other energy needs," the Bureau of Reclamation wrote, "the further development of the vast coalfields of the North Central region of the United States is a certainty."[18] By the time the *study* was released, the chairman and chief executive officer of the Burlington Northern Railroad Company, which shipped coal east from Colstrip, already touted the region's low-sulfur coal as "the most exciting thing happening on the Burlington Northern." "All the mines in the area are running wide open," he told a reporter for the *Chicago Sun-Times*, "and we have rights to an estimated 11 billion tons of known reserves."[19]

Released in 1971, phase 1 of the study proposed the construction of forty-two major coal-fired power plants in eastern Montana, northeastern Wyoming, Colorado, and western North Dakota. Several of these facilities would be the largest coal-fired plants ever constructed, producing 10,000 megawatts (enough to power roughly 10 million homes). Twenty-one of these would be located in three rural counties of eastern Montana, with the balance in Wyoming and North Dakota. These power plants would be mine-mouth generation stations built adjacent to the gigantic coal strip mines at the "mouth" of the mines.[20] Planners based the feasibility of the plants on the economics of scale and the realities of geography. Large power plants were expensive to build, but the price per kilowatt-hour decreased as the size of the plants increased.[21] Montana Power's Colstrip plant would be the pilot project in the study area.

A second strategy the study proposed to make the project economical was to burn coal close to the mine and then transport electricity to distant markets. Unlike most coal-fired plants in the East and Midwest that were built near where their electricity would be consumed, these plants would generate electricity close to the mine and transport the energy over high-voltage power lines hundreds, even thousands, of miles to where it would be used. Shipping coal over wire in the form of electricity was cheaper than sending it over rails. This strategy had the added benefit of reducing air pollution in population centers. Western coal, lower in sulfur than the anthracite coal mined in the East, burned cooler and cleaner and produced less pollution. Long-distance transmission lines were very expensive to construct, however. The cost of building hundreds of miles of high-voltage lines, 765 kilovolt lines running to the east and 500 kilovolt lines to carry power the shorter distances to western cities, was estimated in 1971 at between $44,000 and $230,000 per mile depending on the terrain the lines crossed. This cost reflected the price of materials and labor but also the purchase of rights-of-way across private property. In addition, transporting electricity hundreds of miles meant the loss of energy as heat through transmission, between 3 and 7 percent for electricity making the long trek east and 1 to 2 percent for electricity shipped west. As line capacity increased, transmission losses decreased. As with the coal-fired plants, the larger the line the more economically efficient it became. Because they were proposed for rural, sparsely populated areas, the power plants and transmission lines could be large. If these massive plants produced millions of tons of sulfur oxides, nitrogen oxides, other hydrocarbons, and particulate matter that polluted the air and came falling back to earth as acid rain, it would fall mostly on agricultural soil, cattle, wildlife, and open land rather than on the dense human populations in the East or coastal West. The plants would include smokestacks hundreds of feet tall to maximize the dispersal of pollutants high in the atmosphere away from local residents. The study promised the sleepy rural towns of the northern Great Plains thousands of high-paying construction jobs in the initial years of the plan and a stable industrial economy for an estimated thirty-five years after the plants were constructed. The millions of residents in eastern, midwestern, and western cities would enjoy cheap, plentiful electricity with a minimal cost to their immediate environment.[22]

But that was only part of the plan. While coal was the key ingredient in the *North Central Power Study*, the possibilities of generating electricity through hydropower projects and sending the energy produced by these new and enlarged dams via the proposed transmission system was not lost on planners. The study proposed major new dams in Montana on the Missouri River and its tributaries. The study also proposed to dam the Yellowstone River—the longest yet-undammed river in the nation. The Yellowstone flowed northeast out of Yellowstone National Park for nearly seven hundred miles before meeting the Missouri.[23]

These dams would provide not only electricity—albeit a drop in the bucket compared to the almost 200,000 megawatts to be generated by coal—but also the second essential component in generating electricity from coal: water. The *study*'s massive mine-mouth plants burned coal to heat water to produce steam to turn giant turbines to create electricity. Coal burning of the magnitude proposed in the *study* was going to require a lot of water—approximately 28 cubic feet, or about 210 gallons, per second for every 1,000 kilowatts. The proposed 10,000-megawatt plant planned for Hanging Woman Creek near Birney, for instance, would require about 2,100 gallons of water every second, 125,000 gallons every minute, and 180 million gallons per day.[24] That is equivalent to the amount of water required to satisfy the needs of more than 1,200 American families for an entire year.[25] In an arid region averaging less than 15 inches of precipitation per year, this was a staggering amount of water. Until the coal boom, agriculture was the largest user of water in Montana, using just over 2 billion gallons annually. If the study was fully realized, coal production would require 391 billion gallons every year. Planners estimated that the entire Colstrip-Gillette region of southwestern Montana and northeastern Wyoming yielded 2.8 million usable acre-feet of water annually—about 912 billion gallons. The proposed power plants would consume about 43 percent (1.2 million acre-feet) of all the water in the region.[26]

What the *North Central Power Study* proposed in strikingly understated fashion was an almost complete transformation of the northern Great Plains. Small towns like Birney, Montana (population 15), at the intersection of two dirt roads an hour's drive south of the slightly more bustling Colstrip, were slated for the construction of the largest coal-fired power plants ever built in the United States. Overnight, they would be transformed into boomtowns with thousands of new, mostly male residents. If they were not going to be stripped to supply coal for the massive new plants, the ranches along Rosebud Creek, Hanging Woman Creek, the Tongue River, Sarpy Creek, near Broadus, and in the Bull Mountains would be adjacent to new mines. The mines threatened essential springs as bulldozers and draglines fractured the fragile hydrologic balance upon which ranching depended. Mines, power plants, transmission towers, and new industrial corridors including power lines, busy two-lane highways, and railroads would fragment the region, humming and roaring as they carried off the energy stores from millions of years past to hungry consumers beyond the eastern and western horizons, twenty-four hours a day, every day of the year. Verdant valleys that cradled small but vital streams, islands of abundance surrounded by the scrub and sage of the high desert, would become reservoirs to store water for the thirsty power plants. The region's few major rivers, the Missouri and the still-wild Yellowstone, would be dammed, their energy harnessed and added to the grid. Behind those dams, hundreds of miles from the proposed coal mines and power plants, tens of thousands of acres of productive land would be flooded. Montana Power promised, through full-page advertisements in the *Billings Gazette*, that its new power plants at Colstrip would meet "all federal and state air and water quality standards."[27] These assurances did little to comfort landowners. They saw the dramatic alteration of eastern Montana's land, water, air, regional economy, and society in the course of only a few decades. As far as they could make out, their livelihoods and way of life were being sacrificed.

Landowners Unite

As they had with previous challenges, landowners bonded together for mutual assistance. Ranchers in the Bull Mountains realized that if they had any hope of defending their land, they had to use their common interest to join efforts. In 1971, Boyd Charter and Bob Tully organized a meeting at Tully's ranch. "We decided we all had best work together and stick together and the best way to start was to become an organization," Anne Charter remembered years later.[28] They called themselves the Bull Mountain Landowners Association, and they quickly elected officers. The group elected Bob Tully chairman and Anne Charter vice chairman.[29]

As vice chairman, Anne mostly conducted public relations for the new group. She lived part-time in Billings while her children were in school, which gave her access to media outlets in Montana's largest city. Though living on a remote ranch, Anne was worldly and well-traveled. Originally from St. Louis, Missouri, she had attended Wells College in New York and Washington University in St. Louis. In college, she studied in Germany, toured Western Europe, and lived in the East before meeting Boyd. Her education and experiences up to that point, however, did little to prepare her for the new challenge. "The only thing I could think of doing was to call the *Billings Gazette* and give them the news that we had formed an organization, what our purpose was, and the names of our officers," she remembered.[30] The paper referred her to reporter Dave Earley, who proved to be a valuable ally in the group's first battles. The ranchers' story attracted Earley, who eagerly covered the issue and wrote numerous articles about the group's efforts to protect their land during the early 1970s.[31]

The Bull Mountain Landowners Association (BMLA) also benefitted from the professional expertise within its ranks. One of its greatest assets was Ellen Pfister Withers, the daughter of Louise Pfister, the widowed owner of a large ranch in the Bulls. Although her husband thought that women had no business running a ranch, he had no sons, and his death in 1966 left Louise and her eldest daughter Ellen in charge.[32] According to Anne Charter, Consolidated Coal thought they had found a weak link in Louise and invited her to come to their office in Billings for a consultation. Without informing Consol, Louise brought along Anne and Boyd. When Boyd accused the Consol representatives of trying to take advantage of an elderly woman, they grew frazzled. Consol's Western District Vice President Del Adams emerged from a closet with a tape recorder. According to Boyd, Adams "was going to record this stuff, so that they caught the old woman in a weak moment," and have recorded proof that she had consented to sell her ranch.[33] Experiences like these galvanized daughter Ellen, who was attending law school in Mississippi at the time. Ellen's experience with coal mining extended back to her childhood in the 1950s when she would visit her great-grandfather's farm in Pennsylvania. Coal mining, she remembered, had left nothing of the farm but piles of tailings. "When I looked at the land," she recounted, "I couldn't think how anyone could do that to their land."[34] When the land men first came to the region, Ellen used her legal training to untangle the rights of her family and their neighbors. When she finished her degree, she returned to the Bulls and put her expertise to work. For the young organization, having an effectively pro-bono lawyer on retainer proved essential in the fight against the coal companies.

Over the next year or so, BMLA's members spoke to anyone they thought could help their cause and took every opportunity to publicize the situation in the Bull Mountains. In one instance while Anne was updating her neighbors in Billings about the latest developments, she was overheard by a young and curious Janice Burchell. The sixth-grader had spent time at the Charter ranch and wanted to help. The next day, Janice presented Anne with more than thirty "priceless" letters from her classmates at Billing's Grand Avenue School.[35] BMLA used the letters locally to publicize the issue and to correspond with senators and congressmen in Washington, DC. Burchell also organized her classmates to help turn out attendees for one of Billings' first Earth Day celebrations, and BMLA capitalized on the event. The organization presented a slide show of the Bull Mountains narrated "vivaciously" by rancher Vera Beth Johnson. At the event, the BMLA caught the local chamber of commerce off guard.[36] Johnson effectively nullified the business group, who had few facts to substantiate its ardent support for strip mining in the Bull Mountains.[37]

BMLA also made sure to turn out its members at every public meeting concerning mining in the Bull Mountains whether it was organized by the state, Consolidated Coal, or local business interests. A June 1971 hearing in Roundup conducted by Montana state lands commissioner Ted Schwinden (Montana governor, 1981–1989) regarding Consol's proposal to mine a fifteen-acre test pit was typical. About twenty-five people presented testimony; roughly half were ranchers skeptical of Consol's promises to reclaim its proposed mine. According to the *Great Falls Tribune*, which covered the hearing, "each side had its cheering section and applause was frequent."[38] William Clancy, representing the United Mine Workers of America and a veteran Roundup-area coal miner, spoke in support of the mine, as did

Roundup attorney Charles Maris, who cited the potential economic benefits the mine would bring to Musselshell County. Consol's spokesman Larry Fuller reassured the crowd that it was the company's policy to restore all the land it mined in Montana to a useful, productive condition. BMLA president Bob Tully countered and read a letter from H. Cochran, Consol's public relations director, in which Cochran wrote that the land in question would "be richer for having been strip mined."[39] BMLA became well known for challenging government bureaucrats and mining representatives with questions and comments at these meetings.

Beyond simply publicizing the threat of strip mining in the Bulls, BMLA learned quickly that their success in defending their land from Consol's divide-and-conquer techniques depended on building broad public support that could translate into political power. They built on their public relations successes in the *Billings Gazette*, at Earth Day, and in public meetings to actively recruited new members. They set up informational and recruitment booths at county fairs and rodeos. It was at one of these fairs that a sometimes cantankerous, usually amiable, and ever-persuasive Boyd Charter ran into his old acquaintance Wally McRae and asked him to join the Bull Mountain ranchers' effort.

McRae was reluctant to get involved with the BMLA. After all, his ranch near Colstrip was more than 150 miles east of Bull Mountains, and his fight was with Montana Power and Peabody Coal, not Consol. Moreover, although McRae worked in the same business as the Charters, the culture of the Rosebud County ranchers differed from that of the Bull Mountain ranchers in subtle but important ways. Unlike most of the landowners in the Bull Mountains whose roots in the area dated back to the early and mid-1900s, most of the ranchers near Colstrip were the descendants of pioneers who had homesteaded in the region in the 1880s or 1890s. If anyone fit the romantic ideal of western rugged individualism, it was these people. They lived far from town, traveling occasionally into tiny Colstrip for provisions or for a school sporting event and only making the trip to the regional hubs of Miles City, Billings, or Sheridan, Wyoming, once or twice a season to sell their cows or to attend a fair or rodeo. Their ranches were large, some measuring in the tens of thousands of acres; the most enduring operations had water, either in the form of springs or perennial

streams or rivers to which the operators had senior water rights dating
back to the late nineteenth century. The importance of land to the Colstrip
ranchers contributed to an almost visceral defense of private property. "All
of my life I can remember that the ranch was *the* most important thing,"
McRae told Michael Parfit for his 1980 book on the Colstrip power plant
controversy *Last Stand at Rosebud Creek*. "It was more important than comfort or happiness or anything. It was more important than family. It was
more important than marriage. It was more important than religion. It
was *absolutely* the *only* important thing in the world."[40] To protect their
ranches, whether from fire, drought, blizzards, or low cattle prices, they
relied on their own ingenuity and toughness, and called on neighbors only
when absolutely necessary. Years later, in his history of rural activism *Raising Less Corn and More Hell: Midwestern Farmers Speak Out*, Jim Schwab writes
that this rugged individualism, often more imagined than real, became
the "philosophic cornerstone of rural culture."[41] It tended to leave rural
people unable to admit their need for collective political action; to do so,
he observed, suggested that one was weak or a failure. Schwab noted that
this unwillingness to ask for help continued until an issue erupted into a
full-blown crisis.[42] The situation along Rosebud Creek had not yet reached
this point for McRae and his neighbors in the late 1960s and early 1970s.
They addressed this new threat in the ways they knew how.

When Peabody Coal Company's land men knocked on McRae's door in
1968 to survey his ranch, McRae addressed the issue as he did most affairs
on the Rocker Six Cattle Company ranch. McRae owned almost 30,000
acres of land, which he had bought from his father a few years before.
However, the Rocker Six was a split-estate. McRae's great-grandfather had
bought the land from the Northern Pacific Railroad. He got the surface
rights, but the railroad and the federal government retained whatever
mineral wealth lay beneath it. In 1968, Peabody leased the mineral rights
beneath the ranch. Wally McRae had never owned the coal beneath his
land, but before 1968, he had never had to confront the possibility that
someone might strip mine through his property to get to it. He began to
search for solutions.[43]

Like most of the ranchers in Rosebud County in the late 1960s and
early 1970s, McRae was a conservative Republican. His politics were deeply

tied to protecting his property, family, and way of life, and the three were tightly interwoven. Although global markets and national policies regarding international trade, farms subsidies, meat inspection, monopoly and antitrust regulation, and issues of interstate transportation and energy prices directly affected his livelihood, his politics and those of most of his ranching neighbors near Colstrip were predominantly local. When they sought a solution to an issue that seemed beyond their immediate local ability to resolve, eastern Montana ranchers often turned to the conservative and powerful Montana Stockgrowers Association, which had provided a voice and political clout for ranchers since 1884. McRae looked to the Stockgrowers to address what he saw as fundamentally an agricultural and private property rights issue. At the 1969 annual meeting of the Stockgrowers, McRae successfully ran for director and was able to persuade the association to pass a resolution that urged the Montana legislature to regulate strip mining.[44] However, despite the historic power of the Stockgrowers, its political influence was declining by the 1960s, while Montana Power's clout in the Montana legislature was approaching its apogee. Peabody's lease hounds did not relent and Montana Power continued its plans to build the power plant at Colstrip.

During 1970 and 1971, McRae and his neighbor in Rosebud County, Don Bailey, continued their efforts to inform landowners about Montana Power and Peabody's activities and to strategize how to fight the companies. In early 1971, the landowners decided to form a group and called themselves the Rosebud Protective Association (RPA). In addition to wanting to protect their ranches and water, RPA also voiced concerns about the effects of rapid industrialization on area schools, disorganized and ramshackle boomtown residential development, and the introduction of hard drugs into the community by construction workers in Colstrip.[45]

Like BMLA to the north, RPA sought the ear of anyone who would listen or might be able to help. They recruited members among other ranchers from the countryside as well as residents of Colstrip who were equally concerned about the social costs of building two 350-megawatt power plants in the town. Between 1968 and 1971, McRae made a name for himself as a passionate and articulate opponent of the proposed power plant and strip mines, leading the opposition at countless public meetings in

Colstrip, Forsyth, Billings, and Miles City and in the local newspapers. His "Marlboro Man" image made him an attractive symbol of the last defense of a dying way of life in the narrative portrayed by local newspapers and occasionally picked up by the national press. Nevertheless, by 1972, the confusing system of mineral ownership and leasing and the tangled mat of property, environmental, and health laws and regulations caught McRae and his neighbors in a bad situation. Generations of experience dealing with and, at times, prospering in the harsh environment of southeastern Montana provided little preparation for battle against determined corporations and the federal government, both of whom seemed to have the law on their side.[46]

While the members of BMLA were putting pressure on Consol and looking for help anywhere they could find it, they heard rumors and read newspaper articles about what was going on in Rosebud County. Boyd Charter knew McRae as a popular rodeo announcer. He called Wally and asked him to come to the Bull Mountains and share his experience with the BMLA and possibly even combine their efforts. "Boyd, I can't do it," McRae remembered telling Charter, "I'm just involved with so many things here."[47] McRae

FIGURE 2. Productive ranch land in the Powder River Basin in southeastern Montana, slated for strip mining, June 1973.

National Archives and Records Administration, photo no. 412-DA-6670.

empathized with what the Bull Mountain ranchers faced in the north, but he had his own issue and he was determined to resolve it himself. Who was he to meddle in the affairs of others? Besides, RPA was very different from BMLA. The group reflected the independence and tendency toward local politics and mutual assistance typical of the ranchers in his part of the state. Although membership in RPA typically implied family membership, male heads of households usually attended the meetings and acted as spokespersons for the group. BMLA not only elected women as officers, but also encouraged them to speak for the organization in the newspapers and at public events. BMLA also differed from RPA in where it sought help. BMLA was willing to accept help from anyone who would lend it, including a new player on the Montana political scene—environmentalists. McRae and RPA looked to the group that they thought best represented their interests as ranchers and landowners—the Montana Stockgrowers Association, who had just a few years prior passed resolutions condemning antiwar activism on college campuses. To call the Bull Mountain ranchers radicals would be a gross exaggeration, but to some of the Rosebud County ranchers, the BMLA seemed a little too liberal for comfort.[48] As daunting as the challenge from Peabody and Montana Power seemed, RPA would go it alone—at least for the time being.

A "Resource Council" Is Born

While RPA was busy near Colstrip, BMLA's campaign to save the ranches in the Bulls started down a different path. In spring 1972, the group prepared to take part in a coal symposium sponsored by the state of Montana in Billings scheduled for April 22, 1972. Organizers purported that the symposium would represent all sides of the controversy. Feeling isolated in the Bull Mountains, BMLA hoped that the event would attract landowners facing the threats of condemnation and degraded air and water quality and quality of life from other parts of the state. As the symposium came together, BMLA got word from ally Billie Hicks, a member of the Audubon Society who was on the planning board for the event, that the environmentalist on the panel was from North Dakota's Knife River Coal Company. To BMLA, it appeared that industry would dominate the symposium. Hicks told the BMLA to find their own environmentalist, and she would make sure that the expert got a seat on the panel. Not knowing where to turn, BMLA invited Cecil Garland, one of the founding members of the Montana Wilderness Association, to serve as their environmentalist.[49]

Garland, the owner of a sporting goods store in the small logging town of Lincoln, Montana, about 270 miles west of the Bull Mountains, was a citizen activist. He became politicized during the campaign to pass the Wilderness Act in the 1960s and in 1972 was leading the ultimately success-ful campaign for the first citizen-initiated wilderness designation under the Wilderness Act of an area along Montana's Continental Divide north of Lincoln. Garland accepted BMLA's invitation. When Anne Charter later called to tell him that the panel was full and that planners of the sympo-sium would not add Garland, he decided to come anyway. He would come to Billings a day early and, if BMLA gathered a few interested people, help the group plot their strategy. Eleven people met at Anne's home in Billings the evening before the symposium. They included the Charters, Tullys, Lou-ise Pfister and her daughter Ellen Pfister Withers, a young schoolteacher at Billings Senior High School named Dick Colberg and his friend, Billings native Pat Sweeney, John Redding from Sarpy Creek, and Laney Hicks from the Wyoming Sierra Club. Garland conducted the strategy session.[50]

Over the course of the evening, the idea for a larger umbrella organiza-tion arose repeatedly. The participants worried that it was so much work fighting one coal company—what if other companies leased minerals in the Bull Mountains and wanted to mine? BMLA needed more information, and the ranchers of the Bulls had no idea how or where to get it. They also recognized that the fight in the Bulls was not an isolated issue. Ranchers across the region were facing similar threats; the coal boom threatened not just their land and way of life but the rural character and agricultural via-bility of the entire region. BMLA realized that to fight the boom effectively, they needed to a larger organization to gather information about what was happening in other parts of the state and to combine the experiences and resources of all Montanans concerned about strip mining. Garland finally asked, "Why don't you just form one?" The group retorted, "How?" Garland told them, "All you need is a name, officers, membership dues and a let-terhead."[51] The group discussed the possibility for a long time—would the group be confined to working only on coal issues or defending agriculture, land, air, and water quality in general? Geographically, what would be its

territory? Who would be its members? Finally, the normally reserved Louise Pfister spoke up. She proposed that the northern Plains would be the
new group's territory, and if they called the group a "resource council,"
they would not be confined to coal. The group voted unanimously to form
the Northern Plains Resource Council. Each person present paid five dollars dues to become a charter member and elected officers including Dick
Colberg as president. The next day, the Northern Plains Resource Council
showed up at the symposium. Its members peppered the panel with questions. Charter remembered that they accomplished little except that they
"generated a lot of righteous indignation."[52] Generating righteous indignation was a significant part of the new group's strategy in its early days.

A few months later McRae ran across the Charters at a fair in Forsyth. McRae remembered Boyd Charter hollering from behind the Northern Plains informational and recruitment booth, "Wally, come over here
and join this organization." McRae responded, "Ah, I don't think I want
to, I think I'm doing OK on my own. I think I have more credibility as
a martyr—a lonely individual out there battling the giants of industry."
Charter retorted that McRae was just comfortable because he had received
a lot of publicity. "You're right about everything," Charter told him, "but
we're going to have a staff, we're putting together a staff now, and they're
going to do research; you don't have time to do research." Then, playing
to McRae's pride and independence, Charter told him, "you can still be
a spokesperson, you can still be a lonely put-upon martyr if you want to
be, but you need staff organization and research." McRae considered this
proposition. What Charter said made sense. He could still fight for his
ranch, but maybe the Resource Council could help with the legal wrangling and research that he and the RPA had neither the time nor skill to
conduct. McRae had read newspaper stories about this new group. He was
unsure that he wanted to be associated with these environmentalists, but
the Montana Stockgrowers were proving useless in his fight. He thought
about all of this, and then he signed up.[53]

Conclusion

With the recruitment of McRae and the Rosebud Protective Association,
the concerned landowners along the Tongue River and near Sarpy Creek,

and environmentally concerned residents from the rest of the state, Northern Plains quickly grew into a statewide organization. When its board identified the construction of Montana Power's Colstrip power plants as its top
priority, McRae and the other ranchers of Rosebud County finally found
the assistance they sought. As 1972 came to a close, the new organization
found itself on the leading edge of a growing local environmental movement. NPRC leaders realized that it was going to take a lot more than righteous indignation to stop the strip mines and power plants. To fully enter
into the political and legal arenas where they hoped to find a solution to
the issues of the coal boom, they needed a capable, energetic staff to do
research, more members, and allies. In the next few years, they would find
all three. NPRC looked forward to the 1973 Montana legislative session and
the possibility of passing state and federal laws to protect landowners from
strip mining or outlawing the activity altogether.

3

The Northern Plains Resource Council during the Environmental Decade

For the ranchers, farmers, and other concerned Montanans who came together to create the Northern Plains Resource Council, forming an organization was only the beginning. Founding members' recollections about the group's birth often glow with the nostalgia and inevitability that accompany a shared creation myth. However, whatever respite the formation of Northern Plains provided from the isolation felt by rural people confronting strip mining—whatever hope it kindled in the men and women who had listened fearfully to bureaucrats and politicians and boosters exclaim the benefits of coal development at their expense—it was soon overshadowed by the cold realities of the coal boom.

Northern Plains' founders hoped that the new group could unite landowners facing strip mining across the region and leverage the knowledge as well as the political and financial capital necessary to save the Plains. In many respects, they got what they hoped for. Soon after Northern Plains' formation, a new staff, supported by the meager membership dues, donations from the group's expanding membership, and some small grants, uncovered the full scale of the boom. In a display of the dogged determination that came to characterize the young organization, its staff combed land and mineral ownership records in courthouses across eastern Montana. Their findings were staggering: at least eighty-seven companies had leased more than a million acres of coal lands in eastern Montana and northeastern Wyoming, and applications to lease another 427,000 acres were underway. In total, about one and a half million acres, approximately

2,400 square miles, were slated for strip mining.[1] With so much development, early staff member Steve Charter, son of Anne and Boyd Charter,
described the new group's activities during its first few years as "putting
out brush fires"—desperately rushing to put out whatever flared up, never
knowing where the next blaze would ignite.[2]

To combat the conflagration, the members of Northern Plains developed strategies that defined the group's activities during the 1970s. Chief
among their early strategies was passing legislation to address the threats
strip mining posed to private property, the environment, and agriculture.
Although their tactics evolved within the context of the coal boom on the
northern Great Plains, they were typical of those of many citizens' environmental organizations during this first decade of the modern environmental movement. During this era, groups like Northern Plains tended to
interpret threats to their land, water, health, communities, or ways of life
as unjust failures of the law and government to protect what they often
referred to as the people or citizens. If a law did not exist to protect citizens and communities from unfair damages to property or safety, then the
most logical remedy was to pass a law to correct this oversight. Further,
they undergirded their arguments with the assumption that those most
affected by environmental decisions were those most qualified to take part
in environmental decision-making. Citizens' groups comprised of people
who shared interests in protecting their property, health, and communities
from a common threat tended to reflect the complexion of their membership. They usually were an assortment of people from many different occu-
pations. Few were scientists or experts in environmental management and
few were lawyers. However, they were Americans; they knew their rights,
and they thought they understood how government worked—that it was
supposed to be attentive to the welfare of the people. In their eyes, environmental threats were issues of fairness, justice, and governance. When it
appeared that the law and government were failing, citizens' groups organized to pass new laws. The Northern Plains Resource Council followed
this pattern.

The primary thrust of Northern Plains' early work was advocating laws
to prevent or at least temper the devastating effects of strip mining and
coal-fired power production in eastern Montana. At the state level, they
proposed four legislative solutions. The first was an outright moratorium

on strip mining. The second would amend Montana's eminent domain law to remove the ability of coal companies to use eminent domain to condemn ranches and farms for strip mining. The third would enhance the rights of landowners in split estate situations so that they could better control what happened on their property. Lastly, they proposed a law that would stringently regulate strip mining and require strip-mined lands to be reclaimed so that agriculture could continue after the boom. Although the reclamation issues proved to be very technical, the laws they advocated for mirrored much of the group's rhetoric. They sought legislative solutions aimed primarily at giving citizens a say in the decisions that affected their land, water, quality of life, and livelihoods. They favored democratic reforms that provided citizens access to information and environmental decision-making processes rather than technical, science-based prescriptions to the problems of the coal boom.

Montana's Shifting Political Landscape in the Early 1970s

As Northern Plains members looked forward to the 1973 legislative session, Montana's political landscape was shifting. Prior to 1965, rural landowners in the eastern part of the state held disproportionate power in state politics. Due to the way the state had drawn legislative districts, observers of Montana politics often quipped that eastern Montana cows had more of a vote than the residents of Missoula. In 1962, however, the U.S. Supreme Court's *Baker v. Carr* decision mandated legislative reapportionment to meet the "one man, one vote" requirements of the Fifteenth Amendment of the U.S. Constitution. When the state's legislative districts were adjusted in 1965 as a result of this decision, voters in the rural parts of the state, and especially in the east, lost voting clout. As the power of eastern Montanans waned, corporations like the Anaconda Mining Company and its subsidiary, the Montana Power Company, maintained an inordinate amount of influence in the legislature. Anaconda executives had written the state's constitution in 1889 to benefit the mining industry. In the 1970s, Anaconda and Montana Power continued to wield incredible sway through lobbying and financing political campaigns. Legislative reapportionment, however, had a silver lining for activists fighting the coal boom in the early 1970s. While it altered the makeup of the legislature and shifted power away from

its traditional rural locales to more populous areas in the central and western part of the state, this now more fully enfranchised electorate tended to
be more urban and environmentally aware.[3]

The passage of a number of protective environmental measures by
the state legislature during the early 1970s testified to the shift in political
power toward Montana's cities and the west and the increasing importance of environmental issues in state politics. The Montana Environmental Policy Act (MEPA), sponsored by Republican state senator George
Darrow of Billings, passed the state House and Senate in 1971 by nearly
unanimous votes. Like its federal counterpart, the National Environmental
Policy Act of 1969 (NEPA), it required environmental review and analysis
of state actions that could negatively affect the environment and required
the state to solicit citizen comment in environmental decisions. In addition,
MEPA created an Environmental Quality Council to review and research
environmental issues in the state and recommend policies to the legislature. Environmental organizations including the Montana Wilderness
Association, Montana chapter of the Sierra Club, and Montana Audubon Society joined with the Montana League of Women Voters and what
journalists identified as an especially strong "cowboy lobby" from eastern
Montana to counterbalance the Anaconda and Montana Power companies
during the 1971 session to pass a strip mine reclamation law. Though the
law was weak and never implemented due to lack of funding, this marked
a departure from business as usual in the Montana legislature. After 1972,
Northern Plains and another new group, the Montana Environmental
Information Center, swelled the ranks of the environmental lobby.[4]

Another important development was the state Constitutional Convention of 1971–1972 in which delegates rewrote Montana's constitution and
included significant new environmental and public participation mandates. Lauded nationally as a model of "participatory democracy" because
of its inclusion of people normally shut out of the halls of power, the
new constitution reorganized state government. Many of the convention
delegates—nineteen of whom were women—had never held any elected
political office and were largely independent of entrenched special interests. Montana's new constitution for the first time declared that each resident had an inalienable right to a "clean and healthful environment" and
required the reclamation of all lands "disturbed by the taking of natural

resources."[5] Importantly, the 1972 constitution required an unprecedented amount of citizen participation in the legislative process through public hearings, open meetings rules, and citizen right-to-know provisions. What historians have referred to as Montana's environmental decade was in full swing by the spring 1972, and the effects of environmentalism were rippling through the state. With these new favorable conditions in place, the members of the NPRC set their sights on passing laws to reform coal mining and protect their land.[6]

Looking toward Helena

In the roughly eight months between when Northern Plains' charter members paid their first dues and declared themselves an organization and the beginning of the 1973 legislative session, the group developed at a remarkable pace. Ranch kids Tom Tully, Steve Charter, and Paul Hawks combined efforts with Pat Sweeney and Kit Muller from Billings. Sweeney and Muller were refugees of the counterculture, Students for a Democratic Society, and the New Left who had finished college and then returned home to consider what to do next. They were critical of the war in Vietnam and worried about the real possibility of being drafted. Years later, Sweeney still remembered his draft lottery number. "I felt like the whole time I was in college, I had a bull's eye on my back," he recalled.[7] The young staff members, all of whom initially worked on a volunteer basis, were idealistic and energetic and offered a peculiar contrast to NPRC's conservative ranching members. To Wally McRae, they were a bunch of "wild-eyed, fuzzy-headed environmentalists."[8]

Whether they grew up on farms or ranches or in town, the young staff interpreted the threats represented by the coal boom and the *North Central Power Study* through a lens of Montana history that tied mineral extraction to exploitation. Sweeney graduated from the University of Montana—a regional hotbed of the counterculture and New Left politics during the 1960s and 1970s. He cited Montana historian K. Ross Toole's interpretation of Montana's copper kings, Gilded Age figures who sought to control the state's copper mining industry, and the Anaconda Mining Company's exploitation of the land and people of Montana as influencing how they understood the present threat.[9] Historian Dan Flores refers to an "anti-corporate *zeitgeist*": the Anaconda Mining Company's abuses of the environment and people were a pervasive element in Montana political culture in the postwar era. The early volunteer staff members came of age in this intellectual milieu. The intellectual, political, and cultural environment of the late 1960s and early 1970s, with its protests against the Vietnam War and critiques of industrialized capitalism combined with their experiences growing up in Montana in the postwar era, led them to be almost instinctively suspicious of corporations and to interpret the coal boom in terms of corporate greed and excess.[10]

Initially, Northern Plains was organized loosely around a board led by a chair, Billings high school teacher Dick Colberg. It met at least monthly between April and summer 1972 at Kit Muller's house in Billings. All members were encouraged to attend the monthly meetings where they updated the group on developments in their areas and discussed strategy. Over the course of these few months, the staff moved into Colberg's unused pottery studio on the third floor of the Stapleton Building in downtown Billings across the street from Montana Power Company's imposing office.[11] A skilled novelist could not have better orchestrated the "David and Goliath" symbolism in the situation. Beneath the gaze of this regional corporate giant, the five staff members worked feverishly tracking down coal leases, reading environmental assessments and impact statements, and brainstorming and organizing legal and legislative strategy.

As the staff worked, the ranchers, the leadership of the organization, slowly began to institutionalize the structure of the group. Ellen Pfister Withers returned from Mississippi in the summer 1972 with a law degree in hand and assumed the responsibility of overseeing the new Billings office and staff. By that summer, the board approved bylaws for the organization that clearly delineated roles for members and staff: members were to make decisions regarding issue positions and strategies for the organization through democratic processes and serve as leaders and spokespeople for the group; the staff were to research, organize, and provide information and strategy suggestions to the board as well as implement the board's decisions. Under the new bylaws, the staff was paid two hundred dollars a month from dues and whatever other money the group could raise. When Colberg resigned his chairmanship to run for the 1973 session of the Montana State House, the members elected Withers chair.[12]

Understanding the need to organize its membership and win allies, Withers and the staff went to work in summer 1972. Before forming Northern Plains, BMLA and RPA members found it easy to organize over the relatively small geographic areas they were concerned with through word of mouth and personal meetings. Northern Plains organized a region of the state that stretched hundreds of miles and included thousands of people, usually living in sparsely populated communities or counties. They had phones, although some, like those in the tiny village of Birney along the Tongue River, were still party lines where residents could listen in on their neighbors' conversations. Other forms of communication were difficult. To bridge the gap, Withers and Anne Charter produced the group's first newsletter in summer 1972.[13]

Typewritten on four 8½ by 11 inch pages, the austere form of the first newsletter of the Northern Plains Resource Council followed its practical function. In straightforward terms, it explained what was at issue, unambiguously defined the sides in the conflict, and informed readers how to defend themselves. It maintained a stark sense of "Us" Montanans versus "Them" coal companies. "Did Anybody Ask You If 'They' Could Do This to Montana?" asked one headline.[14] The first issue described the *North Central Power Study* and the coal boom. It took statistics directly from the Bureau of Reclamation's study and interpreted them for readers, tying the coal boom to the national energy crisis and explaining that oil companies were acquiring coal companies due to shortfalls in oil production. Finally, the newsletter informed readers about developments in Congress and explained legislative proposals to expand surface owner rights to defend their land from strip mining and to reclaim strip-mined land so that it could return to productive use.[15]

After explaining the situation in eastern Montana as they understood it, Withers and Charter implored the readership to take action—a strategy that became standard for the organization. An "action needed" section implored members to write or wire their senators immediately and encourage them to support West Virginia senator Ken Hechler's strip mine reclamation bill in Congress. Part of the newsletter informed readers about activities within the organization, including updates on members' trips to Washington, DC, to lobby or Appalachia to meet with other anti-strip-mining groups. Through its language and reporting, the newsletter imparted a vigorous right to participate in the decision-making process despite the challenges wealth, power, and distance presented the Northern Plains ranchers.[16]

In the last two pages of the newsletter, the authors outlined the devices coal companies used against surface owners—what they called "battle tactics"—and how to combat them. They warned, "DON'T lease for any reason," and provided questions landowners should ask of land men, coal company representatives, if they should visit the readers' homes.[17] The newsletter advised landowners to find legal representation independent of the coal companies. They warned members not to talk to land men without witnesses present and not to sign anything "without competent legal counsel."[18] The newsletter encouraged landowners to talk to each other and not allow land men to exploit the "code of the West" that neighbors did not meddle in each other's business.[19] In their list of allies, they named the new, affiliated Birney Land Protection Association, the League of Women Voters, and a handful of environmental groups including the Montana chapter of the Sierra Club and Montana Wilderness Association. They also listed political allies including Senators Mike Mansfield and Lee Metcalf and Representatives John Melcher and Dick Shoup, as well as Wyoming's congressional delegation. Lastly, they made a pitch for membership. Five dollars a year would guarantee one's membership in the organization and receipt of the newsletter, which they described as a "clearing house for spreading information and getting the right people in touch with each other."[20] "Only by standing together," Wither and Charter wrote, "can we live in an unpolluted and beautiful land."[21] By the following January and beginning of the 1973 Montana legislative session, the newsletter, renamed the *Plains Truth*, had become a regular publication and source of information for people concerned about the coal boom.

From its inception, NPRC's members had realized the importance of finding and working with allies. BMLA had relied on help from the Wyoming Sierra Club and the Montana Wilderness Association to organize the young group and had worked extensively with new allies at the Environmental Policy Center in Washington, DC, and citizens' organizations from Appalachia in opposing strip mining at the federal level. In the last months of 1972, in advance of the 1973 legislative session, NPRC members and staff made trips out of state to rally the support of others sympathetic to their cause.[22]

In the next few months, Carolyn Alderson and Anne McKinney, ranchers near the Hanging Woman Creek site of a proposed 10,000-megawatt power plant, busily worked with allies to lobby their cases. Alderson traveled with a group of ranchers facing similar issues across the border in Wyoming to Washington, DC, to lobby for the defeat of a weak Senate surface mining bill and in support of a stronger House bill. McKinney traveled to the state capital, Helena, to lobby the members of the Montana Stockgrowers Association to adopt some of the Northern Plains positions regarding strip mining. On October 6, the traditionally conservative ranching organization voted to call for stronger regulations of strip mining, including requiring that mining companies reestablish forage plants on the lands they disturbed during mining and post a bond of $1,000 per acre to pay for reclamation of mined lands. The Stock Growers also called for a prohibition of mining in lands that were impossible to reclaim or lands that were of historical or archeological interest. Soon after, Alderson traveled to an energy conference in Sheridan, Wyoming, where she warned officials from a collection of oil, gas, coal, and power companies to "not underestimate the people of this area." She told them, "Do not make the mistake of lumping us and the land altogether as 'overburden' and dispense with us as nuisance." With a somewhat ironic reference to the Native Americans who inhabited the land now owned by ranchers, she told the meeting, "We are the descendants, spiritually, if not actually, of those who fought for this land once, and we are prepared to do it again. . . . We intend to win."[23]

Staffer Kit Muller and member Bill Bryan traveled to San Francisco in late November 1972 to meet with allies and potential funders and held a press conference including a film on strip mining in Wyoming in hopes of attracting political and financial support outside the region. In early December, representatives from the Environmental Defense Fund and Natural Resources Defense Council met with NPRC staff and members in Billings for three days to discuss legal strategies and possible policy issues and prescriptions. Representatives from the state Environmental Quality Council and Montana Wildlife Federation met with Northern Plains members on December 12 to advise the group on legislative strategy. The

Montana Wilderness Association passed a resolution calling for a four-year moratorium on strip mining. With the support of their allies both in Montana and out of state, NPRC prepared for the 1973 legislative session.[24]

The 1973 Montana Legislative Session

As Northern Plains began its legislative work in January 1973, all of its work to elevate the coal boom issue paid off. Compared to the previous session in 1971, coal strip mining was a well-publicized issue in the press and in state politics by 1973, and the issue colored Montana politics. During the 1972 state constitutional convention, the chair of the Natural Resource Committee, Louise Cross of Glendive, a region in eastern Montana slated for strip mining, identified the environmental problems associated with the coal boom as her primary concern in advocating for a strong environmental section of the constitution.[25] Delegates to the convention in 1972 were familiar with the debates over coal mining and reclamation in the 1971 legislative session. Over the following year, they read dozens of articles in state newspapers illuminating the prospects of strip mining in the region. By the time the 1973 legislative session got underway, both political parties had taken critical positions on strip mining. In fall 1972, the Montana Democratic party adopted a conservation and environment plank that called for a moratorium on any further strip mining until the legislature passed the following protections: a land reclamation bill that guaranteed restoration of mined lands to their original or higher use including the establishment of self-sustaining vegetation, a law guaranteeing water rights and the protection of water quality from mining pollution, an amendment of the state's eminent domain laws so that coal companies could not condemn private land under the guise that coal mining was a necessary public good, a law regulating air quality, and a commitment by the state and nation to an energy policy reliant on "clean alternative energy supply."[26] The Montana Republican Party, at the instigation of Billings senator George Darrow and with testimony from NPRC's Bob Tully, passed a resolution that called for reclamation and "adequate protections" for surface and groundwater as well as air quality.[27] The Republican resolution also recommended that the legislature give landowners a better ability to protect their private property in split estate situations where the property rights of surface and

mineral owners came into conflict.[28] With the official support of both parties for their general legislative aims, it appeared that Northern Plains was
in a strong position to push for meaningful legislation.

One of the immediate threats landowners faced from the proposed
strip mining was the ability of coal companies to condemn their land
under old eminent domain laws. Originating under English common law
to allow for the condemnation of private land for construction of public
(or royal) necessities or amenities, eminent domain has been used in the
United States since the nation's inception for the building of roads, railroads, dams, and public buildings. During the energy crisis and coal boom
of the 1970s, coal companies used this legal power to remove landowners
whose property overlaid the coal beds by arguing that it was in the public's
interest to mine the coal. Landowners faced an indefensible position in
trying to retain their property: either agree to the coal company's terms or
be condemned and removed, and accept what the courts considered fair
compensation. In 1973, now State Representative Richard Colberg, a Democrat from Billings, introduced House Bill 238, which removed coal strip
mining from the definition of public use in Montana's eminent domain
law. Northern Plains members and legislators argued that it was unjust to
allow private companies to use the power of the state to deprive citizens
of their property. The apparent injustice of the situation resonated with
legislators; the House voted for the bill 86–11, and the Senate concurred
by voice vote. On March 17, 1973, Governor Thomas Judge signed the bill
into law.[29]

Amending the state's eminent domain laws to protect landowners from strip mining had broad support. What position to take regarding strip mining itself, however, was more controversial. Some Northern
Plains members proposed to ban strip mining altogether. The coal in the
Northern Great Plains was low-sulfur lignite that burned cleaner and was
closer to the surface than the coal mined in the Midwest and Appalachia
but because of high transportation costs, it was only profitable for export
out of the state if it was strip-mined. A ban could end large-scale coal mining in Montana. Many Montanans including the Charters and Pfisters near
the Bull Mountains, the McRaes, Baileys, Golders, and others near Colstrip,
and the Hayes, McKinneys, and Aldersons near Birney welcomed the idea
of a ban that would spare the rolling hills and coulees of their regions from

strip mining. The environmental devastation in the Appalachian coalfields provided a vivid illustration of what could happen to Montana if the state allowed large-scale, unregulated strip mining.[30] In a letter to the editor of the *Billings Gazette*, senior Montana senator Mike Mansfield recommended a ban until protective environmental laws were in place.[31] But what if a ban bill failed? Would the landowners go home empty-handed and have to wait another two years to try to convince a new legislature to rein in strip mining? The bulldozers were practically at their doorsteps.

The decision they made proved definitive for how the organization addressed strip mining and other environmental problems in the future and was crucial to maintaining their ability to support meaningful legislation during the 1970s. While most of their members opposed strip mining outright and supported a full ban, the organization itself assumed a middle ground. The NPRC proposed a bill sponsored by Democratic representative Dorothy Bradley of Bozeman that would enact a three-year moratorium on strip mining to give the state and federal agencies time to study strip mining and reclamation and enact regulations to protect the environment and people. Bradley's HR 492 came within one vote of passing in the House. Encouraged by the close vote, Northern Plains redoubled its efforts to pass a revised bill, lobbying hard for provisions that expanded citizen participation rules and gave landowners the power to negotiate terms to protect their property. Over the course of one long night in early 1973, determined Northern Plains members Ellen Pfister Withers, Bob Tully, staff member Kit Muller, and young lobbyist Pat Sweeney hammered out the draft of what would become Montana's first coal mine reclamation bill, House Bill 555, sponsored by Colberg. They studied recent national and state-level environmental laws, including NEPA and the Montana Environmental Policy Act, as well as the recently passed state constitution, from which they borrowed public notice and participation provisions. Colberg eventually merged HB 555 with a similar bill in the Senate to become the Montana Strip and Underground Mine Reclamation Act. It passed by a near unanimous vote, and Governor Judge signed it into law in mid-March 1973. In its final form, the law required that before strip mining could commence, coal companies had to prepare a mining plan that included detailed prescriptions for restoring the land to its pre-mining condition, including native vegetation and the approximate original contour of the landscape; obtain a permit from the state in a process that provided for citizen oversight and appeal; and complete environmental impact statements under both the National Environmental Policy Act and the Montana Environmental Policy Act. To pay for post-mining reclamation, the state required that companies purchase bonds to ensure the reclamation would be completed and stipulated that the cost to restore mined lands could not be shifted to the residents of the state.[32]

Pushing reforms further, Northern Plains worked with other environmental organizations and concerned citizens to help pass a Utilities Siting Act. House Bill 127, sponsored by Senator Francis Bardanouve (D-Fort Benton), created a permitting process to regulate power plant and power line construction. Supporters included representatives from the Department of Health and Environmental Sciences. Don Bailey seconded their support, as did Jim Murray, a representative of the Montana chapter of the American Federation of Labor Congress of Industrial Organizations (AFL-CIO). Regulation, it appeared, served multiple purposes for the different interests. While Bailey, along with McRae and other members of RPA and NPRC from the Colstrip area, hoped that the Utility Siting Act would force Montana Power and Puget Sound Power and Light to follow new environmental laws and possibly even prevent the plant's construction, state regulators and union leadership hoped the law would provide needed regulatory consistency and certainty to prevent the kinds of lawsuits Northern Plains was currently pursuing against the state and Montana Power. Once the bill had the state's support, it was likely to pass; utility companies felt that they could operate within the regulatory structure it created based on their continued close relationships with state regulators. No one opposed the legislation. Representatives from the Montana Farmers Union, a historically progressive farmers' organization, and the American Association of University Women supported the bill because its provisions increased public involvement in the power plant permitting process. The legislature passed the Utilities Siting Act in 1973 to address environmental and social issues associated with the construction of electric power plants, including those fired by coal, and the transmission lines they needed to move their product to consumers. In the next few years, the law provided Northern Plains with a powerful tool to challenge the construction of additional plants at Colstrip and in other parts of the state and their transmission lines, which were proposed to march west across Montana to the Pacific Northwest.[33]

Finally, mining opponents introduced a bill during the 1973 legislative session to ban all strip mining by 1977. Its hearing drew a sizeable and enthusiastic crowd, including ranchers from eastern Montana, representatives from Montana's small environmental lobby and the League of Women Voters, and a handful of concerned voters. Also in attendance was J. W. Bradley, the president of a newly formed anti-strip-mining group from Tennessee called Save Our Cumberland Mountains, who brought warnings of what might be in store for Montana. The hearing did not include any self-identified representatives of the Northern Plains Resource Council.[34] NPRC may have viewed the strip mine ban bill, House Bill 391 sponsored by Representative Barbara Bennetts, a Democrat from Helena, strategically as a radical alternative that could sway legislators to the less radical NPRC-backed reclamation bill, but the organization remained silent on the issue. While never enacted, the strip mine ban added to the chorus of calls to ban strip mining springing up all over the coal mining regions of the United States at the time.

As the 1973 legislative session wound to a close, Northern Plains, a nascent and wily collection of roughly three hundred families from agricultural and urban backgrounds, could claim a number of victories. Land could no longer be condemned for coal strip mining under Montana's eminent domain law, the state now regulated coal strip mining and required mining companies to reclaim the lands they disturbed, the state regulated the construction of major power plants and their transmission lines, and the permitting process was opened to public scrutiny. NPRC had not stopped strip mining. However, their efforts helped ensure its regulation, that mining companies and not the citizens of Montana would bear the external costs of strip mining and coal-fired power production, and that citizens would have a say in environmental decisions regarding the coal boom.[35]

By the end of the 1973 legislative session, Northern Plains had successfully catapulted the issue of strip mining in eastern Montana to the forefront of state public discourse and policy making. In a little less than two years, what seemed like a local issue affecting a few landowners in the Bull Mountains north of Billings or a handful of ranchers near Colstrip had turned into one of the state's biggest political issues. By mid-1973, articles on coal strip mining or coal-fired energy production appeared almost daily in the *Billings Gazette* and other state newspapers. Its trajectory as an increasingly hot topic was aided by a collective recognition of the potential scope of the coal boom by Montana newspapers and policymakers. It just took a few years for the numbers—twenty-one coal-fired power plants dotting the landscape and polluting the air, new dams and power lines, and dozens of new strip mines—to sink in and for the public to react.

"Cowgirls [and Cowboys] in the Capitol": The Campaign for a Federal Strip Mining Bill

Northern Plains members always recognized that the coal boom crossed state borders and that a real solution to the threats it posed to rural communities, the environment, and agriculture required federal action. In 1971, Bull Mountain ranchers Anne Charter, Ellen Pfister Withers, and Vera Beth Johnson traveled to Washington, DC, to testify at a House hearing on strip mining regulation aided by Montana senator Lee Metcalf and Wyoming senator Cliff Hansen, a supporter of the coal industry but long-time friend of Anne's husband Boyd. In her autobiography, Charter referred to the trip as "Cowgirls in the Capitol," and area newspapers remarked on the uniqueness of the women's trip to Washington.[36] As unconventional lobbyists as the women may have been, they made an impression and laid the ground for a lasting relationship between the organization, Montana's congressional delegation, and representatives and senators from other states who would prove invaluable in promoting a federal strip mining reclamation and regulation law. Perhaps equally important as creating personal relationships with powerful members of important committees, Charter, Pfister, and Johnson connected with the Washington-based Environmental Policy Center, headed by Louise Dunlap, who was organizing opponents of strip mining across the country into the Coalition Against Strip Mining. As part of their trip east, the women attended the National Conference on Strip Mining sponsored by Democratic congressman Fred Harris of West Virginia in Middleboro, Kentucky. At the meeting, they came in direct contact with the ravages of strip mining in Appalachia and with miners who had come to the conference with the intent of breaking it up. No disturbances ensued, however, and the women returned to Montana emboldened as members of a growing national movement for strong federal strip mine regulation.[37]

Their efforts began with Montana's congressional delegation. Powerful Democratic senators Mike Mansfield and Lee Metcalf and Montana's congressmen, Democrat John Melcher and Republican Dick Sharp drew support from the state's powerful mining unions and could hardly resist pressure from the Anaconda and Montana Power Companies. However, the dramatic changes proposed in the *North Central Power Study* alarmed the congressmen. The threats the coal boom posed to Montana's agricultural economy and quality of life prompted them to articulate new values for the natural environment as an essential element of the state. In October 1972, reeling from congressional criticism of the *North Central Power Study*, the Department of the Interior shelved the document and morphed its findings and proposals into a regional study process, the Northern Great Plains Resource Program (NGPRP). Unlike the conventional environmental impact statement requested by Montana environmentalists the following year, which was meant to inform agency decision-making of environmental impacts before the damage was done, the NGPRP would attempt to study future impacts while strip mines, power plants, dams, and all other necessary infrastructure were being built.[38] Representative Melcher slammed the proposal immediately. He called the study a farce if Congress failed first to pass strong provisions for strip mine reclamation before mining commenced.[39] In December 1972, Mansfield and Metcalf joined other senators in voting for a resolution calling for a moratorium on expanded strip mining in Montana until a comprehensive study was completed. When the Department of Interior and the Nixon administration dismissed the resolution on the grounds that current laws adequately addressed the issues that concerned the senators, the senators cited a recent study from the General Accounting Office, which found that supervision and enforcement of coal leasing was lax at best.[40] By early 1973, Montana's congressional delegation understood that despite their protests, the Department of the Interior planned to allow extensive development of coal mining without conducting any kind of meaningful study of the environmental impacts. Directed by President Nixon to increase domestic coal production, the department ignored their calls for a moratorium on leasing and mining until a study was completed. Mansfield, Metcalf, and Melcher joined the growing group of congressional representatives led by delegations from Appalachia, who had been fighting strip mining since the late 1960s, who believed that passing federal legislation to regulate the boom was the only solution.

Over the next two years, Dunlap, the Environmental Policy Center, and the Coalition Against Strip Mining continued to organize advocates for federal strip mine regulation and reclamation from Washington, DC. Throughout 1972 and 1973, they recruited Northern Plains members to return to the Capitol to lobby congressmen. Charter made several more trips accompanied by Pfister, Wally McRae, and Carolyn and Irving Alderson. After the successful passage of the Montana Surface Mine Reclamation Act by the Montana State Legislature in 1973, Northern Plains decided to focus more of its efforts on passing national legislation. In addition to their continuing work on the proposed Colstrip plant and responding to new proposals in the northeastern part of the state, the group elected to send staffer Pat Sweeney to the national capital to work with Dunlap and the Environmental Policy Center to promote a federal bill in summer 1973. Sweeney took the newly passed Montana act with him.[41]

Sweeney arrived in Washington when coal strip mining politics were shifting decidedly to the West and away from a ban on strip mining toward stricter regulation and reclamation. It is important to note that large-scale strip mining began in Appalachia a decade before it was proposed in the West. Because of land ownership patterns, geography, rainfall, and a century-long history of coal extraction, the issues surrounding coal strip mining in West Virginia, Virginia, Kentucky, Tennessee, Ohio, and Pennsylvania were very different from those in the West. So were the politics. Most of the people living in the areas proposed for strip mining in Appalachia had long ties to underground coal mining. They were working-class people who often lived on land owned by coal companies; they owned neither their houses, nor the land they sat on, nor the coal beneath them. Living in the valleys below the mines, they were the backbone of the United Mine Workers in the region, and they were Democrats. The transition to strip mining spurred by increased demand and higher prices for coal and enabled by new earth-moving technologies presented real threats to the environment and worker health, livelihood, and lives. Strip mining removed coal more efficiently with far fewer workers than underground mining, and those workers were usually nonunion. When the overburden of the mines, the topsoil, and rock overlying coal seams was removed, it was placed below the mine on steep slopes clear-cut of timber prior to mining. On multiple occasions, prolonged periods of rain or heavy storms, typical in this moist climate, saturated the overburden, which burst through hastily built earthen retaining dams and cascaded into the valleys below regardless of what or who was in its way. This prompted Representative Ken Hechler of West Virginia to introduce a ban on strip mining in Congress in 1971, which garnered seventy-three cosponsors in the House from twenty-four states but failed to pass. The *North Central Power Study*, with its emphasis on coal development in the West, added the new issues associated with split surface and mineral estate ownership and reclamation, new advocates for legislation, and new congressional voices to the debate. By 1973, Montana senator Mansfield was majority leader of the Senate and Senator Metcalf was chair of the Senate Mining Committee, while Representative Melcher sat on the House Natural Resources Committee. Sweeney and Northern Plains, along with the membership of the newly formed Powder River Basin Resource Council in Wyoming, found themselves at the forefront of this expanded strip mining debate.[42]

From their shared offices on C Street near Pennsylvania Avenue in Washington, Dunlap and Sweeney, along with lobbyists John McCormick of the Environmental Policy Center and Brock Evans of the Sierra Club, wrote the first draft of the Surface Control and Reclamation Act in late 1973. On Northern Plains' behalf, Sweeney introduced three objectives for the legislation, two of which were integral in the Montana legislation. The first addressed the issue of surface owner consent that gave landowners a say in how, when, and if coal mines operated on their property when they were extracting minerals owned by someone other than the surface owner. This profoundly western issue was the primary concern for Northern Plains' ranching and farming members: losing control of their property and livelihood. The second objective was to set up a regulation and reclamation process that was transparent and publicly accessible: a permitting program in which the public, including environmental organizations, could review the details of the proposed project, its scope, and environmental impacts, and then comment on the proposal and appeal the agency permitting decisions. Reclamation with standards concerning to what degree of agricultural productivity the land must be returned, including restoring its approximate original contour and the hydrologic balance of area water resources, would be required as part of the mining plan. Lastly, Sweeney introduced a provision that was specific to the Montana situation but would eventually be used extensively by citizens in other regions to protect special places from coal mining. The "lands unsuitable for mining" provision was meant to ban mining in the Custer National Forest, the only national forest in the eastern part of the state and a favorite recreation site for many residents, where many Northern Plains members either had leases to graze cattle or adjacent property.[43]

As the ink from the governor's pen was drying on the Montana Surface Mine Reclamation Act in Helena, the U.S. Senate and House were considering national versions of the legislation in Washington. The Environmental Policy Center had been working with a collection of citizens groups from Kentucky, West Virginia, and Tennessee, in addition to the newcomers from the West, to identify sponsors who would move a strong bill through Congress to the president's desk. Their priority sponsors were senators and representatives from western states who possessed substantial coal reserves and sat on the House or Senate committees that would serve as the primary venue for considering mining bills. In the House, this included Representative Morris Udall from Arizona, site of the expanding Black Mesa coal mine and proposed giant Navajo Generating Station. In the Senate, they fostered a relationship with Senator Lee Metcalf and Senate Majority Leader Mike Mansfield, both from Montana. They ultimately tied their fate, however, to powerful Senator Henry "Scoop" Jackson from Washington State who sat on the Senate Committee on the Interior and Insular Affairs and had championed landmark environmental laws including the National Environmental Policy Act. Meanwhile, the Nixon administration, which increasingly promoted coal as a central component of its energy agenda, realized that strip mining was a growing national environmental concern for the public. If coal strip mining was going to make the United States energy independent, then it would have to be at least minimally regulated or, as Ken Hechler's narrowly defeated attempts to prohibit strip mining had shown, public opinion might be sufficient to ban it altogether. With this in mind, the administration introduced its own language and also recruited Jackson to carry it. In the House, strip mining opponents recruited Republican representative John Saylor from Pennsylvania to introduce and carry a version of their strip mine regulation and reclamation bill.[44]

The bills introduced by Senator Jackson, the administration, and Representative Saylor in 1973 represented three general positions in the national debate over strip mining and how to regulate and mitigate its effects. The process of passing federal strip mining legislation moved between these three poles. The first, represented by Saylor's HR 5988 in 1973, was the environmentalists' option with specific and stringent requirements for permitting, regulation, reclamation, and coal company bonding for damages as well as opportunities for citizen participation and enforcement of the law and standards through citizen suits. Under this option, the law would be implemented by the states under the watchful eye of an agency within the U.S. Department of Interior. Saylor's bill included Northern Plains' highest-priority provisions, including requiring consent of the surface owner in split-estate situations, citizen participation and right to sue during the entire process, and a provision allowing the secretary of the interior to prohibit strip mining on lands deemed unsuitable for mining.[45]

At the other end of the spectrum was the administration's bill, introduced as S 923, sponsored by Senator Jackson, in the Senate and as HR 3 in the House. The administration bill left enforcement of permitting and reclamation standards up to the states except where the federal government controlled both the surface and underground property (i.e., certain tracts of public land such as national forest or those managed by the Bureau of Land Management). The bill did not require a permit from mine operators until an acceptable state or federal program was created, allowing mining companies to operate for up to seven and a half years largely without government and citizen oversight and review. The administration bill solved this potential problem by requiring a permit for prospecting and mining that was good for the life of the mining operation but provided no specific application requirements.[46] In contrast to the Saylor bill, the performance standards contained in the bill were ambiguous and general. Perhaps most disturbing to environmentalists was the fact that the administration bill contained no provisions requiring the states to carry out reviews or provide public notices of permitting decisions or hearings. It did not address the issue of landowner consent or redress for citizens, for example via lawsuits, from coal mine operators or state and federal agencies that failed to comply with the law. Lastly, it ignored the reclamation of mines, an important issue for coal mining communities in Appalachia, except to release mine operators from certain reclamation requirements if the cost of reclaiming an area mined before the passage of the act was financially impractical.[47]

The final proposal, the Surface Mining Reclamation Act of 1973 or S 425, also sponsored by Senator Jackson, lay somewhere between the two extremes. Like the administration bill, it left primary enforcement of mining and reclamation permitting and regulations with the state but with federal oversight by an agency within the Department of the Interior. It required permits within fifteen months of the bill's enactment instead of four and a half to seven and a half years. Until that time, the bill enacted a moratorium on all new surface coal mining unless the mines were the only sources of coal for electric or metallurgical plants or if a contract to supply coal had been made before enactment. Unlike the administration bill, it provided detailed requirements for the permitting process and a performance bond to pay for reclamation. Its reclamation requirements were similar to Saylor's bill except that it considered acceptable highwalls, spoil banks, and water impoundments at the end of the mining operations if they were deemed stable, a point of contention for citizens in Appalachia and the West. Like Saylor's bill, it included provisions to bar mining from lands deemed unsuitable and required the written consent of surface owners in split-estate situations before mining could commence. The Surface Mine Reclamation Act of 1973 included provisions requiring public participation equivalent to those in Saylor's bill, but it lacked a provision allowing citizens to sue to enforce the law. In the House, the Coalition Against Strip Mining, Environmental Policy Center, Northern Plains, and Sierra Club worked with Arizona representative Morris Udall to sponsor a comparable bill in HR 11500. In addition to these four bills, at least eight more were introduced in the House and Senate in 1973 and 1974 that fell somewhere within the spectrum.[48]

By the end of the 93rd Congress in spring 1974, various parts of many of these bills were amended into Jackson's S 425 and Udall's HR 11500 as it became clear that these were the pieces of legislation with the best chance of passage. Northern Plains and the Environmental Policy Center continued to lobby for provisions that would create an effective permitting and

reclamation program that protected surface owners in split-estate situations, require transparency and citizen participation in decision-making,
and preserve the ability of the Department of Interior to prohibit mining in areas of special concern like Montana's Custer National Forest.
The organizations were able to get all of these provisions into the bills in
some form. They then threw their support and their entire professional
and citizen lobbying power behind both measures. Their efforts paid off
in fall 1974. During the floor debates, Senate Majority Leader Mike Mansfield of Montana, who had been invited to tour the ranches of Rosebud
County and Birney, and whom the Charters, Pfisters, McRaes, and Aldersons had lobbied personally and through countless letters and telegrams,
brought Northern Plains' position to the Senate floor in the debate over
S 425. Employing romantic rhetoric that conjured up the mythic western
frontier, the senior senator from Montana told the body, "I rise to speak
not only about the coal situation in general, but also about a minority of
the population in the state which I have the honor and the privilege to
represent, a minority also in the Dakotas and in the state of Wyoming,
a minority which usually votes Republican, a minority which is entitled
to consideration, and a minority which, in many respects, comprises the
last of the rugged individuals in this country."[49] He stressed that the cattle ranchers and wheat farmers of the Northern Plains had homesteaded
the land before, during, and after the era of the railroads and that their
investment in the land should not be sacrificed for coal development. He
continued along this theme: "They want the fresh air to remain. They want
to have a say about whether the subsurface rights on the land which they
occupied and developed is or is not going to be subject to some . . . force
outside the families which developed this land."[50] Mansfield's leadership
helped carry the issue in the Senate. Meanwhile, Udall's HR 11500 passed
in the House, and the two were reconciled through a conference committee in fall 1974 combined as a single bill under S 425. Almost two years after
its introduction, the Surface Mining Reclamation Act of 1973 passed the
Senate and House in mid-December 1974 and was on its way to the White
House for President Gerald Ford's signature. The administration, however,
heeded the protests of groups like the Virginia Surface Mining and Reclamation Association, which described the bill as death to their industry
by slow strangulation. Despite the hundreds of phone calls and telegrams

from concerned citizens across the county, on December 30, the president quietly killed the bill through a pocket veto.[51]

Ford's veto disappointed members of the Coalition and Northern Plains. However disillusioning it was, the bill itself, reflecting months of compromise between sponsors and stakeholders and hundreds of hours of research by the Environmental Policy Center, Coalition, Sierra Club, and Northern Plains, had now been written. The "people power" organized to turn out phone calls and telegrams from citizens to members of Congress and the president remained in place. The organizations' paid lobbyists were more seasoned, and citizen lobbyists emerged in early 1975 energized and committed to pass the legislation again. The acceleration of the Colstrip power plant plans and organization of citizens along the Colstrip transmission routes in Montana as well as a proposed mine and power plant near Circle in northeastern Montana provided even more citizen activists representing a broader portion of the region's constituency to pressure politicians. President Ford, however, announced an expanded version of his predecessor's Project Independence, including the construction of 200 new nuclear power plants, 250 new coal mines, 150 new coal-fired power plants, 20 new synthetic fuel plants that would convert coal to gasoline, and 30 new oil refineries, as part of his State of the Union message in January 1975. Northern Plains responded by ramping up its efforts.[52]

When the new session of Congress began in January 1975, with substantially larger Democratic majorities in the House and the Senate, Northern Plains and its allies in the Coalition Against Strip Mining, now cleverly referring to themselves as the "COALition," debated strategy. The groups and their allies in Congress decided to reintroduce the surface mining bill. Attesting to the support for regulating strip mining and creating a system of reclamation, twenty-two bills were introduced in the 94th session of Congress. Of these, the two that emerged as the most promising were Representative Morris Udall's Surface Mining Control and Reclamation Act HR 25, and a Senate version of the same bill, S 7, again sponsored by Senator Henry Jackson of Washington. Both were quickly passed by early March 1975, and Jackson's bill was folded into Udall's HR 25. It passed the Senate by voice vote and in the House by two votes more than the two-thirds majority required to override a presidential veto. Understanding that he might not be able to veto the legislation, President Ford employed Frank

Zarb of the Federal Energy Administration to lobby against the bill while its two versions were being considered in conference committee. Between the bill's passage and President Ford's threatened veto, Zarb and the coal-utility industry lobby turned five votes. The House vote to override Ford's veto failed, 273 to 143, just three votes shy of the necessary two-thirds needed. For a second time, federal strip mining regulation and reclamation legislation languished on the president's desk. It appeared that passage of federal legislation would have to wait for a change in the White House.[53]

That change came in November 1976, when Georgia's Democratic governor, James Earl Carter, successfully beat incumbent President Ford in the race for president. The election of 1976 also increased the Democratic Party's share of seats in the House and Senate, resulting in a two-thirds majority in the House and a filibuster-proof sixty-one-seat majority in the Senate. Representative Morris Udall, who had championed the Surface Mining Control and Reclamation Act in the previous two sessions of Congress and had lost the Democratic presidential nomination to Carter, became chair of the House Interior and Insular Affairs Committee, a prime position from which to control the crafting and passage of the strip mining bill through the House. On January 4, 1977, as the new session of Congress opened, Udall reintroduced the language that been agreed upon and passed through both houses in 1975. The COALition and Northern Plains turned out hundreds of phone calls and telegrams in support. By April, a large majority in the House passed the Udall bill, and by mid-May, it was merged with its companion bill in the Senate, S 7, sponsored again by Senator Jackson, and passed by the Senate. On July 25, it was ready for the president's signature. A little more than a week later, Northern Plains members Carolyn Alderson and Art and Marilynn Hayes of Birney, Gordon and Helen Waller of Circle, and now-staff director Pat Sweeney joined members of the COALition, Louise Dunlap, sponsors Representative Morris K. Udall and Senator Henry Jackson in witnessing President Carter sign the Surface Mining Control and Reclamation Act of 1977 (SMCRA, pronounced "smack-ra") into law. Now coal mining states, mining companies, and the membership and staff of Northern Plains as well as similar organizations around the country would have to figure out what it all meant.[54]

After SMCRA: 1977–1980

At the end of the 1970s, this still young coalition of ranchers, farmers, and environmentalists had done a lot to make the members proud. By the end of 1979, Northern Plains had fully engaged the coal boom, organizing residents around the state in fifteen community-based affiliate organizations, and maintained two staffed field offices in Billings and Glendive. While its membership grew to several thousand, its work was still largely dependent on the volunteer work of members. The staff had only grown to eleven. The rest of the work—turning out members for hearings, comments for environmental impact statements and other agency studies, and phone calls and telegrams to pressure politicians—was still largely done by volunteers.[55]

The group's tactics in the fight against the coal boom had quickly diversified in the early years of its existence. Northern Plains members soon learned that passing laws was only one part of the solution. Through their work to stop the construction of the Colstrip power plant, they found that making the laws work required persistent citizen oversight and participation in permitting and rule-making processes. Occasionally, it required lawsuits. Northern Plains members understood that preventing the damages associated with massive coal and power developments depended on the ability of citizens to review proposed projects and have a say in whether they were allowed to go forward and how. They wrote these provisions into the laws they advocated in the 1970s. Their experience with these laws informed their future thinking regarding how to solve environmental problems. They continued to argue for the ability of citizens to participate.

Northern Plains' efforts to fight the coal boom brought it into contact with other Montanans facing aspects of the boom but also other environmental issues. NPRC members applied the lessons they learned and attracted new members to the organization. In 1975, the first affiliate not associated directly with coal development joined the group. The Stillwater Protective Association, hailing from a handful of small towns along the Stillwater River that flowed out of the Beartooth Plateau south to the Yellowstone about one hundred miles west of Billings, formed to fight a proposal to expand hard rock mining in the mountains of the region and its associated social, economic, and environmental impacts. For Northern

Plains, the issues were the same—split-estate, water degradation, boom-and-bust growth, and impacts on small towns—and the new group brought new members that increased their people power. By the late 1970s, the board included new members and leadership from more farming-oriented areas in the north-central and east-central part of the state. Wheat ranchers Helen Waller, Charlie Yarger, and Tom Breitbach chaired the organization in the latter part of the decade. They promoted new issues within the organization, arguing that ultimately the group was concerned with protecting family-based agriculture as the most sustainable use of the land and water in the region. They pressured the group to take on other agricultural issues including price gouging of wheat farmers by the railroads and eventually bank foreclosures.[56]

At the same time the group tested the waters working on these complicated agricultural issues, some members in the south-central and western parts of the state began pressuring the organization to work on more traditional environmental issues.[57] Many of these members, from cities and rural areas, initially joined to fight the Colstrip transmission corridor or hard rock mining. In 1974, members increasingly concerned with finding alternative, sustainable solutions to the energy crisis started a new affiliate, the Alternative Energy Resources Organization (AERO), to work specifically on promoting alternative, or soft path, energy production and conservation and to complement the anti-coal-boom work of the larger group.[58] In 1978, the board elected to support state Initiative 80, which would require direct voter approval before any nuclear power facility could be sited in Montana.[59] They also parted with most traditional agricultural groups and voted to support the designation of the Absaroka-Beartooth Wilderness. Northern Plains members used their skills acquired in other fights to organize comments and participation in the wilderness designation process, which resulted in Congress establishing more than 920,000 acres of wilderness bordering Yellowstone National Park and protecting a significant portion of the headwaters of the Yellowstone River in that same year.[60]

The group also began to grow beyond its borders, seeking to spread its successful brand of activism to other states caught up in the coal boom. In 1973, Northern Plains members and staff helped form a sister organization in Wyoming's Powder River Basin, a region that was similarly slated for massive coal mines and power plants and contained the headwaters of the Powder and Tongue Rivers that flowed north into Montana. Initially, Northern Plains included the Powder River Basin Resource Council in its newsletter and provided staff services for the new group, but by the mid-1970s, the Wyoming group stood on its own. In 1978, Northern Plains helped form a similar group in North Dakota, the Dakota Resources Council. By 1979, Pat Sweeney had organized the three groups and similar organizations in Colorado to form an umbrella organization to provide a regional voice in Washington for issues that concerned all the groups crossing state boundaries and as a clearing house for information and resources for the groups. The Western Organization of Resource Councils (or WORC) institutionalized the people-power tactics that had evolved in Montana and Wyoming since the early 1970s and sought to spread them to other states with the aims of empowering citizens to address environmental and community problems. Like Northern Plains, WORC insisted on solutions that realized the participatory democracy ideals of the 1960s. WORC increasingly incorporated the organizing ideas of labor and civil rights organizers Saul Alinsky, Martin Luther King Jr., César Chavez, and institutions like the Highlander Center in Tennessee and Associations of Community Organizations for Reform Now (ACORN).[61]

Conclusion: Northern Plains as a Citizens' "Environmental" Group

By the end of the 1970s, geographic, numeric, and issue expansion caused the Northern Plains Resource Council to reflect on just exactly what it was. Was it an environmental organization? Was it an agricultural organization? In September 1978, Northern Plains chair Bill McKay Jr., a rancher from the southeastern part of the state, addressed this question. In the newsletter, he wrote,

> Northern Plains Resource Council is unique. Our primary direction comes from the rural sector, and most of the membership considers NPRC to be an agricultural organization. Yet, we are not a trade association in the mold of the Montana Stockgrowers or the Montana Woolgrowers. However, we are the only organization in

Montana that stands up for agriculture in the face of massive industrial development. . . . Much of our work deals with the basic essen-
tials for Montana agriculture: land, air, and water. But this doesn't
make us environmentalists. We're still ranchers and farmers.[62]

A quick survey of the group's issues—mine regulation and reclamation, power plant siting and regulation, alternative energy, opposition to
nuclear power, support for wilderness designation—and their emphasis on
passing legislation to require government-led solutions to these problems
supports Northern Plains' classification as an environmental organization.
The resistance of members to being called environmentalists, however,
is instructive and reveals something about the American environmental
movement in the postwar era. It is safe to assume that their reaction to the
term was partially rooted in the culture wars of the era. By the late 1970s,
environmentalism was already being linked to the socially liberal politics
many conservative rural people associated with the antiwar movement and
social and political upheaval of the 1960s. If environmentalism could be
confined to the people Wally McRae called "wild eyed, and fuzzy-headed,"
then Northern Plains members were indeed not environmentalists.[63] The
ranchers and farmers of Northern Plains distinguished themselves from
environmentalists because their activism was rooted in the protection of
private property and their ability to continue to farm, ranch, and preserve
their rural, agricultural heritage from industrialization. They saw these
values as conservative in the culture wars of the era. They understood their
activism as profoundly American. What they were slow to realize, however, was how similar their activism was to what most environmentalists
were doing. Whether they knew it or not, their tactics, based on the basic
assumptions that citizens ought to have access to information affecting
their environment and well-being and a say in decisions that affect their
health, their families, their ability to make a living, and their communities were central tenets of the environmental reform movement in the late
twentieth century.[64] Their activism more closely aligned Northern Plains
members with other environmental organizations than with the agricultural trade organizations with which they also associated. Activism to solve
environmental problems tended to reflect progressive ideals about democratic participation and emphasized the ability of citizens to participate in

government decisions. Northern Plains members worked on environmental issues, but it was their understanding of the energy boom and remedies to it as fundamentally about justice and democracy that aligned them with the environmental movement.

In its organization and work during the 1970s, Northern Plains Resource Council provided an example of the kinds of grassroots environmental organizations that formed in the United States in the last decades of the twentieth century to address environmental issues. Although details varied from community to community, state to state, and issue to issue and depended on the class and race of the activists, NPRC's experience demonstrates a general trajectory of citizen environmental activism typical during the 1970s. People reacted to a perceived threat to their self-interests: their property, their ability to make a living, their health or that of their families. They found others who also perceived the threat and attempted to address it. Although environmental threats are often scientific and technical in nature, these activists typically understand the issue in terms of fairness and justice. In the Northern Plains example, the coal boom threatened to industrialize a vast swath of rural, agricultural land, destroying ranchers' private property and the streams they depended on, irrevocably altering their communities. The ranchers were not consulted and had no means of appealing the proposals. They felt that their sovereignty over their private property and lives and rights as citizens were violated. From this understanding of the issue, they argued for their right to take part in the environmental decisions that affected their property, health, quality of life, or livelihoods.

Before the 1970s, citizens' access to environmental decision-making was constrained. Activists could write letters to the editors of their local newspapers and petition their political representatives. They could stage protests through direct action. For many groups, passing new laws that included agency transparency and citizen input and provided citizens with the ability to appeal agency decisions often stood out as the most expedient way of achieving their goals. In the process of addressing their local issues, they often realized how similar their issues were to those of others. Slowly, these activists became globalized in their thinking; they began to understand their issues as part of larger systems of environmental, economic, or social injustice. In the process, they became more environmentalist, whether they associated themselves with the label or not. If their primary issue was resolved, to their satisfaction or not, they often refocused their attention and efforts on other issues sometimes in other communities. As their involvement with environmental issues and their groups matured, they become more sophisticated. The organizations professionalized institutionalizing tactics and strategy while the staff and some members began to embrace the technical, scientific, and legal aspects of their work and developed new tactics to engage other aspects of environmental decision-making.

This was the trajectory that Northern Plains followed from its inception in the early 1970s and continues to follow to the present day. Another community-based organization formed in Tucson, Arizona, just three years after Northern Plains, and followed a similar path. Though its membership tended to be predominantly urban and college-educated members of Tucson's middle class, the Southwest Environmental Service's efforts to educate citizens about land use, water, and air quality issues to enable them to more fully to participate in environmental decisions reflected many of democratic goals shared by Northern Plains. The story of the Southwest Environmental Service demonstrates the variety of strategies available to citizens groups and the challenges grassroots environmental organizations faced during the 1980s.

4

Citizen Environmental
Activism in the Southwest

Tucson's Southwest Environmental Service

Priscilla Robinson was fastidious. Her studies in anthropology at the University of Arizona and her years working as a lobbyist in the Arizona legislature defending women's reproductive rights taught her to be exact and pay attention to detail. In the tumultuous years after the Supreme Court issued the *Roe v. Wade* decision, she experienced a crash course in forming unlikely coalitions and compromises. She was fascinated with how people solved problems and by creating effective ways of achieving goals. She cared passionately about the issues she worked on, but she seemed equally attracted to the complicated process of democratic decision-making. She thrived on creating and experimenting with new strategies to achieve success. She liked to say that she approached problems through reason and science. Working for the city of Tucson in the early 1970s, she applied this ardor to her work promoting groundwater management in southern Arizona. She was an administrator and a problem solver first, an activist second.[1]

In 1975, Robinson took on a new challenge. As ranchers and environmentalists were joining efforts to fight the industrialization of eastern Montana, southern Arizonans were organizing themselves to address what they perceived as threats to their environment and quality of life. Out of the rapid urbanization and social and cultural ferment in southern Arizona, stimulated in part by popular opposition to two dams proposed for the Colorado River on either side of Grand Canyon National Park during the 1960s, a new environmental organization emerged in 1974. The Southwest

Environmental Service (SES), a citizen-based environmental organization formed with the help of a grant from a Tucson couple, sought to give residents a voice in local planning and land use issues. Within only a few month of its founding, however, it appeared to be floundering. The group's board of directors turned to Robinson for direction, and she went to work. By mid-spring 1975, SES had secured a small office in downtown Tucson, filed its paperwork as a tax-exempt nonprofit organization, revised its budget, begun to identify and prioritize its issues, and planned how it would allocate its resources. Reason, science, and sound administration would be the foundation from which Robinson and the SES would work for planned urban growth, clean water, and clean air.[2]

The story of Tucson's Southwest Environmental Service presents a marked contrast from that of its counterpart to the north. As in eastern Montana, the environmental movement in southern Arizona was galvanized by the emergence of perceived threats—the proposal to build two dams on the Colorado River on both ends of Grand Canyon National Park to pay for the construction of the Central Arizona Project (CAP) during the 1960s and what local residents regarded as uncontrolled urban sprawl.[3] The Grand Canyon dam controversy did not threaten the land or livelihood of the people in Tucson who organized in opposition. Urban sprawl affected their quality of life but not necessarily their livelihoods. One might even argue that with the completion of the CAP, which would transport water from the Colorado River in western Arizona to Phoenix and Tucson, activists in southern Arizona would be the recipients of the material benefits of the proposed dams without incurring any of the tangible harms. In a way, they resembled the residents of Minneapolis or Seattle who would receive cheap, reliable electricity from the developments proposed in the *North Central Power Study* without dealing with the destruction and pollution on the Plains.

Activists in Tucson differed from the people who formed the Northern Plains Resource Council in other ways. They were predominantly middle-class, educated urbanites—the people who typically come to mind when one thinks of environmentalists. SES's members tended to be concerned with what historians, including Samuel Hays, have described as more traditional environmental issues, what sociologist Robert Brulle calls reform environmentalism discourse, having to do with increased interest in quality of life among Americans following the second world war.[4] Their opposition to the proposed Marble Canyon and Bridge Canyon dams had to do with preserving the scenic grandeur, unique ecosystem, and recreational opportunities of the Grand Canyon. They linked their critiques with larger arguments about the sustainability of continued urban growth in the arid Sonora Desert.

SES also formed differently than Northern Plains. It organized in 1974 after receiving a grant from Tucson's Wilson Foundation, created in the mid-1960s by Richard and Jean Wilson with the aims of addressing environmental and land-use issues in the Tucson area. NPRC was primarily a member-funded organization and did not receive its first foundation grants until a few years into its existence. Receiving foundation funding from the onset, SES traveled a different path in terms of its issues and activities. Because it was not dependent on membership dues for financial support, SES did not emphasize membership recruitment to the degree that Northern Plains did. Like Northern Plains, it incorporated democratic principles in organizational decision-making but lodged that decision-making exclusively in a more professional and expert board of directors that met monthly and was closely guided by a paid executive director. It rarely solicited input from its members outside the board on organizational policy and strategy and did not hold membership-wide annual meetings. Within the social and environmental community, SES might be referred to as an advocacy group or a service organization due to its primary strategies of using experts and professionals to advocate positions on behalf of its membership and providing expert services to environmental decision-makers and governing agencies.[5]

Although SES approached environmental protection from a different direction than Northern Plains, it was similar to other citizens' environmental groups that formed around the country during the era. Like their counterparts to the north, the activists that made up SES considered environmental concerns within a constellation of interests and values and sought solutions based on their understanding of environmental issues as fundamentally issues of good governance and fairness. Their efforts were undergirded by the same conviction that informed citizens are the people best equipped to make environmental decisions affecting the health, communities, and quality of life of the people living in Arizona. Likewise, SES members and staff understood and articulated environmental issues in terms of justice and democracy, arguing for the ability of citizens to participate in environmental decision-making processes and for industry to be held accountable to the people. Like Northern Plains, SES built political support for legislative solutions to environmental threats that included an expanded role for citizens in regulating the activity. SES placed more emphasis on educating citizens about air and water quality and land use issues than encouraging them to become involved politically to affect positive environmental change. The group served as an informer and advocate for citizens in various decision-making venues regarding air, water, and quality of life in the region.[6]

SES also resembles Northern Plains and other citizens' environmental organizations during this period in terms of its leadership. Women held a greater number of leadership positions in SES compared to national organizations and conducted most of the group's on-the-ground work. While the board of directors tended to contain academics and professionals who brought some expertise to the organization's work, the women who did the work and really shaped SES were not trained professionals or experts; they learned the skills and acquired the knowledge they needed on the job. They were concerned about the environment, but initially, they were no better equipped to address the complicated issues of land use, air and water quality, and water conservation than most members of Tucson's middle class.[7]

SES provides an example of a different kind of multi-issue, community-based environmental organization that formed in the United States during the first decade of the modern environmental movement. Its work during the 1970s and 1980s demonstrated many of the strategies grassroots groups pursued in their attempts to improve the environment following the passing of the nation's bedrock environmental laws. Public education campaigns to help citizens to engage in more environmentally responsible behavior, to advocate for new protective environmental regulations, and to enforce existing air and water quality laws passed in the previous decade were the primary activities SES employed in their mission to protect and improve the environment in southern Arizona. Its successes and failures during the 1980s demonstrate the possibilities and challenges inherent to citizens' environmental groups while illuminating a degree of continuity in the way citizens understood environmental issues and reform as the movement matured in the late twentieth century.

The Rise of an Environmental Movement in Southern Arizona

In the last decades of the twentieth century, economic, demographic, and cultural changes in southern Arizona conditioned how people understood and related to the region's physical environment. Changes in the regional, national, and international economy altered the social, political, and economic landscape in southern Arizona and opened the way for new voices in debates over the development of natural resources and quality of life in the region.

From its days as a territory following the United States' acquisition of the region from Mexico in 1854 until World War II, southern Arizona served as a sort of colonial outpost providing raw materials for America's industrialization.[8] Prospectors and mining companies backed by eastern and European capital extracted enormous quantities of silver and copper from the rugged mountains, making mining towns such as Tombstone and Bisbee world famous. Technological innovations in mining and smelting, along with the communications and energy revolutions associated with the telegraph, telephone, and electrification, made large-scale copper mining profitable. With the discovery and development of the "Copper Queen" and "Atlanta" lodes by Phelps Dodge, the "copper collar" was yoked to the southern Arizona economy. Meanwhile, folklore and medical science combined to convince tuberculosis-stricken tourists of the healing qualities of the region's dry climate. Thousands of those suffering from the disease descended upon Tucson and Phoenix in the late nineteenth and early twentieth centuries. Into the mid-twentieth century, health seekers continued to flock especially to Tucson, shaping the foundations of institutionalized healthcare in Arizona and adding a popular appreciation for the state's healthful environment to the region's reputation for mineral riches.[9]

The clear, dry climate was equally attractive to a new constituency with the entrance of the United States into World War II in 1941. To the government interested in training army pilots and industrialists committed to building planes for the war effort, year-round flying and cheap and sparsely populated land provided a perfect place for military bases and wartime manufacturing. Outside Phoenix, the War Department opened Luke Williams Air Field—the largest advanced flying school in the world, training more than 13,500 pilots during World War II. In Tucson, the federal government took over the Davis-Monthan municipal airport and built Ryan Field to the west and Marana Air Base northwest of the city, where it trained thousands of pilots. Consolidated Vultee Aircraft attracted thousands of civilian employees to Tucson. While Phoenix was able to attract and retain more manufacturing industries during and after the war, Tucson captured the enormous Hughes Aircraft missile plant in 1951, and its population experienced a proportionally similar demographic surge to that of its neighbor to the north (from under 50,000 in 1950 to more than 200,000 in 1960).[10] While the copper industry continued to prosper, the manufacturing and service industry quickly challenged its dominance in the economy of southern Arizona. Diversification of the region's economy brought with it a new population with new values, as thousands of returning veterans and their families, G.I. benefits in hand, chose the opportunities that the region's cheap land, plentiful jobs, and mild climate provided.[11]

By the 1960s, new voices reflecting the evolving values of a growing population entered the regional conversation about how southern Arizonans should relate to their environment. Whereas the economy of the region was still of pivotal importance to most residents, many began to emphasize the importance of quality of life. Residents of southern Arizona, concentrated primarily in Tucson, organized themselves to address what they perceived as important community issues having to do with air, water, land, and health. Southern Arizonans formed and joined local chapters of national organizations including the Sierra Club, Audubon Society, Nature Conservancy, Friends of the Earth, and recreational clubs including the Southern Arizona Hiking Club and various hunting and fishing organizations. In addition, Tucson residents formed their own groups in the 1960s and 1970s to address issues of specific interest to urban southern Arizonans: Arizonans for Quality Environment, Southern Arizona Environmental Council, and the Southwest Environmental Service. These three collaborated with the others to advocate for the protection of air and water, planned urban and suburban growth, the preservation of public lands and creation of parks during the 1970s and 1980s. Environmentally concerned citizens often belonged to and led many of these organizations at the same time.

Arizonans for Quality Environment was the first of these groups to form. In 1966, it was chartered as Arizonans for Water Without Waste (AWWW) to fight proposals to build Bridge and Marble Canyon Dams on the Colorado River on both sides of Grand Canyon National Park. The dams were proposed to generate revenues to pay for the Central Arizona Project (CAP), which was designed to transport water from the Colorado River to Phoenix and Tucson. The group found itself in a precarious position. It was unable to oppose the regionally sacred CAP, which promised to deliver millions of acre-feet of water to the state's growing metropolises, but the group absolutely opposed the building of the two Grand Canyon "cash register" dams to subsidize the project. With the removal of the objectionable dams from the CAP project authorization in 1968, AWWW lost its foundational issue and branched out to other natural resource issues concerning southern Arizona. By 1969, AWWW had created five new committees covering air pollution, water, wilderness, wildlife, and conservation education. By February 1970, it changed its name to Arizonans for Quality Environment but retained the familiar AWWW acronym during the early part of the decade.[12]

From its inception in 1966 as a single-issue group through its development into a multi-issue grassroots advocacy organization, AWWW was led primarily by citizen activists, many of whom comprised the backbone of Tucson's environmental movement. Responding to national as well as local controversies, the group took on issues as they arose in the Tucson area so long as members were interested and willing to work on them. In October 1969, AWWW responded to the national fervor surrounding the publishing of Paul Ehrlich's *The Population Bomb* earlier that year by declaring population growth the group's top priority and creating a committee to study the issue led by Priscilla Robinson. Likewise, in response to the oil embargo and energy crisis of 1973–1974, AWWW elected to focus on energy issues including conservation, energy mineral extraction, and alternative energy. Responding to the passage of the nation's most protective environmental laws, including the Wilderness Act of 1964, the National Environmental Policy Act of 1969, the Clean Air Act of 1970, the Clean Water Act of 1972, and the Endangered Species Act of 1973, AWWW maintained committees dedicated to wilderness, water, and wildlife issues. Echoing specifically local concerns, they committed resources to transportation issues, Grand Canyon preservation, urban environment, land use, and eventually mining.[13]

AWWW was joined in the region by a second community-based environmental organization in 1971: the Southern Arizona Environmental Council (SAEC). The SAEC was a different kind of organization. Its stated purpose was "to provide an effective and continuing coordinating structure to increase individual and organization ability to understand and respond to environmental problems in southern Arizona." Consisting of representatives of "any non-profit or volunteer Arizonan organization or association with some stated concern for environmental quality," the SAEC was unique among environmental organizations in the region during the period for its attempt to bring often-divergent interests together.[14] Reflecting this effort, the organization's semi-monthly and later quarterly *Bulletin* included articles from Paulette Dryden, mining chair of Arizonans for Quality Environment, who argued against expanded mining in southern Arizona, and articles by Ted Eyde of the Southwest Minerals Exploration Association supporting mining as a "Necessary and Desirable Green Belt Use in Pima County." Although the SAEC was essentially an organization of organizations, it maintained a membership of individuals and attempted to engage the general public and encourage public participation.[15]

"Catalyst for Action": The Southwest Environmental Service

In 1974, a third community-based environmental organization formed in Tucson to fill a specifically local niche in the southern Arizona's environmental community: urban land use. The Southwest Environmental Service (SES) was chartered under the direction of David Hoyt, a local newspaperman, to address regional environmental issues that had so far fallen outside the purview of the region's other environmental organizations.[16] Although Richard and Jean Wilson, who formed the foundation that funded SES, charged the group with working for general environmental protection, the wealthy couple—Richard, a Yale- and Stanford-trained geologist, was heir to a Texas oil fortune—was particularly concerned with the effects of suburban sprawl in and around Tucson. Hoyt organized a board of directors from active members of AWWW and SAEC. In its first year, SES began work on land-use planning in the Tucson metropolitan area and urban water quality and use as well as Catalina State Park, a nature park north of Tucson on the western flanks of the Santa Catalina Mountains designated by the Arizona legislature in 1974 but left unfunded by the state. In early 1975, Hoyt resigned and Priscilla Robinson took over as executive director.[17]

Robinson brought to the nascent SES a degree of organization and professionalism that characterized the group throughout its tenure. By 1974, she was an experienced activist and was familiar with organizing information and people to work on environmental issues. Once she addressed brick-and-mortar considerations, Robinson turned her aim to the heart of the organization: its work and niche in Tucson's growing environmental community. In an April 1975 report to the board, she illuminated some possible issues for the group to engage. Although many of the options were technical, she proposed a variety of activities intended to educate citizens and encourage their participation in local environmental decisions. She briefly explained progress in two Tucson planning and zoning processes and offered her thoughts on possible functions for the organization: primarily serving in coalitions with other groups, organizing citizen comments in government agency decision-making processes, and gathering information and distributing it to stakeholders. She suggested some ways in which SES could contribute to the land-use planning process and environmental legislation the group might promote. She also offered a list of possible future projects for the group including promoting Tucson's "Natural Areas System," a new program designed to designate nature preserves and parks around the city. She also recommended creating school-based environmental education programs, conducting research for interim legislative committees considering water and land use reforms, and monitoring the transfer of EPA's water quality discharge permit system to the state. Within a month, she had prepared a detailed proposal for an "experimental community education project in land use planning" complete with identified objectives, suggestions for how to meet their goals, and a budget of $1,500.[18] In the document, she proposed to bring together citizens living primarily in the northwest section of Tucson to "study, discuss, and evaluate" Tucson's Tortolita Area Plan in a series of "structured workshops" to educate participants about the residential and commercial

land-use plan so they could influence its direction "if they choose to do
so." In the proposal, Robinson emphasized that she understood the project
as an experiment with "innovative educational techniques in implementing community participation in land use planning."[19] From the beginning,
Robinson proved to be a powerful force shaping the agenda and activities of the organization according to her philosophy of affecting positive
environmental change through education, serving the community, and
working "within the system" to facilitate greater public participation in
environmental decision-making.[20]

Within a year, Robinson led the board in building SES into a multi-
issue organization engaging in a variety of environmental problems
in Tucson. As the group expanded and intensified its work on land-use
planning and the creation of Catalina State Park, Robinson's vision of the
organization became more apparent. She envisioned making SES into an
invaluable resource for natural resource managers and environmental
decision-makers in southern Arizona. Even if she did not know exactly
what role SES would play, she aimed to make sure the group was at the
decision-making table. She also understood that achieving such a position
would require additional help and resources. This reflected a transition
that occurred in the environmental movement in the 1970s and 1980s as
environmental issues and regulation became more technical and required
a new level of activist expertise. In this shifting reality, the strategies citizen activists had cultivated in the 1960s and early 1970s grew less effective. Many groups attempted to compensate for changes in the political
and regulatory landscape by trying to recruit more members in hopes of
increasing the organization's political clout through people power. Robinson realized the need for citizens to engage the scientific and technical
aspects of environmental issues to influence policy and governance. She
was an early adopter of this strategy that would become prominent in the
next decade. Robinson guided the board to identify potential new members who could bring particular expertise to the organization—legal and
accounting skills, for instance, or a background in water quality or other
environmental sciences—and she proposed hiring part-time employees to
assist her in managing SES's various activities.[21]

In its first years, the SES board included men and women who were
dedicated to and could help further Robinson's philosophy of educating the

public and working within the system using reason and science to address environmental issues. Leadership passed between presidents Suzanne Wilson and Thomas Pew with Mary Peace Douglas serving as vice president and Colonel John Rice serving as treasurer. Other board members included Bernard Fontana, William Franklin, and Sol Resnick, and many members were academics associated with the University of Arizona who contributed their expertise to SES's work. Wilson was a professor of archeology at the university. Fontana was an ethnologist working with the university and the Arizona State Museum. Resnick, a water resource professional associated with the university, served as the group's resident expert on hydrologic issues. Pew was a horticulturalist and expert on various environmental issues. When it became apparent to the organization that it needed the expertise of an attorney to negotiate the various intricacies of planning and other environmental laws, Colonel Rice suggested that they recruit a lawyer. Within a month in 1977, they had recruited Tucson attorney Richard Duffield to join the board and satisfy this need.[7]

While the board always included a significant number of women, it did recruit more male board members, which probably reflected the desire to recruit experts from professional fields dominated by men rather than any overt preference. In contrast, the paid staff was almost exclusively female throughout the life of the organization. After SES hired Robinson as full-time executive director in 1975 for the salary of about ten thousand dollars a year, she recommended that the group hire other part-time employees to organize and administer portions of the group's campaigns and administrative work. In 1976, the board approved Robinson's recommendation to hire Victoria Dahl to help with its urban planning projects and organize the group's water workshops, a campaign to educate the public and decision-makers about water issues in southern Arizona. Robinson also employed Dahl to organize a follow-up workshop of hydrologists. In March 1977, she hired Elizabeth Ann "Betsy" Rieke part time to organize the group's growing library and files. The library-organizing work soon shifted to another part-time employee, Barbara Winters, and Robinson drafted Rieke to assist with monitoring the state's process of deciding water quality standards for the Gila and San Pedro Rivers and for Sabino Creek north of Tucson. Within a few months, Rieke was traveling with Robinson to Phoenix to meet with state officials at the State Bureau of Water Quality and State Parks Department. A year later, Rieke made a presentation on surface mining and reclamation on behalf of the organization before the National Research Council.[23]

Although men may have dominated the board, Robinson's preference for hiring female employees had the effect of giving the organization a feminine public face. As the group grew in terms of members, issues, and influence in local and state-level decisions regarding land use planning, water, and air quality, the women of SES—Dahl, Rieke, and especially Robinson—became the recognized spokespeople for the organization. Barbara Tellman, who worked for the organization during the 1980s, remembers that SES hired women out of sheer practicality as "we had the time," she explained.[24] The group could not afford to pay wages necessary to hire full-time professionals, and it found it easier to hire women who could learn on the job and work part time. Robinson acknowledged this rationale but, whether explicitly or implicitly, understood hiring women as part of a larger movement to promote gender equality. Three decades later, she relished the memory of watching Dahl, Rieke, Tellman and others grow in confidence and skills as their environmental work propelled them into the public spotlight. She recruited the women out of the League of Women Voters, many of whom, like herself, had college degrees but no formal training or professional experience in environmental advocacy. Like the women Glenda Riley writes about in *Women and Nature: Saving the "Wild" West*, many were empowered by the work.[25] They acquired skills in networking and lobbying and continued some form of advocacy or activism after they left the organization. Tellman served on the city of Tucson water board and the county wastewater board, and went on to work on various political campaigns for primarily Democratic and environmentalist candidates for office. Rieke went to law school and eventually became one of the premier water lawyers in the Southwest. In 1993, she was drafted to serve as assistant secretary of the interior for Water and Science by the Clinton administration. Like Riley's "women environmentalists," the women of SES, "whether consciously or not . . . widened their own sphere of activity and action."[26]

Robinson understood that she and members of her all-female staff were in a unique position within the environmental decision-making system they strove to influence. On various advisory committees from the city to the state level and in meetings of regulators and environmental managers, they were typically the only female participants. Robinson remembers that she was aware of this fact and deliberately conducted herself to maximize her effectiveness. "I intentionally dressed so as not to stand out," she said. "My rule was that I wanted people to remember what I said, not what I wore . . . [n]eat, becoming, but nothing worth noticing."[27] Perhaps hardened by her previous experiences working as a lobbyist for Planned Parenthood, she did not expect any special consideration on account of her gender. "Discussions can get heated, and that's part of the process," she explains. "You can't expect any change in tone just because you showed up."[28] She attributed resentment toward women in professional settings to stereotypes about women's emotionality. "You can deal with this by playing fair and not getting emotional," she said. "It's o.k. to raise your voice to me, even yell a little . . . a sense of humor is essential."[29] In her experience, the men in the committees or meetings she took part in, often lawyers and other technical professionals, were typically better educated or more experienced. Instead of being intimidated, Robinson viewed these situations as opportunities to learn and to engage the men. She remembers, "I did have experience and insight that many of them did not have," including in politics and the media, "so that part usually worked out."[30] For Robinson, working past the potential challenges of gender differences seemed to be just one more interesting challenge to overcome.

In its first five years, SES's expert-led board and female staff embarked on a series of campaigns based on its philosophy of educating the public to protect and enhance the environment and to provide expert advice to environmental decision-makers. The group accelerated its participation in urban and suburban land use and planning issues around Tucson, continued its work to fund the newly designated Catalina State Park, and created a land trust to facilitate the acquisition of environmentally valuable land in the Tucson region to preserve open space from suburban development and shape how the city grew. In addition, it drew on popular and policymaker interest in water issues in and around Tucson—a desert city that was, at the time, the largest metropolitan area in the United States entirely dependent on groundwater. Water, its quality and use, became a primary issue for the organization, especially because the groundwater aquifer that supported Tucson had been steadily and dramatically declining since the population boom following World War II. Moreover, industrial chemicals associated with the military and manufacturing enterprises as well as municipal and unofficial waste dumps scattered along the ephemeral Santa Cruz and Rillito Rivers that flowed through the center of Tucson poisoned that limited and precious water supply.[31] These issues, and the strategies the group pursued to address them, shaped its agenda for the duration of its institutional life and molded how Robinson and the board addressed the group's most important work in the 1980s.

By mid-1976, SES was in the thick of a land use planning debate. Despite a sluggish national economy during the decade, southern Arizona was in the throes of a population explosion experienced throughout the Sunbelt. Tucson grew from a population of about 263,000 in 1970 to more than 330,000 in 1980; Pima County from about 352,000 to more than 530,000. Of the roughly 180,000 new residents in Pima County, almost two-thirds lived outside the city limits.[32] As was the pattern in other Sunbelt metropolitan regions, that growth tended to radiate from Tucson in low-density residential developments sprawling onto former agricultural land and virgin Sonora Desert, straining city and county road, water, and sewer infrastructure. Less tangibly, rapid suburban sprawl threatened some of the amenities that many Tucson residents valued as vitally important to their quality of life in the region—air free of the smog and highways clear of the congestion that characterized Los Angeles to the west and Phoenix to the north. SES joined other groups including the Southern Arizona Environmental Council in arguing that urban planning, transportation, and air pollution were intricately connected and central to the quality of life in Tucson. Additionally, population growth elevated concerns about water supply: whether the metropolitan area could secure enough water to sustain its growth and that water would be safe to drink.[33]

In its attempts to influence the direction of this rapid growth, SES found itself monitoring, gathering research, and organizing citizens on at least eight different planning issues in the Tucson area between 1975 and 1980. To bolster its position, SES employed Gerald Swanson, an economist at the University of Arizona, to research the economic impact of growth. In one instance, SES advocated an ordinance before the Pima County Planning and Zoning Commission and the Board of Supervisors to promote environmentally responsible growth. In another, it advocated an

FIGURE 3. Suburban sprawl was one of the major concerns of Tucson-area environmentalists in the 1970s. Here, developers bulldozed the Sonoran desert to make way
for a new suburban housing development but left a few of the iconic saguaros to be
integrated into the landscaping, April 1974.

National Archives and Records Administration, photo no. 412-DA 555346.

ordinance meant to prevent unplanned suburban and exurban residential development in rural Pima County northwest of Tucson as part of the
Tortolita Area Plan. SES also monitored proposals for the sewage facility
to service the Tortolita development. SES and other groups feared that
pro-growth developers and planning officials would promote a sewage processing plant much larger than was necessary for the development, thus
encouraging additional growth despite the work of these organizations.
Other planning work included monitoring proposals to expand city streets,
improving the Sahuarita Road south of Tucson to serve new suburban
developments, promoting a proposed city ordinance to restrict building
in floodplains, and continuing the Tucson and Pima County Comprehensive Planning Process. Land use planning also provided one of SES's first
entrées into its legislative work; in 1978, Robinson and SES developed a bill
to give counties more power in land-use planning. Planning and land use
in the Tucson area became such a major issue that Robinson hired Victoria
Dahl part time to help keep track of new developments throughout the

region and attend the many county meetings that evaluated these various suburban developments.[34]

To preserve elements of the regional landscape from the developers' bulldozers and to maintain open space where Tucson's growing population might recreate, SES continued its efforts to develop Catalina State Park and investigated creating a new land trust organization to buy existing open land and save it from development. The Arizona legislature had designated roughly 5,000 acres on the southwestern flanks of the Santa Catalina Mountains north of Tucson as Catalina State Park in 1974, but as of 1976, no money had been appropriated for its maintenance or development as a recreational site. As a result, the park had no facilities. The land was protected, but without funding or planning, its future was in question. Environmentalists lobbied the legislature and state agencies and battled pro-development forces over what kind of park it would be: a traditional city park or more primitive nature park. Robinson and SES led a coalition of groups supporting the park on a prolonged campaign to obtain funding through the state legislature and affect a series of land exchanges that expanded the park and secured its borders. Its work on Catalina State Park resembled its work on urban planning: it required Robinson and her staff to attend and testify at numerous city and county meetings, but it also required them to negotiate personally and outside the public spotlight with landowners whose property bordered the park. The park issues also pulled them into the legislative arena. In 1978, SES supported the state parks department's request for a $900,000 appropriation from the legislature to buy private lands adjacent to the northern part of the park and helped further negotiations for the land exchange between the state and an adjacent landowner. The issue was central to the group's legislative agenda until it finally secured funding for the park in 1983. Robinson cited this as one of her and SES's proudest achievements.[35]

SES's other strategy for preserving open space in the face of Tucson's population boom, creating a land trust, was a marked departure from the organization's philosophy of educating the public and providing expertise to decision-makers. In early 1977, the board elected to enlist Ben Carter from the Colorado Open Land Foundation to advise SES on the benefits of creating a trust in Tucson. In August of that year, board member Thomas

Pew visited the Maine Coast Heritage Land Trust, and SES recruited University of Arizona professor Michael McCarthy and his students to research the prospects of starting such an organization. A new and increasingly popular vehicle to protect open space in the late 1970s, land trusts were nonprofit corporations that bought or accepted gifts of land from private individuals and then protected the land through property rights law and contracts rather than regulatory law. After more than a year and a half of research, the SES board adopted the articles of incorporation of the Arizona Open Land Trust and chartered the new land institution as part of the organization.[36] The land trust added one more tool to SES's expanding repertoire of strategies for protecting land, air, and water in southern Arizona. This strategy, which used private property and market forces to protect land, added to what was evolving into a sophisticated suite of activities including providing public education, promoting citizen participation, and using science and expertise to influence regulatory agencies and policy makers.

By the end of the 1970s, SES's work on land use and water and air quality issues had created a pattern that characterized the organization and continued to influence its work until it closed its doors in 1987. The board recognized as early as 1978 that it was too dependent on funding from only one granting organization—Arizona's Wilson Foundation—and needed to develop other sources of revenue. Toward that end, it proposed to expand the board with the aim of recruiting new members who could identify additional sources of funding. They discussed developing other sources of income that were typical for grassroots environmental organizations, individual contributions and membership dues, but the board members were reluctant to rely on new member recruitment as a way to raise revenue. During its fourteen years, several private benefactors donated to the organization. Robinson reported that by the time it closed, SES had 600 individual contributors and claimed that SES could operate on their contributions alone. However, it remained primarily dependent on outside grants for its campaigns. Although this was different from other citizens' groups like the Northern Plains Resource Council, which relied primarily on dues and smaller donations, it was not necessarily a problem. Although board members raised concerns about the situation, there is little evidence that they ruminated much on its effects on SES's work or viewed the condition negatively. However, from a historian's perspective, it is reasonable to judge SES's dependency on grants as the one of the primary factors in its closing in 1987 after a very successful but relatively short life. This reliance on foundation and government funding also appeared to influence its work. Decades later, Robinson insisted that her own personal interest in an issue or campaign was a more important influence on what the group chose to work on, but she acknowledged that the group consciously considered and sought opportunities to provide services to government agencies as a source of revenue. One of the clearest examples of this was SES's entrance into the issue of air quality in 1978 after receiving a grant from the EPA to produce a citizen's workshop to educate the public on changes to the Clean Air Act in 1977. With this work, SES hoped to attract grant money from the National Science Foundation and Shalan Foundation to enlarge the group's public education campaign and produce a citizen's guide to air pollution. This marked the beginning of one of SES's biggest and most definitive campaigns during the 1980s: the fight for clean air in southern Arizona.[37]

Conclusion

Although SES worked on a variety of issues during the 1980s, the air quality campaign, which expanded far beyond public education, combined with an enlarged and more focused drive to protect water quality to form the major thrusts of SES's activities during the decade. These campaigns grew directly from the SES's work in its first five years. They reflected strategies and tactics the group developed while working on land use planning, Catalina State Park, and various public education campaigns. Its efforts during the 1980s mirrored those of other grassroots environmental organizations across the country in the decade following the revolution in environmental and democratic reforms embodied in the state and federal laws passed to protect air, water, land, and to advance citizen participation in environmental decision-making during the 1970s. Their work on air quality, culminating in their nearly decade-long battle to bring southern Arizona's copper smelters into compliance with the Clean Air Act, demonstrates some of the challenges and possibilities for community-based environmental activism during the 1980s—a decade characterized by a popular conservative backlash to the environmentalism of the previous decade and an increase in the technical nature of environmental regulation.

In response to the changing political and regulatory landscape, SES plied a different path than the Northern Plains Resource Council and other groups of the era. It concentrated on obtaining a seat alongside technocrats and environmental managers to influence how environmental laws passed during the 1970s would be interpreted and enacted. SES recognized the changing political and regulatory landscape of environmental decision-making, and that if citizens were going to have a say in those decisions, they would have to engage different strategies than what had worked in the past. In the group's work on water quality and land use, Robinson guided SES in writing legislation and attempting to influence its passage. However, she increasingly believed that what was required to pass laws and what was required to make sure they were enforced were fundamentally different. From her point of view, ensuring that environmental agencies implemented laws and that water and air were protected was highly technical and required activists to understand the law and complexities of environmental science and management. She strove to acquire for herself and SES the knowledge and political capital necessary to participate in important environmental decisions that often took place out of the public's sight. As a result, Robinson, a self-trained expert on water and air quality issues by the mid-1980s, was often the only nonprofessional, female citizen serving on technical environmental rule-making committees in the state. As such, she represented the interests of citizens easily ignored in environmental decision-making.[38]

In working for improvements to air and water quality in Arizona, SES serves as a case study of a citizens' environmental group that formed and came of age in the era following the passage of the nation's landmark environmental laws. Although the strategies SES pursued to address water and air quality issues differed from those of Northern Plains during the 1970s, they were representative of a trend in citizen activism during the 1980s as groups adapted to the changing political and regulatory climate of that decade. Through public education, encouraging citizens to take part in decision procedures, holding the government and industry accountable to environmental laws, and eventually gaining seats at the decision-making tables, SES displayed a continued understanding of environmental issues as intimately connected with issues of democracy and governance. SES's nearly decade-long campaign to clean up Arizona's copper smelters most clearly demonstrates this continuity in the actions and aims of citizen activists but also their transition during the second decade of the modern environmental movement.

5

Reining in the Smelters

The Fight for Clean Air in Southern Arizona

By the end of the 1970s, Americans were more environmentally conscious than ever before. As the decade closed, however, environmentalists learned that, although Congress or states had passed laws to address threats to the environment, problems persisted. Implementation of environmental laws required the continual attention of citizens to monitor government agencies and industry in order to hold both accountable to the public. In Arizona, this was most evident in the fight for clean air.

In 1978, eight years after the passage of the Clean Air Act and an Environmental Protection Agency (EPA) mandate that the sixteen U.S. copper smelters—seven of which were located in Arizona—remove 90 percent of the sulfur dioxide from their emissions, little had changed. Arizona had yet to create plans to control the pollution from its smelters as directed by the federal government. Copper smelters were the largest source of pollution in Arizona and the largest emitters of sulfur dioxide, the chemical responsible for acid rain, west of the Mississippi River. However, the majority of activists focused their attention on urban air pollution created by automobiles. From smokestacks hundreds of feet high, smelters pumped thousands of tons of sulfur dioxide, heavy metals, and other pollutants into the air every day. The pollution drifted over rural Arizona communities, farms, and ranches and into Mexico, causing respiratory problems and damaging crops. By 1978, five of the Arizona smelters had begun to upgrade their facilities to meet the requirements of the Clean Air Act and avoid costly fines from the EPA. However, the final two, the massive Douglas Reduction

Works on the Mexican border owned by the mining giant Phelps Dodge Corporation and the Magma Copper Company's smelter in San Manuel, remained out of compliance and showed no intention of meeting the terms of the law. "Old Reliable," as Phelps Dodge affectionately called its aging smelter in Douglas ("Old Smoky" to many of the people who lived near its belching smokestack), emitted roughly one-quarter of the total smelter pollution in the state.[1] Phelps Dodge appeared more willing to use its political influence and the skill of its lobbyists and attorneys to obtain Clean Air Act exemptions for the Douglas smelter than invest millions to upgrade the almost seventy-year-old facility.[2]

The company reluctantly acknowledged the damage its smelter caused to the land surrounding its smelter. Between the 1930s and 1971, it bought "smoke rights," paying farmers and ranchers owning 112,000 acres in the valley north of Douglas and to the south in Mexico not to sue the company for acid rain damage to their properties resulting from the roughly 100,000 tons of sulfur dioxide the smelter emitted every day. "Old Reliable" dependably turned a profit at the expense of the environment and health

FIGURE 4. Phelps Dodge's Douglas Reduction Works smelter in 1972. The Douglas smelter pumped thousands of tons of sulfur dioxide and other pollutants into the atmosphere and polluted the air and land for miles around the smelter.

National Archives and Records Administration, photo no. 412-DA-543989.

of people living in southeastern Arizona. If forced to spend hundreds of millions of dollars to install pollution controls, Douglas would not be profitable again for many years. Phelps Dodge's plan was to subvert the intent of the Clean Air Act for as long as elected officials and regulators would allow. As it did so, it would smelt copper with a competitive advantage over the region's other smelters, which were investing millions of dollars in pollution abatement technologies. When it could no longer get its way with state politicians and regulators, Phelps Dodge would close the archaic smelter, leaving hundreds of southern Arizonans out of work. It was a ruthless, but economically rational, strategy for a company with a long history of ironfisted corporate behavior.[3] The Phelps Dodge smelter had killed crops, choked residents, and ignored or perverted the law in the region for decades; unless someone intervened to thwart its plans, the company would continue to undermine public health, the environment, and the law in southern Arizona for decades to come. When government failed to act, citizens, emboldened by new environmental laws that included citizen participation provisions, stepped in. Tucson's Southwest Environmental Service (SES) led the movement to hold the smelters and government accountable to the laws, health, and environment of the people.

In the late 1970s, SES expanded its work to include concerns about water and air quality. The organization initially understood both issues in relation to urban growth and land-use planning, but SES's work on water and air quality quickly evolved in response to a variety of developments outside the organization's control. Water quality and air quality each became separate campaigns for the organization, and air quality eventually became SES's chief priority. Changes in federal air quality laws during the 1970s and requirements for the state of Arizona, Pima County, and Tucson to create new air quality standards to bring the region into compliance with the federal Clean Air Act provided a catalyst. In response to the processes created by the 1977 revisions to the federal Clean Air Act, SES's air quality campaign grew from a public education initiative aimed at building awareness about the value of and threats to Tucson's air quality to a focused and sophisticated effort to rein in some of the nation's largest polluters.

SES's air quality campaign illustrates the complexity and trajectory of many local, community-based environmental campaigns during the 1980s.

Like other environmental organizations during this era, SES set out to ensure implementation and enforcement of existing laws and used citizen participation to influence decision-makers to reduce pollution. When this strategy failed to produce the desired results, SES adapted. Its campaign grew more sophisticated and technical. SES actively recruited media coverage to build their case for closing the offending smelters and looked to other decision-making bodies for solutions. Ultimately, their campaign to clean up southern Arizona's air was won through the courts and administrative processes established under the federal Clean Air Act. SES's air quality campaign demonstrates the relationship between environmental laws and citizen participation, the role of the media and politics in influencing environmental decisions, and how citizens' environmental groups adapted to changing regulatory and political landscapes and creatively used all means at their disposal to affect change.

From Smog to Smelters: SES's Air Quality Campaign, 1977–1981

Until December 1977, air quality was simply a subset of Southwest Environmental Service's larger work on land-use planning. While the organization busily monitored various proposals for new suburban developments and attempted to influence county and state regulations regarding growth, events in Washington, DC, changed the context of its work on air quality. In 1970, Congress passed the Clean Air Act with bipartisan support, and Republican president Richard Nixon signed it into law. This success came after more than five years of lobbying by environmental organizations and out of general frustration by certain members of Congress at the failure of previous federal remedies to air pollution. Political scientist Walter Rosenbaum argues that federal environmental laws before 1970—the Water Quality Act of 1965 for instance, or the Air Quality Act of 1967—were congressional experiments in incrementalism.[4] Instead of Congress's legislating a primary role for the federal government in setting standards for environmental quality and then enforcing those standards, it treated pollution as a "uniquely local problem," which could best be solved by a "partnership" between state and local governments. The deference of the federal government to the states was a "prescription for inaction," as few states cooperated and voluntarily created and enforced pollution abatement regulations.[5] The rapid growth in the political strength of the environmental movement during the 1960s, the increasing public awareness of the severity of environmental degradation, and the leadership of veteran conservationists in Congress created the impetus for the passage of a new generation of federal environmental laws. The Clean Air Act of 1970, along with the landmark National Environmental Policy Act, was one of the first of many laws that mandated a new role and responsibility of the federal government in rectifying environmental problems. It made air quality a national priority, created a new national framework for setting standards for pollutants, and established strict deadlines for compliance. Under the law, which Rosenbaum identifies as "one of the longest, most complex, and most technically detailed regulatory programs ever enacted on a federal level," the federal government was to establish national standards for air quality for major pollutants harmful to human health and the environment.[6] The act directed the states to administer the program within guidelines established by Congress and the EPA. The federal government and states were to share enforcement of the standards.[7]

After six years, Congress reviewed the law and revised it in 1977 through a series of amendments. Significantly, the 1977 Clean Air Act Amendments created mechanisms for prevention of significant deterioration (PSD) of air quality in areas meeting the National Ambient Air Quality Standards (NAAQS) enacted by the 1970 law and established new penalties for failing to comply with the standards. Because many states did not meet the standards set in the law, the 1977 Clean Air Act Amendments granted extensions on standards for pollutants emitted from automobiles under the stipulation that standards of carbon monoxide and hydrocarbons would be further tightened after 1980. In an attempt to make coal strip mining and power production more palatable to environmentalists in the midst of the energy crisis, Congress and President Jimmy Carter also wrote into the amendments the New Source Review Program that required operators of large industrial facilities, namely coal-fired power plants and oil refineries, to install modern pollution control technology in new plants and when retrofitting old facilities. Due to pressures from the copper lobby and congressmen representing copper-producing states, however, this provision did not extend to Arizona's copper smelters. Instead, Congress created the Primary Nonferrous Smelter Order (NSO) system that created a process by which copper smelters built before August 7, 1977, could be exempted from complying with pollution standards in the act until as late as 1988.[8]

The Southwest Environmental Service monitored these amendments from afar for most of 1977. In December, however, when Robinson caught wind of rumors that under the amendments the federal government could withhold funding for highway and wastewater projects around Tucson if the state failed to enforce air quality standards, she took notice. Highway and wastewater issues were primary concerns in the organization's land use work. At that month's meeting of the board, Robinson told the members about the amendments to the Clean Air Act. She reported her understanding that the federal government was requiring more action by the states and for the first time, federal funding for other programs would be tied to whether states enforced federal air quality standards. She explained that each state, and regions within each state, were required to prepare a plan to achieve federal air quality standards by January 1979, and public hearings and citizen participation were required in the crafting of the plans that ultimately would have to be approved by the Environmental Protection Agency. "Because this is an area where important decisions will be made within the next year," she told the group, "and because extensive citizen participation is possible, it is an area where we need to become expert."[9] She requested that the board allocate five hundred dollars to hire a part-time researcher to study the changes and how they might affect SES's work. The board approved the request.[10]

From early 1978 until 1979, SES's clean air work consisted primarily of studying the changes to federal law and identifying how the group might positively affect air quality in southern Arizona. Robinson hired Betsy Rieke on an hourly basis to research the issue. The two worked to understand what was required of the state of Arizona in terms of creating regulations or programs to meet the new federal mandates and determine how SES might influence state agency decisions regarding air quality. Following its organizational philosophy, the group embarked on a campaign to educate the public about air quality issues and encourage citizens to participate in any environmental decision-making process that might emerge.[11]

Like other environmental groups in Tucson, SES's principal concerns had to do with urban air quality. In February, SES formed a working group made up of representatives from the Southern Arizona Environmental

Council, Arizona Lung Association, League of Women Voters, Sierra Club, and a handful of other interested individuals. Robinson also traveled to Phoenix that month to meet with representatives from other groups interested in air quality to network and strategize.[12] By March, the working group had eighteen members representing seven different organizations, and they focused on addressing air quality issues associated with transportation planning.[13] In June, SES partnered with the Arizona Lung Association and, with a small amount of funding from the EPA, organized a Clean Air Workshop in Phoenix modeled on the successful Water Workshops SES organized two years prior. It drew seventy concerned attendees.[14] Three months later, SES helped organize a community-wide Clean Air Day at a shopping mall in Tucson sponsored by the Southern Arizona Environmental Council, the Pima County Air Quality Council, and the Sierra Club. In announcing the event, SAEC's newsletter told readers that it was organizing the event because "the environmental well being of Tucson may well depend on Tucson's ability to meet the new federal clean air standards." The event emphasized the effect of automobile emissions on Tucson's air quality and taught residents how to reduce their emissions.[15]

As SES became more involved in its air quality public education campaign, Robinson was forced to learn the scientific and technical aspects of air pollution and air quality laws as well as their enforcement. On the heels of the Clean Air Workshop and in the midst of internal conversations about the financial future of SES, the organization succeeded in getting a small grant from the EPA for a public education campaign to produce a citizens' clean air handbook in conjunction with a smaller publication about smelter pollution to be produced by the Arizona Lung Association. The project required the group to delve deeper into the details of air quality. Understanding the Clean Air Act, its 1977 revisions, the standards they created, and what they required of state and local government was a challenge even for technocrats trained and practiced in law and environmental management. The SES staff had to decipher the meanings of attainment and non-attainment areas, stationary and mobile sources of pollution, particulates, photochemical oxidants, carbon monoxide, sulfur dioxide, and other pollutants. In addition, they had to navigate an ever deepening pool of acronyms: NAAQS (National Ambient Air Quality Standards, pronounced "knacks"), NESHAPs (National Emission Standards for Hazardous

Air Pollutants—there is no record of this being pronounced "kneeshaps"),
SIPs (State Implementation Plans), and NSPSs (New Source Performance
Standards). If this were not enough, they had to unpack the differences
between Class I, Class II, and Class III air quality areas and where the EPA
had located each in the state. Their research drew them into meetings concerning the Pima County Air Quality Regulations and hearings on the EPA's
proposed boundaries for non-attainment areas, areas that did not meet
the agency's NAAQS and thus had to be managed differently under the
Clean Air Act. They reviewed the potential impact on land use and transportation planning in Tucson of zoning the Saguaro National Monument
as a Class I airshed and of proposed state air quality regulations. Amid all
of this, one acronym came to stand out more than the others: NSOs.[16]

In January 1979, SES was notified that the EPA was holding a series of
hearings in Tucson concerning rule making for something called Nonferrous Smelter Orders. Nonferrous Smelter Orders, or NSOs, were an exemption written into the Clean Air Act Amendments of 1977 to shield existing
copper smelters from penalties resulting from their inability or unwillingness to meet the sulfur dioxide standards established in the act and the
EPA. Much of the popular fervor surrounding new air quality standards and
enforcement mechanisms for stationary, industrial sources of pollution in
the amendments revolved around emissions from coal-fired power plants
and oil refineries; this was a response to the plans of government and the
power industry to build dozens of major coal-fired electrical generating
plants and oil refineries during the 1970s. As a result, Congress created the
New Source Review Program, which required new plants and refineries to
incorporate the latest pollution abatement technology in their facilities.[17]

Copper industry lobbyists and politicians from copper-producing
states, including Arizona's Democratic congressman representing Tucson
and southern Arizona, Morris Udall, worked to protect the industry from
new air quality regulations as the amendments took form. Copper lobbyists from international mining corporations like Phelps Dodge, Magma,
ASARCO, and Kennecott argued that if they were forced to comply with the
Clean Air Act standards, they could not compete with government-owned
foreign competition like the recently nationalized mines in Chile. Fearing
a loss of jobs, Udall and the Arizona delegation pushed for the exemptions. NSOs created a process that made official what had been a de facto

exemption of certain copper smelters from the requirements of the Clean Air Act by the EPA's inability to compel states to force facilities into compliance. However, in April 1978, the EPA told Arizona that after eight years of failing to meet Clean Air Act standards, the state must create a plan to bring the smelters into compliance. If Arizona failed to do so, the federal government would step in. For smelters to continue to receive the exemptions, they had to apply for a Nonferrous Smelter Order by demonstrating that pollution abatement technology was either not available or too expensive. If granted, the smelter could continue to operate exempt from air quality standards until a designated date. In 1979, the two most polluting smelters in Arizona, and potentially the entire United States, Phelps Dodge's facility at Douglas and Magma's facility at San Manuel, applied for NSOs. If granted, the smelters would receive an exemption until January 1, 1983, at which time they could reapply for a second NSO that would extend the exemption to January 1, 1988. As required by the Clean Air Act, the EPA scheduled hearings to gather public input on the regulations for issuing NSOs for Phelps Dodge's and Magma's applications.[18]

When Robinson received the notice of the upcoming hearings, she scrambled to get SES involved. She feared that the Tucson-area environmental community was so focused on urban air quality and the regulations that accompanied the notice from the EPA were so technical that the SES had to do something or no one else would. She read the proposed rules attempting to understand the issue as best she could and prepared a mailing to her list of more than three hundred people interested in air quality encouraging them to testify at the hearings or at least submit comments. At the hearings, twenty-three other speakers joined Robinson; SES recruited at least seventeen of these speakers. Robinson testified on the proximity of Douglas and San Manuel smelters to Tucson and to the Saguaro National Monument, Aravaipa Canyon primitive area, and other wilderness areas eligible for designation as Class I air quality areas under the Clean Air Act and the effects granting NSOs to Phelps Dodge and Magma might have on air quality in these areas and the region as a whole. After the hearings, she reported to the board that the EPA staff appreciated SES's work in "helping to provide some balance at the hearings."[19]

At the hearings, she met a man named Michael Gregory from Bisbee, approximately thirty miles west of the Douglas smelter. Located in the rugged Mule Mountains just north of the U.S.-Mexico border, the town was one of the capitals of the southwestern copper empire during the twentieth century. When Phelps Dodge's Lavender Pit closed in the 1970s, the company moved its western regional headquarters out of Bisbee. In 1979, Bisbee was in the process of transitioning from a mining town to a refuge for artists, counterculture types, and, increasingly, tourists. Gregory alerted Robinson after the hearings that there was a group of people in Bisbee who stridently opposed Phelps Dodge's application for an NSO exemption. He described clouds of sulfurous smog rolling northeast from the smelter into the mountains and asthma attacks among the young, elderly, and infirm. Robinson's interest was piqued.[20]

Throughout 1979, as Robinson and Betsy Reike worked on the citizens' clean air handbook, smelter pollution absorbed more and more of their attention. SES became aware of other groups concerned about smelters and began to broaden its alliance. In the fall, SES connected with a new group of concerned residents near McNeal, twenty miles north of Douglas and with the Arizona Department of Health Services (ADHS), who contacted the group to review the EPA's proposed regulations regarding NSOs for Douglas and San Manuel for the department.[21]

In December 1979, SES's smelter work found a new and unexpectedly potent ally. Dick Kamp, a self-described "quasi-hippy with a non-career" who managed an auto-wrecking yard and worked part time at the Bisbee post office, approached SES about smelter smoke problems in both Arizona and Sonora, Mexico.[22] He was concerned with not only the NSO proposal for the Douglas smelter but with a proposal for a massive, 930-foot-high smelter smokestack in Nacozari, Sonora, and the expansion of the Cananea smelter in Sonora, Mexico. Years later, he remembered, "The air quality in the area was horrid."[23] He proposed to take photos of the Douglas smelter from the ground and from the air and correlate them with emissions reported by the smelter and EPA for information to use in the NSO process. The prospect of having an ally on the ground who could gather empirical data to use in SES's arguments against granting the NSOs immediately appealed to Robinson. Allying with Kamp marked a turning point in the group's clean air campaign. The citizens' air quality handbook was completed and under review by the EPA by late 1979. The state, the EPA, the SES and other groups found it "enormously useful." However, by the time of its publication in 1980, SES's air quality work had decidedly shifted toward reining in the pollution of Arizona's dirtiest smelters.[24]

SES Fires Up Its Smelter Campaign

With newfound allies in Kamp and Gregory, SES moved quickly in 1980. The loose coalition formed the Cochise Smelter Study Group to arrange a workshop on clean air, smelter pollution, and the NSO process during February 1980 that attracted about seventy-five interested people. SES organized Kamp's photographs and information into factual summaries and mailed them to its air quality mailing list of more than three hundred Arizonans encouraging them to submit comments to the EPA regarding the NSOs. Robinson and Kamp traveled to Salt Lake City, Utah, in July to testify on the EPA's proposed visibility regulations. During a labor strike at the smelters in the fall of 1980, the group worked with members of the Southern Arizona Hiking Club and Sierra Club to take clean-air baseline photos of the Galiuro Wilderness and other areas while the smelters sat idle. Phelps Dodge had already informed the EPA and the state that it would close down the Douglas smelter rather than upgrade its facilities to comply with the law if it failed to obtain an extension of its exemption from the Clean Air Act under the NSO system. Kamp remembers Robinson telling him that she was confident that by using the NSO process, the state's most polluting smelter would close within three years.[25]

The Southwest Environmental Service's leadership on air quality and especially the smelter issue began to attract broader attention by mid-1981. In February 1980, Robinson was asked to take part in the Four Corners Study Information Group created under the National Commission on Air Quality by the 1977 Clean Air Act amendments. When she attended the first meeting of the group on March 15 in Durango, Colorado, she found that she was "a national expert on smelters" because of her written testimony during the NSO hearings in Tucson.[26] She continued to take part in the group, which was reviewing and advising the National Commission as the commission prepared its final recommendations to Congress for reauthorization of the Clean Air Act scheduled for 1982. From the meetings, she gleaned technical knowledge about the Clean Air Act, EPA regulations, and air quality in general.[27] "It is an excellent educational process for me," she reported to the SES board in December 1980.[28]

Robinson's education in air quality took a new direction the next year when the National Clean Air Coalition asked SES to join its organization. Although she was familiar with the workings of county and state government in Arizona, this experience offered her a crash course in national environmental politics. In March 1981, she attended the coalition's meeting in Washington, DC. There she discovered that smelters were woefully absent from the coalition's agenda. From her perspective, the coalition was dominated by national groups like the Sierra Club that were primarily interested in urban air quality issues affecting the eastern United States. When she inquired about smelters, she was advised by other attendees to talk to Robert Yuhnke, a Boulder, Colorado-based attorney working with the Environmental Defense Fund (EDF). Yuhnke was the resident expert on smelters in the coalition. The two instantly hit it off and agreed to work together on the NSOs for the Douglas and San Manuel smelters.[29]

Robinson returned to Tucson after the meeting and continued to organize the local campaign with Rieke and tend to SES's other issues, but she was not home for long.[30] In June, the National Clean Air Coalition recruited Robinson to testify about smelter pollution before the Senate Committee on Environmental and Public Works that was considering revisions of the Clean Air Act. The coalition contacted Robinson on June 1 to testify just four days later on June 5. She gathered information from her work with the Four Corners Study Information Group and caught a plane to Washington. Robinson arrived to find that she was the only non-industry speaker on the panel presenting alongside representatives from the American Smelting and Refining Company (ASARCO), Phelps Dodge, Kennecott Copper, and Newmont Mining, of which Magma Copper, the owner of the smelter in San Manuel, was a subsidiary. Despite the unbalanced nature of the panel, Robinson felt that "the session went well."[31] She returned home to news that the Reagan administration intended to, in her words, "gut" the Clean Air Act, including extending the exemption of smelters from the air quality standards until at least 1993.[32] Robinson quickly drafted a response to the administration's position. The clean air campaign began to dominate her work and SES's agenda.[33]

SES Elevates the Smelter Issue in the Clean Air Debate

In the midst of these activities, Robinson realized that if SES hoped to do anything about pollution from the Douglas and San Manuel facilities, it was going to have to draw more attention to the smelter issue. In Arizona, she experienced firsthand how little people understood about smelters and the kinds and amount of pollution they produced; in Washington, even committed air quality activists knew little about the smelters that belched out many times more pollution than the power plants and refineries that received most of the attention. To rectify the situation, Robinson contacted a few reporters she knew at the *Arizona Daily Star* and the *Tucson Citizen* to attract them to the smelter issue. This inaugurated a sustained media campaign for the organization. Jane Kay, with whom Robinson had cultivated a relationship through SES's earlier work, wrote the first series of articles in the *Daily Star*. On June 14, Kay's two-page spread, "'Old Smoky' Is Not All That's Fuming in Douglas," told the story of Frank Grisby and Clyde McGatha, who farmed land near Douglas. "You should have been down here last week," Grisby said in the vivid exposé. "You couldn't even see the Mule Mountains." "When they start firing it [the Douglas smelter] at high, you can smell it at night so you can hardly breathe. Lots of times you can taste it," added McGatha.[34] The following week, the *Daily Star* printed another Kay piece that compared copper smelting to a recent natural disaster, adding a new element to the evolving discourse about air pollution in the region. The headline read, "Arizona Smelters: Mount St. Helens-Size Issue: Acid Rains Bitter Story Told by Dirty Air, Dead Lakes."[35] In subsequent months, the pages of the *Arizona Daily Star* and *Tucson Citizen*, the two major daily newspapers in the region, published articles tying copper mining and smelting to increased birth defects in mining towns.[36]

The media campaign raised public awareness among Arizonans, but politicians did not immediately feel its effects nor did it shape debates over smelter exemptions and revisions of the Clean Air Act. In September, Representative Morris Udall met with members of the Bisbee clean air group to hear their concerns about the Douglas smelter and extending Clean Air Act exemptions for smelters.[37] If smelters were far from the limelight in the national air quality debate, they were more than familiar to Udall. Known for his sense of humor and consensus-style of politics, the

FIGURE 5. This pollution pictured here, produced by smelters in Globe-Miami east
of Phoenix, was typical of that produced by the Douglas smelter during the 1970s.

National Archives and Records Administration, photo no. 412-DA-546749.

congressman was caught between his environmental ethics and the fact
that Phelps Dodge and Magma were two of the biggest employers in his
district. As chair of the House Committee on Interior and Insular Affairs,
Udall also held significant power to influence the Clean Air Act revisions in
Congress. At the meeting, Robinson reported that Udall was unusually rude
and dismissive, and made it clear that he supported the extension of the
smelter exemptions until 1993.[38] Following the meeting, Robinson decided
to concentrate her efforts on Governor Bruce Babbitt, with whom she had
a better relationship. Robinson had been Babbitt's first appointment to the
Arizona State Parks Board, and she had worked with his administration on
water issues. Babbitt was an easier target, but she knew that ultimately the
group would have to gain Udall's support to end the smelter exemptions.[39]

Robinson further realized the political difficulties Arizona clean air
advocates faced when the National Clean Air Act Coalition recruited her
to testify at another hearing in Washington in December 1981. When she
arrived to testify before the House Committee on Energy and Commerce
on potential revisions to the Clean Air Act, she found that the coalition
had failed to notify her that the committee room had been changed. She

arrived late for the hearing but still managed to testify. She attempted to shrug off what appeared to be an honest mistake until she realized that the national groups, particularly the Sierra Club, had been meeting with Udall and had already agreed to the continued exemption for smelters. Udall had championed the Alaska Lands Act in 1980 that designated millions of acres of wilderness in that state, which was one of the group's top priorities. The Sierra Club hoped that conceding the smelter exemptions would help maintain their relationship with the congressman and secure his support for the rest of the Clean Air Act.[40]

Although Robinson found the trip "fairly miserable," it was also instructive and ultimately beneficial.[41] Beyond providing another opportunity to meet with and lobby members of the Arizona delegation, it revealed the complex power dynamics of the clean air debate in Washington. In addition, she found unlikely allies in SES's work on the NSO issue—representatives from ASARCO, which operated the Inspiration smelter in Arizona, and Kennecott that operated a smelter across the border in New Mexico. Although the companies preferred to avoid any further regulation, they were already improving pollution abatement technologies in their smelters to meet the requirements of the Clean Air Act. Investing in this technology put them at a competitive disadvantage with Phelps Dodge and Magma if the companies continued to operate under exemptions provided by the NSO process. They offered Robinson the opportunity to tour their facilities and provided SES technical information to use in its work against the Douglas and San Manuel smelters.[42]

Collaborating with ASARCO and Kennecott was one element in what Robinson would later recount as SES's strategy of building "unlikely coalitions."[43] This unlikely coalition continued to grow in 1982 to include more radical environmentalists. On New Year's Day, Robinson met with Jonathon Western, a member of Greenpeace, an international environmental organization with a history of using direct action tactics in their campaigns. Western described his proposal to Robinson: a media event that involved activists climbing the smokestack of the Douglas smelter to unfurl a banner illuminating the relationship between the facility and acid rain. The potential benefits of such publicity intrigued Robinson. Acid rain had become a growing public concern during 1981 and 1982 and increasingly attracted media attention. For the most part, articles from the Associated

Press stressed the danger of acid rain in the East, but newspapers in the Southwest were also beginning to cover the issue. At the same time, Bob Yuhnke at the Environmental Defense Fund linked smelters to acid rain in the West as part of EDF's air quality work. Robinson thought that the Greenpeace media event might give the issue the push it needed to awaken the National Clean Air Coalition and Arizona politicians to the seriousness of smelter pollution, but she also worried about how SES's involvement with such a controversial action might affect the group's reputation. She decided to help Western plan the event but keep a low profile.[44]

Worried that the Douglas smelter was too remote from media centers and that law enforcement in Douglas "was pretty much still in a Wild West mode," she advised Greenpeace to climb the San Manuel smelter instead.[45] She contacted Kay at the *Arizona Daily Star* and Tony Davis at the *Tucson Citizen*. On the morning of February 8, Greenpeace activists David Stewart, a tree trimmer from Colorado, and Clare O'Brien, a rock climber from New Mexico, climbed the thin metal ladder that clung to the side of the Magma Smelter three hundred feet off the ground and unfurled a sixty-by-twelve-foot banner. In the frigid whipping wind, it proclaimed "For Our Children, For Our Land, For Our Future—Stop Acid Rain." The activists spent the night on the stack before coming down. Magma's lawyers told reporters that the company considered the event an obvious case of trespassing and might press charges. Greenpeace representative Alfred Quarto responded to reporters, "We told them we thought Magma is trespassing on clean air."[46] Quarto told the press that Greenpeace was not trying to shut down the smelter with the action. "We're doing this," he said, "because we see the Reagan administration trying to weaken an already weak [environmental protection] act. . . . We want to preserve at least what we have now."[47] Robinson managed the press at the event, directing reporters to Greenpeace spokespeople. She did not appear in news coverage and quietly reported the event to the SES board.[48]

The Greenpeace action was followed by a second round of hearings on Phelps Dodge's and Magma's applications for exemptions for their smelters held in San Manuel, Phoenix, and Douglas in late February and early March 1982. The Arizona Department of Health Services (ADHS), the state agency charged with enforcing federal air quality law in Arizona, organized the hearings. If the ADHS approved the smelters' applications, they would be sent to the EPA for review. SES recruited people to testify in person or submit comments through the mail. Robinson and Kamp attended all four hearings that were livened up by a few Greenpeace members who remained after the smelter action. The majority of attendees opposed the smelters receiving NSO exemptions. Despite this strong local opposition, however, Robinson expected ADHS to grant the NSOs. When they did, SES, EDF, and Kamp's Smelter Crisis Education Project (SCEP) would challenge the decision, taking it to court if necessary. She was convinced that with their technical knowledge about smelters and pollution abatement technology as well as Yuhnke's legal ability, they could win and shut down the smelters in the next year. The truth was on their side. It was only a matter of time before it prevailed.[49]

Things did not unfold exactly as Robinson predicted or as quickly. The Arizona Department of Health Services did approve the NSOs for Douglas and San Manuel, but the EPA's Air Quality Division did not take action on the NSOs because Arizona's sulfur dioxide emission limits were not scheduled to start until the following year. Phelps Dodge and Magma were challenging the NSO regulations in court. Pressure by the Reagan administration and mining interests may have also influenced EPA's delay. While clean air advocates waited for the EPA to take action, Robinson went back to work trying to influence the ongoing congressional review of the Clean Air Act, including lobbying Representative Udall on smelter exemptions.[50] By April 1982, it appeared that the press coverage of the smelter issue and intensive lobbying by many of Udall's supporters from Tucson were starting to turn the congressman's opinion. He received dozens of letters from constituents, many prompted by SES's mailings. Dr. Frank Lewis and his wife Udiko, for example, wrote that "extending the exemption will do nothing to aid the industry with its present financial problems. . . . Extension would only demonstrate that those smelters which have made no effort to comply with the goals of the Clean Air Act will be rewarded, while the people who live in the surrounding areas can continue to breathe toxic air and contend with acid rains."[51] T. A. and G. A. Korn told Udall that extending the exemption would give smelters like Douglas and San Manuel a ten-cent-a-ton competitive advantage over Arizona's five other smelters who complied with the law. They wrote, "What this situation says to everyone is: if you don't like the rules of the game, ignore them or make up your own rules, because the good guys always lose."[52]

After meeting with Udall, Robinson reported to the board that "Mo" was not committed to any position, but that it was her impression that he would probably not support the copper industry's proposal to extend Clean Air Act exemptions until 1993.[53] The apparent progress Robinson observed with Udall was accompanied by some success in persuading the National Clean Air Coalition to make the smelter issue a priority. For the duration of 1982, neither the ADHS nor the EPA gave any indication of movement on the NSO applications for the Douglas and San Manuel smelters. Despite the seemingly stalled state of this aspect of SES's work, the political component of the smelter campaign continued to strengthen. So did the working relationship among Robinson, Yuhnke, and Kamp.[54]

New Coalitions and New Dynamics in the Fight for Clean Air

SES's smelter campaign entered a new phase in 1983. All of the group's work during the previous years to make smelter pollution part of the larger conversation about air quality began to bear fruit. In August 1982, the National Clean Air Coalition finally identified the smelter exemptions as one of its top priorities. When a bill supported by the Reagan administration that included amendments extending the exemption until 1993 reported out of committee in September, the coalition led the charge against it. With the election looming, Congress let the bill die in the fall of 1982 only to pick it up the next year. The November 1982 elections swept a more environmentally aware Democratic majority into Congress and tilted the makeup of key committees in environmentalists' favor. When the new session of Congress opened in January 1983, the Senate resurrected the bill as a starting point for the Clean Air Act revisions that were now a year overdue. The House started from scratch. However, neither side moved a bill that session, with or without the smelter exemption extension.[55]

Before the new Congress began, however, SES worked to build new coalitions and new relationships with Arizona's political leaders to advance the smelter issue. Robinson met with representatives of the United Steelworkers Union to craft a compromise on the Clean Air Act exemption that would extend it only to smelters that were in the process of upgrading their facilities to comply with the law by a set deadline. With the Steelworkers, she convinced Arizona's Democratic senator Dennis DeConcini to support this proposal. She met with Representative James "Jim" McNulty Jr., a Democrat representing the new Fifth District, which covered parts of Tucson and southeast Arizona, including Bisbee and Douglas. The drawing of this new district and election of McNulty rearranged smelter politics in southern Arizona. Udall was released from representing the mining and smelting regions of the southeastern part of the state. McNulty made smelter pollution a priority and was especially concerned about the proposal to build a new smelter across the border in Nacozari, Sonora. The Mexican smelters would more than double the air pollution that drifted over southern Arizona creating what critics labeled the "Gray Triangle." With all three smelters running in this border region, residents of the triangle could expect their air to be clogged with up to 2,700 tons a day of sulfur dioxide and particulates.[ ] This was more than three times the pollution that spewed from the Douglas smelter alone and roughly twenty times as much as the massive coal-burning Navajo Generating Station in northern Arizona emitted, which produced enough electricity for roughly 2 million homes. At the same time, it would undercut production costs at a time when copper prices were painfully low, threatening hundreds of jobs in the state. McNulty opposed the Mexican smelters on both fronts because of pollution and overproduction and helped catalyze popular opposition on the issue in Arizona. Despite the fact that hundreds of thousands of tons of harmful sulfur dioxide and other pollutants had drifted south from the Douglas smelter onto Mexican farms, ranches, and communities for decades, Arizonans cried out against the unfairness of foreigners polluting the southern part of the state. With allies like McNulty, environmentalists fended off attempts by business groups and the Reagan administration to extend smelter exemptions and maintained the Clean Air Act as it was amended in 1977.[57]

In addition to the Mexican affair, clean air advocates benefited when Phelps Dodge copper workers around the state went on strike in 1983. The conflict began with negotiations over a three-year contract between the United Steelworkers and Arizona's mining companies. All of Arizona's copper mining companies—Asarco, Inspiration, Magma, and Kennecott—accepted the union's offer except Phelps Dodge, which claimed that with the prolonged slump in copper prices, it could not afford to accede the union's demands. At one minute after midnight on July 1, thousands of workers at Phelps Dodge operations in Ajo, Bisbee, Douglas, and Clifton-Morenci walked off the job. The situation quickly escalated into one of the ugliest labor conflicts of the late twentieth century. It ended only after Governor Bruce Babbitt, at the request of Phelps Dodge, called in the Arizona National Guard to remove strikers who physically blocked doors and gates and shut down the mines at Clifton and Morenci. Nature also intervened in the form of a catastrophic flood that wiped out one-third of the workers' homes in Clifton.[58]

The tactics employed by strikers, the callous corporate behavior of Phelps Dodge, and the apparent collusion of the state government with the company were all enormously unpopular with Arizonans and ruptured the relationship between Phelps Dodge and Arizonan politicians. Since the early 1900s, the corporation had flexed its muscle throughout the state with campaign contributions and the promise of jobs and economic development. The strike forced politicians like Bruce Babbitt and Morris Udall, who had tried to protect and promote the copper industry—and particularly Phelps Dodge—to go against an essential part of their base: organized labor. As the strike progressed, public sentiment mostly fell with the workers. Bruce Babbitt resented the position Phelps Dodge put him in and completely distanced himself from the company to rebuild his relationship with organized labor in advance of his eventual presidential campaign in 1987. He directed the Arizona Department of Health Services to enforce water and air quality laws pertaining to the company with unprecedented vigor. Similarly, Udall, who had done everything in his power to shield the copper industry from environmental regulations while copper prices were so low in the early 1980s, committed himself to ending the exemption for Phelps Dodge's Douglas smelter.[59]

The strike, coupled with the Mexican smelter issue, changed the political dynamics of SES's smelter campaign. By the end of 1984, Udall agreed that he would not support extensions beyond December 1987 for the Phelps Dodge and Magma smelters in the revisions to the Clean Air Act that were still winding through Congress. Governor Babbitt was more than enthusiastic about forcing Phelps Dodge to comply with air quality laws. All of these developments boded well for SES and clean air advocates.

From this strengthened position, however, SES and its allies initiated a new tactical move.[60]

Moving to the Offensive: Citizens Use the Courts

While attending the Western Acid Rain Conference in Gunnison, Colorado, in July 1984, Robinson met with Robert Yuhnke to discuss the smelter campaign. Yuhnke explained to Robinson that, after working on the smelter issue for more than five years, the Environmental Defense Fund, had collected enough evidence to file a lawsuit with the Southwest Environmental Service and Smelter Crisis Education Project. "I was delirious with joy," Robinson wrote later of her reaction to the news.[61] When Robinson and Kamp first testified at the NSO hearings for Phelps Dodge and Magma, Robinson had predicted that the NSO process would spell the end for the smelters. If the Arizona Department of Health Services (ADHS) and EPA granted the NSOs for the smelters, the environmentalists would challenge the decision and, she believed, they would win. The swift conclusion that Robinson envisioned was thwarted by the EPA, which was practically standing still on the NSO applications. The EPA's inaction allowed Phelps Dodge and Magma to continue to pollute beyond the specifications of the Clean Air Act while the agency considered their NSO applications. In Robinson's view, "the whole thing was headed toward a vast legal tangle and it was time for us to sue to push the thing along."[62] Yuhnke's lawsuit indicted Phelps Dodge and Magma Copper Company for failing to comply with the state's plan to implement sulfur dioxide standards under the Clean Air Act. If the smelters had received final approval of their NSO applications from the EPA, they would have been exempt from the sulfur dioxide standards until 1983 and potentially 1988. However, until the EPA acted, the smelters operated in a legal limbo. Citizens' ability to review or appeal the EPA decision hinged on EPA action. The lawsuit would force the EPA to act. Once the agency did, citizens could appeal the decision in the courts. At a bare minimum, the smelters would be forced to clean up or close down by January 1, 1988, at the latest.[63]

On November 28, Yuhnke filed the suit in federal district court in Tucson. The plaintiffs were the EDF, Priscilla Robinson, and Dick Kamp. Robinson and Yuhnke organized a press conference about the suit.[64] "This is not an attack on the entire copper industry," Robinson told the press. "There are seven smelters in Arizona and five of them have either completed their modernization or will be within a matter of months . . . these are the only two western smelters that are continuing to operate and have not met the emission standards."[65]

With their legal challenge slowly working its way through the federal court in Tucson and Phelps Dodge and Magma's NSO applications still tied up by the EPA, Robinson, Yuhnke, and Kamp aimed their efforts toward continuing to sway the opinion of politicians and the public against the offending smelters. Throughout 1985, negotiations continued between the United States, Mexican, and Arizona governments and the World Bank and the Inter-American Development Bank concerning the new and expanded Mexican smelters. In March, SES, EDF, and SCEP learned that the EPA was moving toward an agreement with Mexico in which the Mexican smelters would operate without air pollution controls until 1987 in exchange for allowing the Douglas smelter to continue to operate out of compliance with the Clean Air Act until the same year. The environmentalists and Representative Dennis DeConcini opposed this plan because they believed that once the plants began operation without air pollution controls, it would be very difficult to force them later to comply with standards. At the same time, the Arizona Department of Health Services began considering the renewal of the operating permit for Phelps Dodge's Douglas smelter. The renewal process gave the groups and concerned citizens the opportunity to comment on the renewal and demand that the smelter comply with the Clean Air Act. The two processes happening at once provided SES and its allies the opportunity to focus more attention on swaying the opinion of the public, politicians, and administrators.[66]

Kamp, who had already been working to explicate the dangers to air quality posed by three uncontrolled smelters operating in the Gray Triangle, jumped on this development. For the remainder of the year, from April 1985 into 1986, every time he discussed the Mexican smelter issue, he tied the need for the Nacozari smelter and Cananea expansion to include pollution controls to the need for Douglas to comply with air quality laws or shut down. The newly elected Arizona Republican congressman Jim Kolbe understood the great concern over the Mexican smelter issue among his constituents. Like McNulty before him and DeConcini, he understood the

Mexican smelter as connected to the Arizona smelters. If he called on Mexico to build a modern, cleaner smelter, he had to condemn the Douglas smelter and support its closure if it did not modernize. Robinson, Kamp, and Yuhnke decided that SES, which was increasingly tied up in issues of water quality, could best use its talents to lobby Governor Babbitt in the hope of convincing him to deny Phelps Dodge's pending permit. They reasoned that if the state denied the renewal, the EPA would be encouraged to take a stronger stand in negotiations with Mexico about the Nacozari and Cananea smelters. As Robinson reflected, "It was a lovely strategy in every way, and a truly virtuoso performance by Dick."[67]

The governor's office did not deny Phelps Dodge's permit renewal for the Douglas smelter during 1985. Instead, the ADHS issued the permit in August with a list of conditions designed to force Phelps Dodge to modernize its smelter and move toward compliance with the law. Phelps Dodge appealed the decision to the Air Pollution Control Board. SES, EDF, SCEP, and members of the Bisbee group, which had resurrected the name GASP (Groups Against Smelter Pollution) from a 1970s era environmental organization based in Tucson, intervened on behalf of the department in the appeal. The governor's strategy worked in leveraging political opposition to the continued exemption of the Douglas smelter from air quality regulations. Babbitt directed the Arizona Department of Health Services to enforce air quality laws on the state's smelters more vigorously. Equally important, SES finally made progress with Representative Udall. Robinson met with Babbitt in September 1985 and asked the governor to contact Udall about the Mexican smelter issue and the Douglas permit. Udall agreed with Babbitt that, as part of the international agreement with Mexico concerning the Nacozari and Cananea smelters, the Douglas smelter would have to clean up or close. Within three months, a bipartisan group of Arizona congressman and senators, including Representatives Jim Kolbe, John McCain, Morris Udall, and Senator Jim DeConcini, encouraged the EPA to work with Mexican officials on a policy that would consider the Douglas smelter emissions together with the pollution from the Nacozari and Cananea smelters and give the agency the power to shut down the Douglas smelter if it failed to meet clean air standards in two years.[68]

As Kamp and Robinson worked in Arizona, Yuhnke shifted his strategy. The environmental lawyer was becoming something of a celebrity in air quality activist circles for his work on acid rain in the West and his pending lawsuit to force EPA action on the Douglas and San Manuel NSOs. In late 1985, he changed direction to emphasizing the health risks of sulfur dioxide to asthmatics. This added a new dimension to the campaign: beyond harm to the natural environment caused by the acid rain produced by sulfur dioxide in the atmosphere, he argued that the smelter was a tangible danger to public health.[69] At the Air Pollution Control Board hearing of Phelps Dodge's appeal of the ADHS's decision on the operating permit for the Douglas smelter, Yuhnke argued that EDF ought to be granted intervener status in the appeal to help defend "the people whose lives are being crippled" by smelter pollution.[70] He intended the message to resonate with the public and politicians, but it had its greatest effect on EPA administrators. On December 6, Yuhnke and the EDF joined seven states and four other environmental organizations in filing suit against the EPA for failing to establish standards to protect the health of asthmatics.[71] Much of the data used in the lawsuit came from the Douglas area. Yuhnke's emphasis on asthma put further pressure on the EPA to take action on the Douglas smelter.[72] Governor Babbitt also increased pressure on the agency when he threatened in early 1986 to sue Phelps Dodge or the EPA if they failed to act to protect asthmatics.[73]

The Douglas Smelter Closes, Citizens Claim Victory

By the beginning of 1986, all of the pieces were in place for the final round between environmentalists and the Douglas and San Manuel smelters, but there was little for anyone other than the lawyers to do but wait. Robinson spent most of her time working with the governor's office and the Arizona legislature to pass the Arizona Environmental Quality Act to address water quality issues. When she could, she worked with Kamp writing letters or lobbying on the Mexican smelter issue.[74]

Then, without announcement or fanfare, on July 10, 1986, the smoke stopped. Yuhnke's most recent lawsuit still sat in the federal district court in Tucson; the Arizona Department of Health Services had yet to make any formal decision on Phelps Dodge's 1986 air quality permit; the Environmental Protection Agency had issued no decision on extending the air quality exception for "Old Reliable." Nonetheless, the subtle roar of the smelter furnaces and the iconic plume that had been part of life for residents in Douglas for more than eighty years ceased.[75]

In the most anticlimactic of endings, the smelter closed because after six years, the extensions of the stay of enforcement of the Clean Air Act granted by the EPA while it considered the NSO application ran out. As unexpected as it was, clean air advocates had precipitated the situation. The EPA had to either act on the NSO application or extend the stay. The motion filed by Yuhnke earlier that year argued that the continued stays of the law pending determination of the NSO application were illegal. It forced the EPA to act on the NSO—either grant another stay, which would require them to go into federal court and respond to Yuhnke's motion, or do nothing. The EPA chose the last option. Hounded by continual bad press and financial difficulties, Phelps Dodge did what it had promised to do for years: close the smelter and put roughly three hundred people out of work in a town of 15,000.[76]

Phelps Dodge justified its decision based on economics, but the closure of the smelter was a huge victory for advocates of clean air. Activists prevented the company from continuing to profit while violating the Clean Air Act and damaging the environment and public health into the 1990s. The company recognized that without an extended stay or the exemption provided by the NSO, it would have to operate at a dramatically reduced capacity to avoid exceeding air quality standards or accrue hundreds of thousands of dollars in fines from the EPA. Operating at quarter capacity undermined any kind of economy of scale for "Old Reliable" and drove production costs above those of other smelters, including the company's Clean Air Act–compliant smelter at Playas, New Mexico. After the closure, the state, the EPA, and Phelps Dodge entered a consent decree, an agreement filed in federal district court, on July 29, which stipulated that the company could reopen its smelter and operate it at a reduced rate so that it did not violate air quality standards under the Clean Air Act without incurring penalties before it closed permanently on January 15, 1987. SES, EDF, and SCEP filed to become partners in the consent decree. Although the state would not settle the issue of the San Manuel NSO for another year, that smelter was eventually also forced to shut down and modernize to comply with the Clean Air Act under a similar consent decree between the state and Magma Copper Company. This battle for clean air in Arizona had been won. For environmentalists, all that remained was the celebration.[77]

Bob Yuhnke flew into Tucson from Boulder, Colorado, on an unusually snowy evening the night of January 16, 1987. Robinson met him and the two drove through the storm to Bisbee. When they arrived after 10 P.M., the party was well underway. Robinson kept the celebration out of her reports to the SES board. They partied late. The next morning was still overcast, the sky heavy with winter. Yuhnke, Robinson, and Kamp pulled themselves together and made their way through the windy, icy Bisbee streets and the haze of hangovers down to Douglas and the smelter covered with a fresh blanket of white snow. The smelter was quiet, its stack cold. A photographer from Tucson took pictures. Robinson wrote that she thought they "looked confused but happy."[78] Although the Magma NSO remained unresolved, Yuhnke took a prolonged sabbatical. The campaign, which Robinson described as "three people without a net," and "the most fun and scariest" of her life, was over.[79] Kamp continued to organize on air quality and other environmental issues in the Southwest. Robinson returned home to Tucson. Less than a year later, Southwest Environmental Service closed its doors.[80]

A Bitter Consequence of Success

The closure of Southwest Environmental Service was as much a surprise to those involved in environmental issues in Tucson and Arizona as was the shutdown of the Douglas smelter. The group played a pivotal role in the writing of the Arizona Environmental Quality Act in 1986 and in shutting down the largest single sources of air pollution in the southwestern United States. Administrators from state and federal agencies, politicians from Pima County to Washington, DC, and environmental activists at all levels respected Robinson and her staff as an effective voice and force for environmental protection. But what made the group so successful also contributed to its closure. Such technical work required expertise acquired over years of working with agencies and committees. Other staff members— Barbara Tellman, Victoria Dahl, Betsy Rieke—supplemented Robinson's work and largely covered SES's other campaigns in the final years of the smelter campaign, but Robinson bore the brunt of the organization's work, including writing grants and soliciting funds. From the early 1980s through early 1987, as Robinson became increasingly involved with the water quality and smelter campaigns, she had less time to devote to organizational development. SES did not consider what to work on after its two primary campaigns ended. When the group won both in a relatively short amount of time, it floundered without clear direction and without a compelling issue to pitch to funders. Although it received some financial support from individual benefactors, it had never developed an alternative solution to its reliance on foundation or agency grants. During 1987, it accelerated its grassroots fundraising, soliciting money from supporters through mailings, but this effort proved to be too little, too late. When four of its most reliable foundation supporters denied funding to SES in late 1987 and early 1988, Robinson acknowledged the obvious. On March 31, 1988, she wrote a letter to SES's contributors and supporters. "We have come a long way together," she began, and she listed off the group's many accomplishments: achieving 100 percent compliance with the Clean Air Act by Arizona copper smelters and passage of Arizona Environmental Quality Act, the creation of Catalina State Park, the implementation of household hazardous waste collection days in 1987, the passage of conservation easement legislation in 1986, the Sole Source designation for the Tucson Aquifer in 1984, the cleanup of Sabino Creek from 1977 to 1983, and a variety of public education campaigns. "When SES closes its doors on March 31, we can all feel a great deal of pride in our accomplishments." The organization then disbanded.[81]

Conclusion

Despite dire predictions by local residents and Phelps Dodge that Douglas would collapse if the company followed through on its threat to close the smelter, five years after the giant smokestacks went cold and were toppled, the town appeared to be on the rebound. Indeed, census figures showed that only a little fewer than four hundred people left the city between 1980 and 1990. By 1992, the Chamber of Commerce reported that the population was actually growing as the town developed into a tourist destination and a major supplier of goods and services for its booming Sonoran sister city, Agua Prieta. Agua Prieta, bolstered by the location of U.S. factories ("maquiladoras") in the Mexican city, grew to 80,000 residents.[82] With the region's open desert vistas unobscured by smelter smoke, Arizona newspapers touted the historic town as a picturesque gateway to Mexico for tourists and the drive from Tucson to Douglas as scenic. "The smoke and steam wafting from the company's ore processing smelter was said to be the most scenic view around, because it meant jobs," said one article.[83] Instead, like its neighbor Tombstone that became a prime destination for tourists looking to experience the Old West, Douglas proved too tough to die.

As for SES, Priscilla Robinson applied the skills she had acquired during her nearly fourteen years working on environmental issues in southern Arizona to other environmental campaigns, including working with mining companies to find more efficient and environmentally sound ways to mine in the state. Other employees went on to work for progressive and environmental causes across the country and for the Arizona Democratic Party. Through its staff and members and environmental victories, SES's legacy rippled through Arizona environmental and progressive politics and its cleaner air and water into the twenty-first century. Additionally, its experiences offer lessons for those interested in environmental activism and solving environmental problems.[84]

The Southwest Environmental Service, from its inception in 1975 to its closure in 1987, demonstrates the ways in which citizen activists engaged environmental issues in the decade after passage of landmark environmental laws at the federal and state levels. While its story and organizational structure are unique, its tendency to gravitate toward the technical aspects of environmental decisions and its work to gain a voice in the inner circle of decision-making was typical of grassroots environmental activists during this era. This new form of activism may have evolved as a logical evolution of activists' work in relation to an increasingly technical regulatory landscape or as a product of Robinson's preference for using science and reason to address what she viewed as threats to quality of life, community well-being, and good governance. However, the group's successes were not scientific. Like other local and community-based environmental organizations, their ability to learn how to influence environmental decision-making was central to their success. When science and reason failed to produce results, Robinson targeted politicians using traditional means of persuasion in a democratic society—pressure from constituents who framed arguments based on fairness and justice. Robinson understood that environmental issues were political issues that could be addressed by democratic means.

The filing of the lawsuit in 1984 represented the apex of SES's involvement in the technical aspects of environmental advocacy and a progression in SES's work to assert the rights of citizens to participate in environmental decision-making. When the organization first engaged the air quality issue, it did so with the aims of educating the public and encouraging citizens to take part in the administrative processes created by environmental laws to influence environmental decisions. As its air quality campaign became more focused, not only on smelters but on the legal processes by which smelters were regulated or exempted from regulation, SES's work became more technical. Robinson, her staff, and the SES board continued to educate Arizonans about the issue and encouraged them to testify at hearings, submit comments to agencies, and write their elected officials, but this part of the campaign took a back seat to the group's increased involvement in the specialized activities of affecting federal legislation and suing the smelters in court for failing to follow the citizens' laws.

This was a logical response to the nature of environmental decision-making in the 1980s—an era when citizens responded to laws that had already been passed and attempted to enforce or improve them. This reflected Robinson's view, expressed in a 2011 interview, that "organizations that formed to pass laws [were] not suited to enforce them because the issues are highly technical."[85] Engaging the technical sides of environmental protection was another tool Robinson and SES, and many other environmental groups during this era, added to their repertoires. The Northern Plains Resource Council also understood using the courts as part of their larger efforts to affect change by giving citizens an increased role in environmental decision-making. Citizens' environmental groups came to view appealing to the judicial branch as part of the democratic process. American government was made up of a system of checks and balances between three equal branches of government—if the other two failed to address environmental degradation and abuse of the public interest by private entities, then citizens could appeal to the third. The lawsuit filed by the Environmental Defense Fund, Robinson, and Dick Kamp, the first in SES's history, opened a new chapter in SES's work on environmental issues. It complemented the group's growth in public credibility and political influence during the mid 1980s. SES used the courts alongside traditional citizen organizing to achieve its goals.

At the same time that SES was learning how to affect environmental change, members of another, but very different, community-based group two thousand miles to the east were learning similar lessons about how to adapt to changing political and regulatory conditions to protect their land, water, health, and quality of life.

6

Citizen Environmental Activism in Appalachia

Save Our Cumberland Mountains

The bright yellow of sodium lights lit up the wet pavement of the Lake City Elementary School parking lot as cars and pickups slowly began to fill its spaces. Bodies wrapped in wool and down jackets, denim and scarves, emerged from the vehicles and made their way toward the building's entrance in ones, twos, and threes. Although the sun had only just set, the ridges of the Cumberland Mountains stole any last light the narrow valley around Lake City might have enjoyed on this January night in 1972. PTA, basketball games—the human inhabitants of this valley had any number of reasons to meet at the school after dark. The gurgle of Coal Creek muffled the closing of car doors and footsteps as it meandered through the town and around the school. A light pungent smoke hung in bare tree branches above rooftops.

Inside, the steam heat warmed the bodies of retired and currently employed coal miners, teachers, subsistence farmers, and a TV repairman as they awkwardly tried to fit their legs under desks made for children. Mountains of jackets grew on the classroom's perimeter, and the windows began to sweat. Most were "valley people"; some were "mountain people" who came in from the various hollows in the surrounding hills. After the initial scuffle, confusion, and familiar conviviality, the meeting was called to order. At the front of the classroom, energetic in a plaid flannel shirt, jeans, and work boots, J. W. Bradley laid out the evening's agenda: what to do about coal mining. Specifically, what to do about coal strip mining.

For the better part of a century, coal mining was the lifeblood of Appalachian Tennessee. It left its marks on the land, in the names of creeks, towns, and hollows, and on its people. Until the completion of Norris Dam on the Clinch River by the Tennessee Valley Authority in 1939 and its resulting reservoir, Lake City had been known as Coal Creek. Nearby was the town of Coalfield near Coal Hill. Since the Civil War, coal miners and their families built lives in the mountains near the mines. During the day, men and boys worked deep underground pulling the ancient energy to the surface while their wives and families tended subsistence gardens and farms. Some of these towns—Briceville and Wartburg—were still around. Others were only known by the remnants of overgrown cabins and clusters of delicate tiger lilies and mimosa trees, nonnative ornamental plants transplanted by homesteading and coal mining families in the nineteenth century. Old cemeteries kept silent record of the descendants of those families, going back two and three generations. Occasionally, clusters of tombstones recorded in cold, objective fashion great tragedies in the mines like the Fraterville disaster of 1902, where methane gas exploded and killed 216 miners, or the Cross Mountain mine explosion of 1911 that killed 84 men and boys.[1]

The people who met in the elementary school that night in 1972 knew well the history of coal mining in eastern Tennessee, the disasters and the labor struggles of the 1890s, and they were proud of their heritage. The coal mining that they were meeting to discuss on this winter night, however, was not the underground variety with which they were intimately familiar. This night, they were concerned with coal strip mining, the same practice that was prompting ranchers, farmers, and environmentalists in Montana to form the Northern Plains Resource Council. However, geography, climate, and history of land use and ownership in the region made strip mining in Appalachia a very different animal than what it was in Montana.

In the 1960s and early 1970s, changes in mining technology and demand for coal prompted a shift in coal mining in Appalachia from traditional underground mining with all of its various safety, health, labor, and environmental issues to strip mining. By 1966, the proportion of coal produced by strip mining had risen to roughly one-fifth of the total mined in the region, and forecasters predicted further increases in strip mining. By the 1970s, Tennessee's biggest buyer of coal, the Tennessee Valley Authority (TVA), was mostly dependent on strip-mined coal. Strip mining presented a direct economic challenge to underground coal mining and the workers and families who depended on it.

Underground mining, where miners would find a vein of coal and then follow it down into the ground or horizontally into a mountainside, was inherently dangerous work. Mineshafts could collapse, methane and other gases from the coal seams could cause asphyxiation or deadly explosions, and coal dust caused long-term problems such as coal worker's pneumoconiosis or "black lung," which led to many premature deaths among miners.[2]

Due to these dangers and harsh working conditions, Tennessee miners, who had migrated to the region in the decades after the Civil War, had fought hard against mine owners and state politicians in the 1890s and early twentieth century to unionize the mines, and they continued to struggle to improve their working conditions into the mid-twentieth century. Tennessee passed right-to-work legislation in 1947; unless a mining company had a contract to supply coal to a consumer who stipulated that it be mined by union labor, most of the new underground and strip mines after mid-century were open shops employing nonunion labor. Strip mining threatened underground miners' work opportunities and challenged the few existing unions to maintain and improve safe working conditions. The new strip mines tended to employ far fewer workers, maybe one-tenth of what a comparable underground operation employed. Because it required fewer employees and could be nonunion, strip mining was more economical for mine owners, allowing them to undercut the prices of their underground competition. By the early 1970s, only one underground mine still operated under a union contract. For the retired unionized underground miners, strip mining presented a direct threat to the jobs of their sons and to the advances in workplace safety, wages, and benefits unionized underground miners had achieved in the past seventy years.[3]

It also threatened their communities. While they fought to protect their jobs and their ability to organize for better wages and working conditions, many miners still lived on land that was owned by coal companies. During labor struggles, coal companies would intimidate workers by threatening and, at times, carrying out evictions. Because the companies

FIGURE 6. Coal miner deep underground in a three-foot shaft typical of nonunionized underground coal mines in Tennessee, August 1974.

National Archives and Records Administration, photo no. 412-DA-556514.

owned most of the land near the coalfields, miners and their families were vulnerable to such tactics. When strip mining began, this history of land ownership had multiple consequences. First, when a company proposed to strip land on which miners and their families lived, sometimes for generations, residents had little legal recourse to prevent their dislocation. Unlike their rancher or farmer counterparts in the West who owned the surface property and fought the mining companies by asserting constitutional protections of private property, residents of the coal mining communities of eastern Tennessee simply had to get out of the way.[4]

The history of landownership further compromised residents' security when strip mining in an adjacent area, on slopes above their homes, for example, spilled over onto the land on which they lived. When mine tailings, the waste rock and dirt produced by mining, cascaded down through a small subsistence farm or house, occupants had few protections under the law; the mining company owned the property and often the buildings on it. Strip miners hastily deposited the "overburden," soil removed from above the coal seams, on the slopes below the mines cleared of trees prior to mining. These slopes ranged in steepness from 20 to over 40 degrees.

During periods of prolonged rain, the overburden became saturated, heavy, and viscous and could break through the poorly built earthen dams intended to hold it back. It then rushed in great mud and rock avalanches over county roads and other infrastructure and into the homes of residents below.[5]

The most tragic avalanche occurred in February 1972 in Logan County, West Virginia, when a Pittston Coal Company coal slurry impoundment dam, certified satisfactory by a federal mine inspector just four days prior, burst. The rupture unleashed a flood of 132 million gallons of wastewater, mud, and debris cresting over thirty feet high on the homes of roughly 5,000 people in Buffalo Creek Hollow below. The flood killed 125, injured more than 1,100, and left over 4,000 homeless. Similar smaller incidents occurred in northeastern Tennessee.[6] In one event, a flood caused by the collapse of the walls of a strip mine pit ripped through the home of Effie Birchfield in Stonyfork, killing five members of her family and leaving only her and her son alive.[7] In Lake City in 1969, a man driving his truck across a bridge near town was killed as he was swept up—truck, bridge, and all—in the torrent from a breached impoundment upstream. In April 1972, a flood of water, mud, and trees swept through Lick Fork in Campbell County, destroying the home of Alonzo Norman.[8] In the Northern Great Plains, strip mining caused conflicts over property ownership, competing ideas about land use and aesthetics, and the possible degradation of water and air quality. In the narrow valleys of Appalachia, it could be a matter of life and death.

Although strip mining was a relatively new activity in the 1960s, the federal government was already taking notice of its impact on Appalachia by 1966. By that year, the Department of the Interior reported coal strip mining had already disturbed eight hundred thousand acres in the region. These disturbances exposed sulfide-rich earth to the elements, which produced acid that leached heavy metals from the soil and rocks into streams and washed them down from the mines. The acid and metals mixed with sediment that washed off the mines to turn once-clear streams toxic and rust colored. In addition to stream degradation, the department described "massive slides along outslopes, destruction of forests, damage to watersheds, thousands of acres of land isolated or made hazardous by highwalls, wasted natural resources, health and safety hazards, and impaired

aesthetic and economic values.'" Secretary of the Interior Stewart Udall
recommended that if the coal mining states failed to remedy this problem
"within a reasonable period of time," Congress should step in to "protect
the public interest."[10] Despite the secretary's urgings, however, the federal
government failed to act for another decade.

The January 1972 meeting in Lake City was not the first time that
members of the communities of the coal mining region of eastern Tennessee had come together to discuss problems of health, safety, land ownership, and apparent injustices stemming from the control of the region's
land and resources by coal companies. In the previous decade, residents
of some of Tennessee's poorest counties along with medical and nursing
students from the Vanderbilt University Student Health Coalition, led by
Professor Bill Dow, organized a series of community health fairs and
opened sorely needed health clinics to provide people living in isolated
places basic health care and health education. In the process, they uncovered, in the coal-producing counties of northeastern Tennessee, a degree
of poverty, malnutrition, and poor health unrivaled in the state. Dow and
his students wondered how the region that was richest in mineral wealth
could contain the poorest people. Possibly inspired by the attempts of the
anti-strip-mining group Save Our Kentucky to reform property taxes in that
state to make coal mining companies pay taxes commensurate with the
value of their property, the Vanderbilt students began to investigate
the relationship between land ownership and tax assessment. They found
that the largest landowners, a handful of large, out-of-state, and multinational coal companies who owned roughly one-third of all the land in
Campbell, Anderson, Scott, Claiborne, and Morgan Counties, were paying less than 4 percent of the property taxes.[11] Meanwhile, the counties'
residents, who owned only a fraction of the land, picked up the balance.
These taxes supported not only public schools and other services, but the
roads and other infrastructure on which the coal companies depended.
According to Tennessee's constitution, the state was supposed to count all
minerals in property tax assessments. The researchers found that instead
of paying taxes on their mineral properties, the companies had been making generous contributions to the campaign funds of county tax asses-
sors, who were elected officials in Tennessee, thus avoiding assessment
of much of their mineral wealth. Using a Tennessee tax law that allowed

residents to appeal a neighbor's property taxes, thirteen petitioners, local residents who had been involved in the health clinic and education program, appealed various coal companies' property tax assessments in 1971. In November 1971, the State of Tennessee Tax Assessment Board sided with the petitioners and reassessed the coal companies' properties in eastern Tennessee. This contrast between the poverty in their communities and the wealth being hauled out of the region in coal trucks radicalized many of the region's residents in the early 1970s. By the time of the state assessment board's decision, several hundred residents from the coal counties of northeastern Tennessee had signed petitions calling for the coal companies to pay their fair share of taxes. The introduction of strip mining and its challenges to unionized underground coal mining and community health and safety added to an evolving critique of land ownership, poverty, social services, and general fairness. This was the climate in which the concerned residents met in Lake City on that cold January night in 1972.[12]

The meeting included people representing a wide range of interests and opinions concerning coal strip mining. There were people who had witnessed firsthand the dangers of strip mining when their homes, or the homes of relatives or neighbors, had been damaged or destroyed by floods and landslides of overburden. Predictably, these attendees ardently opposed strip mining. The meeting also included retired union underground miners, some of whom had sons employed by the strip mining companies but who opposed the strippers because they employed few workers and were nonunion. They talked jobs, wages, and benefits, but their arguments also included implicit concerns about the deterioration of their communities. Then there were "valley people" from towns like Lake City, Caryville, or Jacksboro who were store owners or teachers or other people not directly involved in mining who feared what strip mining would mean for their communities. And there were miners, some of whom worked for the strip mining companies and came to speak in favor of strip mining, and still others who wondered about the job prospects associated with strip mining or the threat it presented to underground mining.[13]

Despite divergent interests, the meeting stayed peaceful. J. W. Bradley of Petros, a charismatic character who had worked in the underground mines and was an outspoken critic of strip mining, emerged as a clear leader in facilitating a productive conversation about the concerns of the people at the meeting. He welcomed the opinions of everyone there and then, as he sensed the sentiment of the group moving one direction or another, called for a simple vote on what course of action to take. In this dramatic demonstration of direct democracy in which all people at the meeting had a vote, whether they opposed strip mining or supported it, the majority of those present decided a course of action. Those who supported the expansion of strip mining lost the simple election; the group decided that they would oppose strip mining and begin to work to mitigate the problems associated with existing operations.[14]

As Chad Montrie observes in his study of strip mining opposition in Pennsylvania, Ohio, Kentucky, and West Virginia, attendees articulated opposition for environmental and conservation reasons like their urban and suburban middle class environmentalist counterparts—for the damage it would do to the natural beauty and ecological integrity of the region and the waste of valuable minerals and timber. Their most passionate arguments revolved around the threat of strip mining to homesteads and jobs. Once the group decided to oppose strip mining, twelve of the people present voted to form an organization and elected J. W. Bradley its first president. According to Montrie, this small charter membership included "two young miners recently fired for signing UMW union cards, several working men employed in Oak Ridge plants, a former county weight inspector who quit his job in protest against the failure to prosecute overweight coal trucks, a local college student, a community worker, and several local women."[15] In this way, a democratic, grassroots community organization was born in Lake City, Tennessee. Bradley proposed that they hold a contest among the new members to choose a name for the new organization. By their next meeting, they had made their decision. The charter members hailed from the five coal producing counties—Campbell, Claiborne, Morgan, Anderson, and Scott—that accounted for 80 percent of the coal mined in Tennessee. These counties either straddled or included parts of the Cumberland Mountains, a range in the southeastern section of the Appalachia Mountains, so they called their group "Save Our Cumberland Mountains." Within a few weeks, Bill Dow had found two young organizers, Vanderbilt students Heleny Cook and Jane Sampsons, both in their early twenties, to assist the organization on a quasi-volunteer basis.

Dow was able to provide money for about half of their expenses through Vanderbilt's rural health initiative; Save Our Cumberland Mountains' members passed the hat at its meetings to make up the rest.[16]

Saving the Cumberlands from Strip Mining: The 1970s

Over the next few years, Save Our Cumberland Mountains (SOCM or "Sock 'em") became more sophisticated in its organization and its tactics. In May 1972, SOCM formalized and voted on a group constitution and bylaws. It maintained its grassroots democratic character under the leadership of Bradley, who acted as a de facto staff director in addition to president. SOCM grew quickly from its twelve charter members to 400 members by 1974. In its early days, SOCM's staff remained largely volunteer, and early efforts quickly exhausted its first two organizers. The group then enlisted two young locals, Johnny Burris and Charles "Boomer" Winfrey. In 1973, SOCM obtained its first source of outside funding in the form of two grants from the Episcopal Church and the Unitarian Universalist Youth Project.[17] Winfrey became SOCM's first paid employee, earning a meager two hundred and fifty dollars a month. The grants also allowed the group to hire its first full-time organizer, a young high school history and social science teacher from East St. Louis, Illinois, named Maureen O'Connell, who had become familiar with the organization during the summers she spent in the Cumberland Mountains.[18]

The group made decisions regarding everything from tactics to hiring and paying staff through simple votes of the members present at the monthly meetings. Meetings were moved each month from town to town to incorporate the interests of the group's expanding membership in all of its geographic areas. This form of decision-making sometimes led to inconsistent positions. For example, in October 1973, members sympathetic to organized labor at a meeting in Marion County voted to donate half of SOCM's funds to support a United Mine Workers strike in Kentucky. The next month when SOCM met in the southern part of their territory, where members were less sympathetic to unions, the members present rejected a motion to support a local strike in spirit. During the group's first five years, its dedication to democratic practice also led to a lack of

FIGURE 7. J. W. Bradley speaking at a "Deep Mine Benefit" in the mid 1970s.
Private collection, Statewide Organizing for
Community eMpowerment, Lake City, Tennessee.

turnover in leadership as the membership was content to continue nomi-
nating and voting for J. W. Bradley to serve as SOCM's president.[19]

During its first decade, SOCM achieved several notable successes.
Building on the state property tax assessment victory of late 1971, the group
organized campaigns to hold coal mining companies accountable for the
damages they caused to the rural communities of Campbell, Anderson,
Scott, Morgan, and Claiborne counties. The organization tended to link
health and safety with economic and environmental issues, arguing that
coal companies had an obligation to behave responsibly toward residents,
communities, and workers. To this end, in 1972 they worked with the Tennessee Citizens for Wilderness Planning to promote a ban on strip mining.
In 1967, the Tennessee General Assembly had passed a strip mine regulation and reclamation law with the intent of keeping track of the new
strip mines and preventing unregulated "wildcat" mining, but the law was
weak. It allowed mining on slopes steeper than 20 degrees, which contributed to massive and deadly landslides. Dependent on self-reporting by
coal mining companies and enforcement by political appointees with very
little transparency or opportunity for public oversight, the law was largely
toothless. By 1972, the inadequacy of the 1967 law was obvious to anyone
concerned with strip mining in Tennessee.[20]

In the minds of SOCM's members and the Tennessee Citizens for Wilderness Planning, so little of the coal country of eastern Tennessee was less than 20 degrees steep that strip mining was not practical. At most, it represented a fraction—some estimates were as low as 4 percent—of the total coal mining possibilities in the state; the damage strip mining caused undermined its relatively small positive economic impact in terms of new jobs and economic development compared to underground mining.[21] These were the basic arguments offered by state Senate sponsor William Bruce, a Democrat from Memphis, and House sponsors Democrat W. J. "Willie" Neese of Paris and Democrat Keith Bissell Jr. of Oak Ridge when they introduced the strip mine ban in Senate Bill 1707 and House Bill 2038 The ban in these pieces of legislation failed to make it out of committee In 1972, but the issue did not go away. In the next two sessions (1973–1974 and 1975–1976), the ban was reintroduced in various forms. SOCM also eagerly supported attempts by Representative Ken Hechler, a Democrat of West Virginia, to ban strip mining at the federal level, and members made numerous trips to Washington, DC, with the help of the Washington-based Environmental Policy Center organized by Louise Dunlap to testify and lobby on this issue after 1972. Congressional support for Hechler's strip mining ban reached unprecedented support in 1971 but fell victim to pressure from coal companies and the United Mine Workers, who hoped to unionize new strip mines outside Tennessee.[22]

The proposed ban articulated the extreme side of the negotiation for legislators, activists, and coal companies. While SOCM and other groups advocated for a ban, they were able to affect the passage of other coal strip mine regulations, including the Tennessee Surface Rights Act in 1977, which required the consent of surface owners in split-estate situations before their surface property could be strip mined.[23] They also worked with the consortium of similar groups from Appalachia and the West directed by the Environmental Policy Center in Washington, DC, to help pass the 1977 Surface Mine Control and Reclamation Act.[24] At the last minute, compromises on wording that allowed strip mining on slopes steeper than what SOCM and other Appalachian groups sought to prohibit prompted the organization to retract its support before it passed. Reflecting the group's continued linking of the social, economic, and environmental issues associated with strip mining, SOCM advocated for and helped pass Tennessee's first severance tax on coal that levied a ten-cent tax on each ton of coal mined and provided roughly a million dollars to each of the coal-producing counties to be used for road maintenance, stream improvement, and education.[25]

Like other environmental groups at the time, SOCM engaged in a number of strategies in conjunction with legislation to hold coal companies and government agencies accountable to the people and communities of the coal-producing counties. Building on the 1971 study of land ownership and taxation in the five coal-producing counties of northeastern Tennessee, the group was able to win a ruling by the state tax assessment board that mineral tracts had to be assessed as part of land value for purposes of taxation. Their campaign to keep the coal companies and regulators accountable extended to prodding state agencies to enforce Tennessee's 1967 strip mine law and its amendments. As part of this effort, SOCM published a study of strip mine regulation enforcement and mine compliance in the late 1970s.[26] They also attempted to use the courts to hold coal companies and government accountable to existing laws. In fall 1972, the group joined the Tennessee Citizens for Wilderness Planning, Save Our Kentucky, the Sierra Club, and the Environmental Defense Fund in filing its first lawsuit against the Tennessee Valley Authority, arguing that as a publicly supported utility the TVA needed to complete environmental impact statements for each of their long-term contracts for strip-mined coal. In their words, the members of SOCM sought to use the lawsuit to remind TVA, which purchased one-half of all strip-mined coal in the state, "that it must be responsible to the citizenry of the Tennessee Valley" and consider the social, economic, and environmental costs of its coal purchases to the communities of northeastern Tennessee.[27] This lawsuit was ultimately unsuccessful; SOCM president J. W. Bradley understood the need for the group and its members to have qualified legal representation but also that it was very difficult to find attorneys in the coal counties that did not have ties to the coal industry.[28] In response, in late 1973, SOCM formed the East Tennessee Research Corporation, a public-interest law firm funded by a grant from the Ford Foundation, to carry out its legal work. Its handful of lawyers and staff remained busy exploring new ways to use existing laws to combat strip mining until the foundation funding dried up in 1978. By the end of the 1970s, SOCM had learned to use environmental laws passed earlier in the decade, including the National Environmental Policy Act and Surface Mine Control and Reclamation Act, to defeat several proposed mining plans, including AMAX Coal Company's massive plan to mine twenty thousand acres on the Cumberland Plateau.[29]

Growing Out and Growing Up: New Issues, New Strategies, and Organizational Development

As their first decade drew to a close, SOCM diversified geographically to begin organizing in the coalfields of the Cumberland Plateau south of its original territory. It also began to diversify its issues and was commencing work on environmental and health hazards associated with toxic waste dumping. As the group grew, it took stock of its past and prepared for the future. In response to apparent member and staff burnout—fewer members attending monthly membership meetings as well as overcommitted staffers with a high turnover rate—members organized SOCM's first leadership retreat in August 1979. During the daylong event, the SOCM leaders and staff engaged in structured discussions about the organization itself, how to build its strength, how to identify winnable issues, and how to recruit members and funding to maintain an effective and powerful organization including a paid staff. These retreats became annual events and led to innovations within the organization. SOCM also increased its work with other similar organizations regionally and nationally. Like Northern Plains, it worked with other groups concerned with coal strip mining to advocate federal strip mining legislation and then became one of the founding groups in the national Citizens Coal Council to help coordinate the efforts of many local and regional grassroots groups on national coal issues. "We accidentally did a few things right," Maureen O'Connell recalled decades later about the group's growth and its instinctive sense that SOCM should be a member-run organization.[30]

In the 1980s, SOCM continued its work on its bedrock issues: coal strip mining, reclamation, and coal company tax policies. They researched landownership and taxation for the state's sixteen coal-producing counties and published a study demonstrating that, despite the tax reforms of the 1970s, coal companies still paid less than their share of taxes. SOCM used the study to support its work in the central and southeastern part

FIGURE 8. Maureen O'Connell at an SOCM strategy meeting, early 1980s.
Private collection, Statewide Organizing for
Community eMpowerment, Lake City, Tennessee.

of the state in the Cumberland Plateau. It won a precedent-setting court ruling that prohibited the mining of coal seams laced with toxic heavy metals, which would degrade water quality, unless the coal companies had a proven-effective plan for handling the toxic by-products of such mining. SOCM also successfully advocated for legislation in the state assembly that rectified the split-estate situation in certain parts of the state that reunited surface and mineral properties. In addition to their mining work, they engaged oil and gas development in eastern Tennessee, prevented the permitting of toxic and hazardous waste facilities in the rural and often economically depressed parts of the state, and began to oppose the construction of giant landfills for out-of-state urban waste.[31]

While SOCM cultivated new county-based chapters and sought new issues threatening health, the environment, and communities, the group also began to shift its tactics. During their first decade, the members of SOCM, primarily from the five coal-producing counties north of Knoxville, tended to rely on three forms of action. First, they sought to research the present situation. SOCM members sought answers to several questions. Who was mining where? Do they have permits? Where will they mine next? Who owns what land and what taxes do they pay? Can we make them at least pay their fair share of taxes to compensate for the damage they're doing? Can we stop them? Local residents sensed that they needed to know as much as they could about the situation, so they went to work researching these questions. Once their research was complete, they advertised their results in newspaper articles and at the State Assembly; their second tactic was to seek legislative solutions to the problems associated with coal strip mining. SOCM proposed a ban in 1972 and 1973, lobbied for amendments to the ineffective 1967 Tennessee strip mine reclamation law, and advocated for a federal law to regulate strip mining and require reclamation of mined land. Third, SOCM promoted increased citizen access to and participation in environmental decision-making alongside requirements for permits, monitoring by state and federal agencies, and specific standards for what lands could be strip-mined and mine reclamation in the legislation they promoted. Their organizing and lobbying efforts proved successful with the passage of a number of laws in Tennessee and the passage of the federal Surface Mine Control and Reclamation Act of 1977.[32] When providing the truth to decision-makers and lobbying to pass a law failed to stop a proposed project, they appealed to the courts.

By the 1980s, due in part to their efforts and the efforts of environmental organizations across the country as well as bipartisan support for environmental legislation by Congress and Presidents Nixon and Carter during the previous decade, the rules of the game had changed. Most basically, the passage of the National Environmental Policy Act (NEPA) in 1970 gave citizens a voice in reviewing and contesting any development that was likely to have a significant impact on the human environment. This measure gave citizens a new means of monitoring environmental issues in Tennessee and created new venues for organizing public participation. NEPA provided a level of disclosure that had not existed in the 1960s, and by the mid-1970s, SOCM was learning how to use the information uncovered in the NEPA process to challenge projects. They could also organize their members to write comments critiquing a proposed development and to turn out at public hearings to make their opinions heard. NEPA was not a voting process or a popularity contest, and agency officials claimed that they made their decisions based on hard science and not the number of comments or passion of commentators. But for people who drove from all over the state to speak their mind, testifying was a powerful experience; it could be cathartic and also incredibly empowering.[33] After the passage of the federal Surface Mine Control and Reclamation Act (SMCRA) in 1977, all applications for permits to strip-mine prompted a NEPA review from the federal Office of Surface Mining (OSM) or state Department of Environment and Conservation. NEPA also provided citizens with the ability to appeal decisions when they felt that government agencies had illegally granted a permit. By 1980, SOCM was learning to play by these new rules. They began applying what they learned to issues other than strip mining.[34]

As a result, their activities looked much different in the 1980s and 1990s than they did in the 1970s. Chad Montrie argues that after the passage of SMCRA, SOCM's primary activities were concerned with enforcement of the law.[35] In the early 1980s, the group monitored and documented the inability of the Tennessee Department of Environment and Conservation to adequately enforce the amended Tennessee strip mine reclamation law and the federal Surface Mine Control Reclamation Act. Their findings prompted the federal Office of Surface Mining to take over jurisdiction of strip mine regulation and reclamation from the state agency under provisions in SMCRA in 1984. This embarrassed state regulators but resulted in more rigorous evaluation and permitting of mining in the state.[36] When a new strip mine was proposed for an area on the Cumberland Plateau known as Rock Creek, SOCM creatively used the untested "Lands Unsuitable for Mining" provision in the new SMCRA law that had been added to the legislation to prevent strip mining in Montana's Custer National Forest. The provision allowed citizens to petition the federal OSM to prohibit mining on a large portion of the land in the Rock Creek proposal because it had significant environmental, scenic, or cultural value and was unsuitable for mining. In 1987, their petition was successful. SOCM pioneered the use of the "Lands Unsuitable for Mining Petition" (LUMP) and used it more extensively than any other group in the country in the following decades. These strategies, which were heavily reliant on staff expertise rather than member involvement, challenged the organization's grassroots foundation, forcing it to develop alternate avenues of recruiting new members, of keeping them involved, and of cultivating new leadership. Rule-making hearings were not as alluring as mass protests or marches outside the state capitol. The group had to learn how to create opportunities for member participation in ways that furthered its campaigns. In addition, the group's tactic of holding industry and government regulators accountable, a strategy that evolved organically in SOCM's early battles, had become more sophisticated and effective by the 1980s. Finally, SOCM applied what it had learned to successfully challenge air and water quality permits and construction permits for toxic and hazardous waste facilities.[37]

As their membership, issues, and tactics evolved, SOCM's leaders also made structural changes to the organization. After a period of experimentation, SOCM adopted a new decision-making structure. They tempered the inconsistency of making decisions "town meeting" style at monthly membership meetings by simple voice vote by creating a board made of members representing each of the organization's county-based chapters and four permanent committees: finance, personnel, membership, and legislative. County chapters, organized once a county contained twenty or more members, still organized their own monthly meetings, but organization-wide decisions were made by bimonthly meetings of the board according to strict adherence to democratic principles. General membership meetings

FIGURE 9. SOCM members pack a hearing in the early 1980s.
Private collection, Statewide Organizing for
Community eMpowerment, Lake City, Tennessee.

took place twice a year. SOCM also determined that the group would be a multi-issue organization. Chapters could propose new issues to become official issues of the larger organization entitled to requisite organizational resources including paid staff work and volunteer time. If more than one chapter was working on a particular issue, the chapters could petition the board, which would consider the issue according to a series of criteria: did it fit SOCM's mission and goals? Was it winnable? Did it build the organization in terms of membership, financially, or in political power? If the issue met these standards, it might become an official SOCM issue.[38]

As a result, SOCM worked on a number of issues by the 1990s ranging from coal mining to oil and gas development to the building of toxic and hazardous waste facilities, the clear-cutting of forests, pesticide spraying, protecting the health and rights of temporary workers, and antiracism campaigns to try to build coalitions with Tennessee's African American population. This diversity of issues caused new chapters to emerge in new parts of the state and created new standing committees that added more people to the group's board. By 1992, the number of chapters had grown from four to twelve, increasing board membership from eleven to nineteen, while the number of standing committees jumped from four to ten. As SOCM's third decade got underway, its membership numbered roughly 1,500 families.[39] Along with these changes, the board developed the organization's first five-year, long-range plan and its first major fundraising campaign. Like the Northern Plains Resource Council did in the West, it expanded its scope beyond Tennessee and helped form the Southern Empowerment Project to train new organizers to work in similar groups. SOCM also helped to create Community Shares, a federation of Tennessee-based community groups to raise funds cooperatively through voluntary payroll deductions to address social, economic, and environmental issues in the state. While attempting to remain as close to its democratic roots as possible, SOCM became more institutionally formal and professional.[40]

Conclusion

At first glance, Save Our Cumberland Mountains looks like a representative example of a membership-based environmental or conservation

FIGURE 10. The "Under 30 Crowd" in the annual tug-of-war with other members and staff at a SOCM annual meeting in the early 1980s. Maureen O'Connell is third in line.

Private collection, Statewide Organizing for
Community eMpowerment, Lake City, Tennessee.

organization that formed in the 1970s and traveled the trajectory of the environmental movement to the early 2000s. In the 1970s, it formed to address dangers associated with an industrial activity. To remedy the situation, SOCM primarily sought legislative solutions—first to ban strip mining altogether and, when that was unsuccessful, to regulate it to mitigate its most egregious effects. It paired these efforts with research, public education, and, when necessary, litigation. During the 1970s and 1980s, the group grew geographically and numerically, and as it did, it expanded the kinds of issues it worked on. In response to its larger membership and more expansive ambitions, SOCM institutionalized and professionalized aspects of its operation. It moved from being a potentially temporary single-issue grassroots group concerned with banning strip mining to a more permanent multi-issue organization. SOCM integrated its environmental work with capacity-building efforts to increase its power in environmental decision-making and to ensure its endurance beyond immediate issues whether they were satisfactorily resolved or not.

Like most citizens' environmental organizations, however, SOCM's work was about more than just environmental concerns. In their activities, they retained an almost instinctive sense that environmental issues were really issues of justice and democracy and the best way to solve them involved allowing the citizens affected to have a say in those decisions. This sense was not atypical; other citizens groups including the Northern Plains Resource Council and, to a degree, the Southwest Environmental Service shared this instinct. It was both implicit and explicit in the organizing strategies of hundreds of citizen's groups around the nation in the last decades of the twentieth century. Whether as a result of its rural and working-class roots or conscious decisions of leaders within the organization, SOCM's emphasis on justice, fairness, and a purer ideal of democratic governance caused the organization to more clearly articulate an understanding of the connectedness of social justice, environmental protection, and democratic action.

In the last decade of the twentieth century, scholars identified the emergence of a new movement that recognized that environmental degradation and toxic contamination disproportionately affected people of color and the poor, and that a community's success in rectifying these issues often depended on the race and class of those affected. These emerging groups combined environmental concern with a simultaneous commitment to social justice and racial and class equality. In some cases, environmental justice activists and scholars leveled criticisms against the mainstream environmental movement, whose memberships tended to be white and middle class, for ignoring or neglecting the environmental issues affecting the nation's most vulnerable members in favor of protecting wilderness and wildlife or for advocating policies at the expense of racial minorities and the economically depressed. The divisions between the mainstream environmental and environmental justice movements articulated by scholars begin to blur when examining grassroots environmental organizations.[41]

During the 1990s, SOCM was involved with myriad campaigns. The fight to stop the construction of massive mega-landfills in economically depressed areas of rural Tennessee to store garbage from urban centers outside the state demonstrates how the group blended its focus on justice and public participation in environmental decision-making to protect and improve the natural and human environment within the changing legal and political conditions of the era. This campaign offers snapshots of the intricacies of grassroots environmental organizing and offers glimpses into the connections between the mainstream environmental movement and environmental justice movement.

7

Dumping in Tennessee

In 1990, two Save Our Cumberland Mountains members traced a trail of garbage a mile up the Tennessee River to a collapsing 100-foot side wall of the county landfill in Witt, east of Knoxville, in Roane County. After discovering the source of the trash, they met with the head of the regional division of the state solid waste management agency, Jack Crabtree, who acknowledged water pollution problems stemming from the landfill. Crabtree advised that residents should not eat fish from the river. To raise public awareness, SOCM members posted signs along the river stating that the fish were unsafe to eat, which attracted coverage from local television news stations. SOCM followed this action with a protest on the road to the landfill on March 27 and a protest at the Division of Solid Waste Management office in Knoxville in May.[1]

On May 9, about forty residents, including pregnant women, great-grandmothers, and a teenager dressed as Mother Nature "with tire tracks smeared across her blue and white dress," picketed outside the state agency office.[2] They protested the failure to enforce waste management laws at the Witt landfill (which had been cited for over 125 violations since 1982), the proposals for new landfills in Roane County, and the abandoned strip mine pits of Anderson County. The protestors, who hailed primarily from Hamblen, Roane, and Anderson Counties, congregated outside with signs and then walked into the building to present a bottle filled with polluted green water to Crabtree.[3] They sang an adaptation of the civil rights–era standard: "We are fighting for our rivers, we shall not be moved."[4]

SOCM member Gerry Bellew accused the state agency of failing the citizens of the state. "We have seen garbage left uncovered for months, black water running from landfills and trash scattered along county roads. . . . The law is written to protect the citizens," Bellew said, and she insisted that the agency stop issuing new permits for landfills until the issues were resolved.[5] Guy Collins, Hamblen County commissioner and chairman of the county landfill board, asked Crabtree why the state had failed to take action against the operators of the Witt landfill.[6] The protest elevated the issue in the press and led to local results. The Roane County Commission soon adopted a zoning ordinance to stop private commercial landfills in April 1990 and accelerated its efforts to rectify problems with its own troubled waste dump. At the state level, however, the protest resulted in little more than a verbal assurance by Crabtree that the solid waste division would continue working with counties to enforce the law, and that new landfills would be "state-of-the art."[7]

Americans produced a lot of trash in the late twentieth century. By the mid-1980s, Americans threw away more than 260 million tons of garbage annually—more than a ton per person per year and nearly ten times as much per capita as Canada, the world's second highest waste-producing nation.[8] Population growth, economic expansion, and revolution in the production and marketing of consumer goods following World War II resulted in a very real problem of what to do with all of the trash. States with large urban populations were vexed to find new locations to inter their solid, hazardous, and medical wastes. Enterprising waste management companies offered an attractive solution to cities like Chicago, New York, and Atlanta, and to communities in rural areas linked by rail or highway to the metropolises. Their idea: to open enormous "state-of-the-art" landfills in the rural parts of Tennessee and other isolated rural places and export the waste there. Since most of the proposed receiving areas were economically depressed, the landfills and their jobs would be a boon to local economies.[9] Moreover, Tennessee and its landfill counties would reap tax revenues and impact fees, surplus money to help pay for basic services including roads, health clinics, and education. At first glance, the landfills seemed to solve a serious problem. The big cities outside of Tennessee would have a solution to their trash problem, the shareholders of multinational and publicly traded companies like Waste Management and Browning-Ferris Industries would profit from handling the trash, and the state Tennessee and a few fortunate counties would enrich their public coffers. To many in the state in the early 1990s, landfills were a win-win proposition.

The only problem was that in the late 1980s and early 1990s, landfill operators in Tennessee did a poor job keeping track of their facilities and regulators were lax in enforcing Tennessee's already weak waste management and environmental laws. For many residents of small towns like Oliver Springs in Campbell County in the coal fields of northeastern Tennessee, or in Hamblen or Roane Counties near Knoxville, the assurances from waste management companies and the state that new landfills would not pollute their land, water, and communities were far from convincing. The proposed construction of mega-landfills hundreds of acres in size, sometimes sited on lands previously disturbed by strip mining, meant much more than increased revenue for their counties and the state. Of course, it meant millions of tons of garbage being trucked into their communities, some of it hazardous, that would be a nuisance at its most benign and a real danger to the water quality and health of residents at its worst. In addition, the landfills meant increased traffic; dozens of garbage and semi trucks a day made rural roads more dangerous and expedited the decay of existing roadways, increasing repair costs and causing traffic delays. If that were not enough, the locations of the landfills and incinerators could depress property values in the receiving communities and permanently retard the development of other sorely needed economic activities. The waste management companies chose impoverished and sparsely populated areas as possible sites for landfills because the land was cheap and these areas were starved for economic activity. Many residents saw the landfill as patently unfair and unjust. Why should the residents of other states get to dump their waste on rural Tennesseans just because they were poor? And why should a few giant waste management corporations be allowed to pollute rural communities for profit?

The out-of-state waste issue arrived in Tennessee in the midst of what historians of American environmentalism identify as the "toxics movement." Rachel Carson first alerted Americans to the insidious nature of chemical contamination and its danger to the environment in her landmark *Silent Spring* in 1962.[10] It was not until the late 1970s, however, that Americans realized the full threat of industrial and chemical waste to human health. The 1978 exposé of the wholesale poisoning of the Love Canal neighborhood of Niagara Falls, New York, by the Hooker Chemical Company opened a new era in the public's awareness of industrial pollution. Love Canal, and revelations of other toxic disasters, prompted the federal government to take decisive action. In some cases, the federal Environmental Protection Agency evacuated residents of polluted communities, bought their homes, and paid to relocate them to safer locales. In 1980, the federal government enacted the Comprehensive Environmental Response, Compensation, and Liability Act (CERCLA), providing funds through a new superfund and directing the Environmental Protection Agency to clean up sites contaminated with hazardous and toxic substances.[11] In 1990, Robert Bullard revealed in *Dumping in Dixie: Race, Class, and Environmental Quality* that African American and poor communities in the South were especially likely to be exposed to toxic pollution in the postwar era. Bullard demonstrated that as a consequence of the environmental movement and the federal government's recognition of the dangers of toxic waste, polluters increasingly, and sometimes illegally, shifted their dumping of hazardous materials away from white and more affluent areas to minority and economically depressed communities—the people with the least economic and political power to defend themselves. This revelation ushered in the environmental justice movement.[12] It was within this context that citizens interpreted proposals to dump garbage and hazardous wastes from faraway urban areas on Tennessee's rural and working-class communities.

Citizens had historical experience that caused them to distrust the waste management companies and state regulators. Members of Save Our Cumberland Mountains organized to fight the landfills using the democratic tools they had struggled to acquire in the previous decades. In response, waste management companies and their allies worked to remove these tools, first by trying to repeal county government's ability to deny new landfills and then by trying to alter provisions in Tennessee's waste management laws to concentrate environmental decision-making in the hands of the waste management industry and politically appointed government bureaucrats. In response, SOCM found itself, once again, fighting to protect the environment and human health while at the same time defending and advancing the ability of citizens to participate in the decisions that affected their health, environment, and quality of life. For the organization's members, these two battles were one and the same, and they pursued them with vigilance and persistence.

SOCM Takes On Trash

As the decade of the 1990s opened, out-of-state waste had become a salient issue for thousands of residents living in rural areas of Tennessee. In May 1989, the Tennessee General Assembly repealed a part of Tennessee's solid waste laws that required local approval of hazardous waste landfills, incinerators, and storage and treatment facilities in an effort to streamline permitting and construction of new waste management developments. With this act, the assembly hoped to attract out-of-state waste management companies. Supporters of the provision, such as the Tennessee Association of Businesses, argued that the revocation was necessary to prevent other states, specifically Alabama and South Carolina, from refusing to accept Tennessee waste in reprisal for Tennessee local governments using the local approval law, or local veto, to block the importation of their waste. In April 1989, the Tennessee attorney general claimed that the local veto represented an unconstitutional delegation of power by the legislature to county and municipal bodies. The assembly reluctantly repealed the local veto under the stipulation that the state Solid Waste Control Board, made up of political appointees and administered by the state Department of Health and Environment, would create new regulations for locating waste facilities. Local control was not completely lost, however. During debate on the bill, Democratic representative Doug Jackson of Dickson County successfully led assemblymen from districts confronting new landfills in amending the law so that local governments in counties and unincorporated municipalities that did not already have zoning to deal with landfills—that is, most of the state's rural areas—retained the final say over landfill permitting and locating until the Solid Waste Control Board established the new rules and regulations stipulated in the law.[13]

In June 1989, the Solid Waste Control Board's Division of Hazardous Waste held a meeting in Nashville to gather input from interested parties about new regulations. According to the accounts of attendees, about half of those present were concerned citizens or representatives from environmental groups.[14] When the board issued its draft regulations roughly six weeks later on August 9, citizens and environmentalists found few, if any, of their recommendations included. The Department of Health and Conservation scheduled three public hearings to be held in September in Nashville, Knoxville, and Jackson to gather citizen input on the proposed regulations before making the rules permanent. Feeling ignored and outraged, members of SOCM and other groups interested in the rule-making process redoubled their efforts to turn out citizens to these hearings.[15]

In preparing for the rule-making hearings, the SOCM staff and members argued against the construction of massive commercial landfills on grounds of basic justice and fairness and called for rules that maximized the involvement of local residents who would be most affected by decisions regarding locating and permitting of waste management facilities. Dr. Michael Crist, a public school administrator from Dickson County, cited the dangerous nature of the waste as a primary concern. Crist wrote a letter to the *Tennessean* of Nashville explaining that the proposed rules permitted known cancer-causing agents and other hazardous materials as close as 200 feet to flowing streams, within 500 feet of scenic, cultural, and recreational areas, and within 1,000 feet of private drinking water wells and 2,000 feet of public drinking water wells.[16] These hazardous substances included polychlorinated biphenyl (PCB), Agent Orange, and other industrial wastes containing lead and heavy metals. Crist echoed a common sentiment of local people who felt helpless against the forces of capital: "Commercial waste means out-of-state waste," he wrote, and once commercial waste facilities were located within Tennessee, "waste-as-a-commodity cannot be regulated or prevented from coming into Tennessee any more than the State or a citizen's group could prevent a certain type of automobile from being shipped to Tennessee from Detroit." "Commercial," he insisted, "also means for profit, and the operators of these facilities are certainly not going to turn away business, regardless of its source or life-endangering characteristics."[17] In turning out members to testify, SOCM provided literature that echoed Crist's concerns and emphasized further the injustice of the decision-making process embodied in the proposed rules. "Those MOST AT RISK are CONSULTED LEAST!" insisted one of their informational fliers. "This is our land," it continued. "We have the right to be heard, to be in on decisions that affect how we will live, what environment our children will be raised in, what dangers they will be exposed to."[18] As with almost all the literature SOCM generated surrounding the issue, the flier emphasized the unfairness of other states dumping their garbage in Tennessee.[19]

Citizen testimony at the hearings reiterated these themes. In their written testimony for the Knoxville hearing on September 7, SOCM members Paul and Sylvia Morrill of Fairfield Glade emphasized the injustice of the legislative action that, in their opinion, "deprived local citizens in their communities throughout the state of the democratic veto power or control of the waste dumps."[20] In addition, they contended that the proposed rules allowed too many loopholes for managers of waste facilities to operate without accountability to the state or residents. As they interpreted the draft regulations, the Morrills complained that they relied "too much on the operator's answers to information," and thus "neglect[ed] the safety of the citizenry."[21] Finally, the Morrills called for increased transparency to help citizens understand what exactly was being proposed. They encouraged the Solid Waste Control Board to include in their regulations a summary of the number of dumps already in the state in 1989, exactly how many new facilities were proposed, who would operate the proposed facilities, the reasons for building new facilities, and the scientific assessments of their safety.[22] Longtime SOCM member Betty Anderson of Knoxville charged, during the September 7 hearing in that city, that the proposed specifications for how far waste facilities must be built from drinking water supplies were inadequate and unfair. "Many rural people have no other source of water than their well or spring. . . . Their loss would be very serious. . . . Many of them do not have the resources to sue."[23] In her testimony, SOCM supporter Carol J. Spiller, PhD, argued for involving local communities in the waste management facilities siting decisions. She referenced a recent report to the Massachusetts Hazardous Facility Site Safety Council, which stressed the importance of local host community and abutting community influence in the siting process and compensation to residents for losses.[24] Spiller recommended that Tennessee consider adopting stronger regulations than the federal government with regard to waste management because the Massachusetts report found that such regulations inspired greater public confidence and credibility. Lastly, she cited recommendations from the Massachusetts report that "exclusionary criteria" prohibiting the building of facilities in certain areas "make facility siting easier because they remove the potential objection that a proposed project is on a physically inappropriate site."[25]

Supporters of the proposed rules such as the Tennessee Association of Businesses, which claimed to represent more than one thousand businesses in the state, characterized the testimony of landfill opponents as subverting the intent of the 1989 repeal of the local veto. They objected to proposals to ban the building of waste management facilities near scenic, cultural, or recreational areas, fault areas, wetlands, or floodplains. The business group testified that the waste management proposals advocated by citizens and environmental groups went "far beyond what is required to provide protection to human health and the environment."[26] As an alternative, the business community advocated "site-specific" and "case-by-case" review of siting criteria and "responsible management."[27] Citizens feared that these recommendations would create a siting and permitting process controlled by business people with direct financial interests in building commercial waste facilities and government-appointed bureaucrats tied to those interests. They continued to work for fairness and ensuring local resident participation in environmental decision-making by making the process of siting and permitting waste management facilities transparent and accessible to the public. In the end, more than four hundred people attended the hearings and one hundred people spoke on the proposed rules, with the great majority opposing the draft regulations. In response, the Solid Waste Control Board scrapped their draft regulations and substituted draft regulations from the federal Environmental Protection Agency without resoliciting public input as required under Tennessee law. SOCM and the Tennessee Environmental Council appealed the board's decision not to hold hearings on the substitute regulations.[28]

The 1989 repeal of the local veto and rule-making hearings and proposed solid and hazardous waste facilities in rural counties galvanized residents, who organized themselves in a variety of community-level groups. Organizations like Citizens Against Pollution in Humphreys County west of Nashville, the site of ten sanitary and industrial landfills, and Stop Trashing Our Premises (STOP) in Union City in northwestern Tennessee emerged in response to the threat. In the eastern part of the state, many concerned residents were already members of Save Our Cumberland

Mountains, which quickly took up the cause. In fall 1989, the prospect of importing thousands of tons of out-of-state waste had emerged as a serious issue among SOCM's members. After much consideration, the board elected to make it one of SOCM's campaigns. By January 1990, the board had named a "Toxics Committee" to address solid, hazardous, and medical waste issues.[29]

The thirteen-member Toxics Committee first met on January 13, 1990. Their work was infused with the language of citizenship, including rights, justice, and responsibility. One of the basic problems they identified was that the waste management industry, rather than the state, was responsible for monitoring its own activities. In addition, they argued that the state had as yet only offered Band-Aid solutions to the problems of landfills. The committee also faulted the state for failing to question whether it was in the interests of Tennessee to accept waste flows from outside the state. Further, it argued that the state had not addressed the lack of enforcement of existing waste management and water and air quality laws and had no remedy for the absence of institutions that allowed citizens a voice in siting and permitting decisions. SOCM's general solutions, far from the technical prescriptions that someone involved in the siting or regulation of waste facilities might have proposed, revolved around massive campaigns to educate the public and actions to hold the industry and government accountable to the citizens.[30]

The Fight for Local Control, Environmental Justice, and the Right to Say No

When it appeared that federal and state authorities were not inclined to act quickly enough to stop the importation of garbage, SOCM pursued local solutions. They pressured county commissioners to set fees on imported waste to discourage dumping in those counties, employing people power by organizing dozens and sometimes hundreds of citizens to turn out for county commission and town council meetings to testify and lobby. SOCM based this local aspect of their campaign, fighting landfills county by county by promoting greater authority for town councils and county commissions to regulate activities within their jurisdictions, on what became known as the Jackson Law. Because the Department of Health and Environment's

Solid Waste Control Board had failed to enact new rules that fulfilled the requirements of the 1989 solid waste management law, local governments representing counties and unincorporated municipalities retained their power to approve or deny proposed new landfills and landfill expansions. To SOCM members, county commissioners, and legislators debating the issue in Nashville, this law became known as the Jackson Law after its 1989 legislative sponsor, Doug Jackson. As the law was written, local governments did not automatically gain the authority granted by the legislation; they had to vote to opt in to enjoy the local control it provided. The law also included an expiration date of July 1, 1991. SOCM saw great potential in the Jackson Law but also worried about its limitations.[31]

In Campbell County, concern over a landfill proposed for an abandoned coal strip mine near the community of Wooldridge prompted dozens of residents to join SOCM in mid-1990.[32] This provided the group its first opportunity to test the utility of the Jackson Law. In August, after learning about the possibilities of the law at one of their first meetings, the local chapter of SOCM gathered eight hundred signatures on petitions asking the Campbell County Commission to adopt or opt in to the law. SOCM also lobbied individual commissioners, providing each with a copy and summary of the law, and ran ads on local radio stations. About thirty SOCM members attended the county commission meeting in August. Led by local resident Connie McNealy, they testified about the dangers of massive landfills for water quality and the inadequacy of government regulation of such facilities. They insisted that it was incumbent upon counties to protect themselves because the state and federal governments, unduly influenced by urban areas and corporate lobbyists, failed to do so. The commission voted unanimously to opt into the Jackson Law at its September meeting. Soon after, Campbell County refused to allow the construction of the contentious landfill.[33]

Following its success in Campbell County, the group went on to organize members in other counties to persuade their local governments to opt to be covered by the Jackson Law. Members in Oliver Springs at the intersection of Anderson, Roane, and Morgan Counties northeast of Knoxville successfully convinced the commission of Anderson County to adopt the law and then sue to enjoin Remote Landfill Services from constructing a landfill without county approval. On January 29, 1990, Anderson County won the suit, resulting in the permanent halting of construction until Remote obtained the approval of the Anderson County Commission.[34] SOCM then successfully convinced the Morgan County Commission to opt into the law.[35] This was one more local manifestation of the group's dedication to ensuring that citizens had a say in decisions that affected their communities, the health of their families, and the quality of their environment. In their efforts to address the mega-landfill issue at the statewide level, they would operate on the same philosophical basis.

In tandem with their county-by-county campaign, SOCM crafted legislative solutions to the problem of solid and hazardous waste management. At a meeting of the state senate's Energy and Environment Committee at Cove Lake State Park in Caryville, approximately thirty miles north of Knoxville, in October 1990, SOCM members from the Morristown, Campbell County, Roane County, and Oliver Springs chapters made their demands known. They called on the assembly to "give us local control of our own counties and what comes in, stop out-of-state waste from coming into Tennessee, improve enforcement of current laws and regulations, and impose stiffer fines on violators."[36] Attendees offered the committee ways to achieve these objectives. Those testifying included a University of Tennessee professor who worked with the university's Waste Management Institute, and Peggy Douglas, a representative of the Tennessee Environmental Council, who described options available for Tennessee to restrict out-of-state waste without violating the U.S. Constitution's interstate commerce clause. Other speakers included Ruth Neff from the State Planning Office, who spoke about possible laws that would allow the Division of Solid Waste to have access to a waste facility operator's past history and compliance reports as part of permitting decisions. Assistant Commissioner of Health and Environment Wayne Scharber testified about the importance of citizen participation in solid waste management processes.[37] SOCM's recommendations at this October meeting—the ability of Tennessee to restrict out-of-state waste, to review a permit applicant's past compliance with the laws of Tennessee or other states, and to ensure that citizens played a vital role in decisions regarding the locating and permitting of waste facilities—became the basis for group's legislative work on the issue.

Publicity surrounding and public opposition to proposals for new landfills and the General Assembly's attempts to deal with the waste issue catapulted out-of-state waste to such prominence that in 1991 Tennessee's governor, Ned McWherter, made it a top priority for his administration. In advance of the 1991 assembly, SOCM drafted language for a waste management bill, solicited assemblymen from the most affected areas to introduce it, and cultivated relationships with a variety of allies including the Tennessee Environmental Council, the Sierra Club, and other citizens' organizations and local governments. SOCM also attempted to influence McWherter as the governor's office wrote its own waste management bill. SOCM advocated for legislation that would provide citizen's a right to appeal permitting decisions; extend the expiration date of the Jackson Law from July 1, 1991, to July 1, 1995; expand the Jackson Law to include all counties regardless of whether they had adopted landfill zoning regula tions or not; and provide the authority of the Jackson Law to local governments immediately without each county having to opt in. In addition, SOCM supported new fees on waste facility permit applicants to pay for enforcement, a requirement that applicants provide fourteen days' public notice before applying for a permit, the addition of citizen members to the Solid Waste Board, and restrictions on the role of board members who had significant economic interests in the permits being considered.[38] The administration agreed to consider these proposals if SOCM could gain the support of county governments for the provisions. SOCM then embarked on a successful campaign to drum up the endorsements from the state's county commissioners. McWherter, however, balked. SOCM members fervently lobbied assemblymen in Nashville to amend the administration's bill to include their provisions; in some instances, they had face-to-face contact six or seven times with the senator or representative. In the end, McWherter's Comprehensive Solid Waste Management Plan included little that SOCM proposed. It did, however, extend the termination date of the Jackson Law. The only other proactive SOCM-supported legislation that passed in 1991 was the so-called Bad Boy Law drafted by the Tennessee Environmental Council. The Bad Boy Law prohibited any waste management company from obtaining a permit to open and operate a landfill under the governor's comprehensive plan if it had a record of environmental violations in Tennessee or another state.[39] In their lobbying and testimony before subcommittees of the assembly, SOCM members talked about such bad boys as corporate criminals and framed their arguments in the language of justice and responsibility. SOCM members were also successful in opposing a series of bills that sought to restrict the rights of local governments to set fees for imported solid wastes and to terminate the Jackson Law, introduced by Senator James Kyle, a Democrat and attorney from Memphis.[40]

SOCM's legislative agenda, although it did not ban out-of-state waste or impose any new environmental regulations, was vigorously opposed by the waste management industry and legislators who saw economic opportunity in the proposed landfills. In hearings before the Tennessee Senate Natural Resources Committee, which was considering both SOCM's and the governor's bills in March 1991, Sandy Johnson of the Tennessee Association of Businesses insisted that any new laws "create mechanisms for scientific and technical reasoning to be the major source of authority in siting landfills" rather than the concerns or opinions of residents.[41] Johnson—whose organization represented more than a hundred manufacturers in the state, who created slightly more than half of all the waste that made its way into non-industrial landfills—argued that the creation of regional solid waste authorities that would coordinate waste management decisions among a variety of local governments would provide yet another obstacle to navigate in what was an "already near-impossible task."[42] Further, she argued that because manufacturers represented more than half of the waste produced, the solid waste board ought to represent manufacturers proportionally by including more representatives from industry in its membership even though those representatives might not live anywhere near the site of a proposed landfill.[43]

SOCM achieved few of its legislative goals in 1991. Other than the extension of the expiration date of the Jackson Law to June 30, 1994, and passage of the Bad Boy Law, SOCM was unable to expand the ability of citizens to participate in or appeal permitting decisions for solid waste facilities, and the membership of the Solid Waste Board remained unchanged. Two decades of lobbying the General Assembly, however, had taught them to be patient; passing legislation often took multiple sessions. Through a series of articles in the SOCM newsletter and workshops, the Toxics Committee and county-level chapters spent the months leading up to the next legislative session educating the membership on what the laws passed in mid-1991 actually did and how SOCM might use them in their continued work on the issue. Although their proactive solid waste management bills failed to pass in 1991, SOCM successfully helped to kill attempts by Browning-Ferris Industries to weaken parts of the comprehensive solid waste law that had passed the previous year, including provisions designed to reduce local controls for counties during the second part of the Ninety-seventh General Assembly in 1992. As they did this, they evaluated their previous legislative efforts, worked to build momentum for the next session, and continued their efforts to advance the power of residents to influence landfill-permitting decisions in their communities.[44]

By the eve of the ninety-eighth session of the General Assembly, the Toxics Committee had refined the language of its proposed legislation. For the 1993–1994 session, SOCM combined its demands for local control and citizen approval of landfills and importation of garbage from out of state into a single flagship bill with three main provisions. First, it sought to strengthen the Bad Boy Law passed in 1991 by leaving less discretion to the state commissioner of environment and conservation to decide what constituted an unacceptable pattern of performance on the part of a landfill operator seeking a permit. The proposed bill would define specifically what constituted bad behavior. Second, the bill authorized a citizen referendum by which citizens could decide whether to allow a landfill in their community or to allow an existing landfill to expand if the proposed landfill accepted more than ten thousand tons of waste a month, changed the kinds of waste it received, or expanded by more than 10 percent. Finally, the bill provided citizens the right to appeal solid waste permits just as they could other permitting decisions regarding air and water quality and strip mining.[45]

SOCM's work on this bill in the Ninety-eighth General Assembly marked a turning point in how the organization understood and publicly explained its work. In introducing their bill, SOCM used a term that was becoming increasingly popular in the world of environmental and social activism in the late 1980s and early 1990s to describe how they understood the solid and hazardous waste issue in the state: environmental justice. Maureen O'Connell, who served as executive director of the organization during the period, remembers that the organization may have first come into direct contact with the term while working with a predominantly African American group from western Tennessee on toxic waste issues in

1991. She recounts that "environmental justice" seemed to permeate conversations regarding waste issues in the early 1990s.[46] In introducing and explaining the proposed legislation to SOCM members, the January 1993 issue of the *SOCM Sentinel* described the issue in terms of justice. It asked readers whether a company that contaminated a community's water supply, had been repeatedly convicted of federal crimes, or had been found to repeatedly illegally dump hazardous waste into a landfill should be allowed to operate a waste facility in the state. SOCM members had always at least implicitly wrapped justice into how they understood and described environmental issues, but the explicit use of the phrase environmental justice with regard to the waste issue indicated a transition in how the organization understood itself and its work. It called its 1993 waste management bill the Environmental Justice Bill. Subsequent legislative proposals to address out-of-state waste would carry the same moniker. By the end of the decade, SOCM had clarified its mission to reflect its dedication to advocating social, economic, and environmental justice.[47]

The Environmental Justice Bill of 1993 was the embodiment of an organizational philosophy that insisted that the best natural resource decisions should involve all interested parties and that citizens should have a right to participate in those decisions. Nevertheless, by July 1993, the bill had met the same fate as its predecessors. A 3-3-1 vote in the Senate Energy and Natural Resources Committee kept it from advancing to the Senate floor, and SOCM's Toxics Committee was already preparing to try again in the next session and strategizing how to influence the rule-making process for the as-yet-unenforced 1991 Bad Boy Law. With the legislative defeat barely over, the Toxics Committee brainstormed how to turn people out for the public rule-making hearings.[48]

While they were navigating the legislative maze in Nashville, SOCM members were also working with similar groups in other rural states to introduce and pass a federal bill that would enable states to prohibit the importation of waste from outside their borders. In September 1991, the SOCM Board endorsed federal legislation written by the Western Organization of Resource Councils (WORC), a consortium of citizens' conservation organizations in the Plains and Rocky Mountain states that grew out of Montana's Northern Plains Resource Council.[49] In a 1991 edition of the *SOCM Sentinel*, one of the bill's authors, Will Collette of WORC, described

FIGURE 11. While SOCM tried to persuade the assembly to pass the environmental justice law, it continued applying pressure through direct action. SOCM action and press conference about illegally dumped waste in Greene County, 1993.

Private collection, Statewide Organizing for
Community eMpowerment, Lake City, Tennessee.

the legislation in patriotic terms as advancing freedom: "Some people call it a nimby [not in my backyard] thing to say 'no' to waste from outside your community. . . . Instead, we consider Not In My Backyard to be another term for democracy. . . . The right to say no is a bedrock grass-roots principle."[50]

For the next four years, SOCM incorporated the federal Right to Say NO bill into its campaign to prevent the importation of solid, hazardous, and biomedical wastes from out of state through an assertion of the rights of citizens to participate in the decisions that affected their communities. In 1994, WORC and the groups supporting the legislation were able to pass what they considered a strong bill out of the Energy and Commerce Committee in the House of Representatives. The State and Local Government Interstate Waste Control Act of 1994, H.R. 4779, sponsored by Representative Rick Boucher, a Democrat from West Virginia, maintained the ability of states to prohibit out-of-state garbage and preserved local, community-level approval for new landfills. The Senate bill, sponsored by Senator Max Baucus, a Democrat from Montana, was weaker but still included much of what the groups wanted, including provisions that enabled states to

control the flows of trash across their borders. Both bills required public hearings or public comment before local governments could approve
the building of a landfill. In varying degrees, both defined a role for local
governments in determining whether they would allow the importation of
waste, and both expanded the ability of state governors to ban the importation of waste but only with the approval of local governments. The House
bill included a bad actor provision similar to what Tennessee passed in
1991; the Senate bill did not.[51] When the Senate bill stalled, SOCM and the
other groups flooded the mailboxes and voicemails of senators asking to
move the bill.[52] Both bills made it through both houses before dying in the
last hours of the 1994 congressional session.[53] The next year, the groups
got an earlier start, flying in citizen lobbyists to Washington. This time
they were a bit more successful as the Senate passed a limited bill by a
vote of 94–6 on May 18. SOCM and WORC then tried to push a stronger bill
through the House. Ultimately, opponents' arguments against the bill, that
it violated the interstate commerce clause of the Constitution and that it
imposed unnecessary and onerous regulations on the industry, led to the
same fate as SOCM's legislative proposals in Tennessee.[54]

A Seat at the Table

When SOCM's efforts failed to produce strong laws at either the state or
federal level, the group pursued another course grounded in its grassroots
philosophy. After the passage of the Bad Boy Law in 1991 and extension
of the Jackson Law, members worked to monitor existing landfills, oversee
the enforcement activities of the Tennessee Department of Conservation
and Environment, and participate in the state rule-making processes to
make sure the new laws were effectively enforced.

In 1992, SOCM employed a practice they had learned in their battles
against the coal strip mining companies in the previous decades: it com-
missioned and published its own independent study of solid waste, landfills, and enforcement ("or lack thereof," in their words) in the state.[55]
During the 1970s and 1980s, they had developed this tactic as a way to
get a grasp on what was actually happening in the coal mining counties.
Through independent research, they assessed how much land coal companies owned, how much the companies paid in property taxes and how

it compared to taxes paid by other residents, which mines had permits, and how effectively the state was enforcing its laws. They used the studies to rally public opposition to strip mining or support for regulation, and to prompt state action. The group applied this same tactic to waste. As they had with the coal mining taxation and enforcement studies, SOCM used the expertise and labor of its members and staff.[56]

While they conducted the waste study, they continued to elevate awareness of the issue through creative direct actions. To illuminate what they considered a lack of enforcement of the Bad Boy Law by the Department of Environment and Conservation and its commissioner, J. W. Luna, they held a mock trial at Legislative Plaza in Nashville on March 1, 1994. About forty SOCM members participated in the event. Standing in front of an easel displaying a state map that included twenty-four dump trucks representing proposed landfills or landfill expansions, Janice Morrissey of Roane County articulated the group's position. "The citizens of this state are under siege from the waste industry," she declared, "and the Department of Environment and Conservation has done nothing to protect us from this siege."[57] State officials cited revisions to Tennessee's waste management laws made in the last three General Assembly sessions to assure citizens they were more protected than they had ever been from the dangers associated with landfills. Rose Ingram of Oliver Springs was not convinced. "We have been fighting an unneeded private megadump for more than four years," she told reporters. She pointed to repeated violations by the company that had taken over the proposed landfill from Remote Landfill Incorporated, Chambers Development Corporation in West Virginia and Pennsylvania, and called on Commissioner Luna to enforce the Bad Boy Law.[58] Chambers, which operated landfills in thirteen states and was under investigation by the federal Securities and Exchange Commission, dismissed the event as just another example of "NIMBYism," but SOCM kept up the pressure.[59]

After three years, SOCM released a report of its findings. According to the *SOCM Sentinel*, the Toxics Committee conducted the study in response to "hundreds of complaints from citizens about problems at landfills in their communities, and countless horror stories of the state's refusal to take any action against the operators."[60] The report—fifty-five pages long without appendices—reflected the group's dedication to holding government and

FIGURE 12. SOCM members from the Oliver Creek chapter meet with Governor Ned McWherter's representatives to urge the state to enforce the new Bad Boy Law.
Private collection, Statewide Organizing for
Community eMpowerment, Lake City, Tennessee.

industry accountable to residents. Alvin Miller, a member from Greene County in the far eastern part of the state, wrote in the introduction of the report, "They [the state] have good guidelines. . . . If they went by the rules, there wouldn't be much problem. . . . Restrictions are no good unless somebody enforces them."[61] The study found that the existing laws were sound but that the state was not adequately enforcing them. It identified four problem areas: inconsistent or only partial enforcement of state regulations; poor agency record keeping that was often inaccessible to enforcement staff and citizens; enforcement policies that were unclear for industry, agency officials, and citizens; and a lack of effective fines to act as deterrents to breaking the law.[62]

Prompted by the findings and allegations of lax state enforcement in SOCM's publicized study, the Tennessee Department of Environment and Conservation agreed to meet with SOCM members on February 9, 1996. At the meeting, agency officials listened attentively to SOCM members Janice Morrissey, Todd Shelton, and Ethel and Clyde Spiller and conceded many of SOCM's findings were correct, including inconsistent enforcement practices, poor communication among the offices, lack of public accessibility to information, and inadequate record keeping. The department staff agreed that there was a need to formalize policy but maintained that the department did a better job than indicated by the SOCM study. However, the department acknowledged that because record keeping was so poor, there was no way for the citizen-researchers to know this. By the end of the meeting, the department and SOCM agreed to a detailed list of commitments for progress, a timeline for accomplishing them with specific dates and benchmarks, and scheduled a follow-up meeting later that year to assess progress.[63]

For its part, the Department of Environment and Conservation agreed to direct its inspectors to document the reasons why they deemed violations minor or serious enough to warrant enforcement activity and to require that they indicate a target date when the violation would be corrected. SOCM agreed to provide the state with information on which field offices it found the most citizen-friendly in their accessibility and record-keeping, so the state could begin to make all of their field offices more accessible. In addition, the director of the Solid Waste Division agreed to meet with field office managers and individual inspectors to address inconsistencies in record keeping and enforcement at the office, and to create a certification process for landfill operators and an educational program for inspectors. Finally, the state agreed to begin implementing a comprehensive inspection records program by July 1996 that would summarize inspection, enforcement information, and the resolution of violations in an accessible computer database. All of these agreements served to make information more accessible to citizens so they could more easily hold the state and waste management companies accountable and prevent pollution from landfills. As pleasantly surprised as SOCM members were with the outcome, they understood that these agreements were only the beginning. Over the next several months, the organization expanded the size of its enforcement campaign, disseminated the findings of its solid waste study, and monitored the Department of Environment and Conservation to make sure it followed through on its promises.[64]

In August 1996, members of SOCM's Toxics Committee again met with the Tennessee Department of Environment and Conservation to review progress in the commitments it made earlier that year. SOCM found that some of the commitments were indeed being implemented while others limped along more slowly. The state had begun creating its certification process for landfill operators and was close to implementing its inspector-training program to standardize enforcement procedures. When SOCM members complained that citizens were still having trouble gaining access to information despite promises by the department that it would make information more available, the director committed to fixing the problem. Disappointingly, the inspection record database was far from complete. The meeting ended with renewed commitments by the state to fulfill its promises from the February meeting and an invitation for SOCM members to present their concerns about citizen access to information to a field office managers' meeting. The Toxics Committee members were pleased with the tenor of the meeting but feared that all of the changes they had worked to achieve might simply be cosmetic. "I think it's a really good first step that we're having these conversations," said Janice Morrissey, adding, "It's something that we're not in the habit of doing, and something they're not in the habit of doing either." Morrissey worried, though: "I hope it makes a difference to the whole enforcement effort, that it's not just fiddling around with paperwork."[65] The only way to ensure that these changes had real effects on enforcement of landfills and made tangible improvements to the environment depended on whether SOCM members and other citizens remained involved in monitoring the agency and ensuring progress occurred at the local level. The Toxics Committee, according to the organization's newsletter, had "forced important changes and given local people the tools to achieve better enforcement at landfills in their area," but it was up to citizens to "make it happen."[66]

Conclusion: The Power of Persistence

By the end of 1996, SOCM's campaign to prevent the importation of out-of-state waste and the construction of mega-landfills had transitioned from an intense, multifront battle into a cooler scenario in which citizens took an active role in monitoring and supporting state regulation and holding landfill operators accountable to the people and existing laws. Other more pressing issues—the prospect of housing radioactive waste in Roane County west of Knoxville, clear-cutting forests, the organization's new campaigns to dismantle racism, and a proposed major strip mine on the Cumberland Plateau—soon overtook the threat of out-of-state waste, and members directed the organization's energies elsewhere.

Since they did not pass any of their flagship legislation that would have given citizens an expanded and decisive role in awarding permits for landfills, or state or local governments the "Right to Say NO" to out-of-state garbage, it is difficult to assess SOCM's campaign against out-of-state waste and mega-landfills. Part of this ambiguity might be attributed to the diffuse nature of the issue. Environmental decision-making regarding waste issues was messy, involving as it did multiple venues including the legislature, state agencies, and county commissions, and multiple and confusing laws and regulations. If their goal was a revolution in solid waste management and democratic participation, then members enjoyed at best only minor success. But if their goals were to stop the mega-landfills that threatened their communities and maintain or expand the ability of citizens to participate in landfill siting decisions, then they can claim victory. In the General Assembly, their preservation and extension of the ability of local governments to veto landfill permits proved vital in allowing citizens to determine what happened in their communities. In addition, the passage of the Bad Boy Law and its enforcement by SOCM members kept the most irresponsible landfill operators out of the state.[67]

Opponents of SOCM's proposed legislation argued that the kinds of public notice and citizens' appeal provisions the group proposed in the legislature would shut down the industry in Tennessee. It appears that it took even less than that; by the end of the 1990s, few of the mega-landfills had materialized and the multinational waste management corporations had abandoned their grandiose proposals. Citizen monitoring of industry and government agencies, which increased enforcement of existing laws at the local level and use of the Jackson Law, proved effective. SOCM members, through a vigorous commitment to grassroots democracy, had formalized their roles as citizen-guardians of the people's interest in solid waste management. After using every strategy they could dream up to influence landfill permitting at every level, citizens had succeeded at achieving increased power in the decision-making process.[68]

8

Conclusion

Participation, Perseverence, and Rethinking Environmentalism

When I first conceived of this project, I failed to fully understand its potential importance. I set out to illuminate an overlooked but ubiquitous form of political participation. I wanted to shine a light on the incredible work of everyday citizens who sacrificed much to address threats to their land, air, water, health, and communities in the late twentieth century. For many observers, these activists are often hidden in the background, holding signs in photos or behind quotes in the local section of the newspaper or on the nightly news. I was interested in how they understood environmental issues and wanted to show how their actions at the local, state, and national levels shaped environmental policy and further democratized American life. I wanted to demonstrate how environmental engagement itself transformed activists and their organizations.

As I researched the project, I realized I was doing so in the midst of a resurgence of grassroots environmental activism. Thousands of people all over the country and from all walks of life, organized through traditional means and social media, were taking part in protests and petition drives to oppose the construction of the Keystone XL pipeline. At the same time, Americans were joining forces to fight natural gas development through the technology of hydraulic fracturing, or fracking. Like the coal boom of the 1970s, the Keystone XL issue and natural gas boom of the 2010s are focusing public attention on the short- and long-term environmental and social costs of energy development. The news in 2014 reads like an epilogue to the stories recounted here. In fact, many of the activists profiled in these pages are actively working to address fracking and climate change today. Since 2010, Northern Plains veterans have led the group's opposition to the Keystone XL pipeline because of the danger it poses to private property, rural communities, and the climate.[1] In the spring of 2013, members of Statewide Organizing for Community eMpowerment [sic] (formerly "Save Our Cumberland Mountains," SOCM) joined other organizations in Tennessee to organize a people's hearing to draw attention to lax oil and gas regulations and to demand that the state of Tennessee protect the environment and people from natural gas development.[2] In the fall of 2013, Northern Plains began an active campaign to fight fracking along the Beartooth Front in south central Montana.[3]

This resurgence of environmental activism has not escaped the media or Hollywood. But even in fictional depictions such as the 2012 film *Promised Land*, big-name actors and dramatic plot lines obscure the stories of citizen activists. Writers and actors John Krasinski and Matt Damon invented an environmental organizer who—spoiler alert—turns out to be a stooge for the natural gas industry. Audiences wait in suspense to see if Damon's character, Steve, will do the right thing and denounce fracking and its damaging consequences for the environment and rural communities. The real story, however, is hidden in the actions of local skeptic Frank Yates, played by Hal Holbrook, who organizes his neighbors to oppose fracking in their town.[4] I wanted to help tell Frank's story because it is the real story behind the headlines and the Hollywood scripts—the story lived by Wally McRae, Priscilla Robinson, and Maureen O'Connell.

During the 1980s and 1990s, the Northern Plains Resource Council grew in every direction: in terms of geography, members and issues, and organizational sophistication. As it did, it confronted the difficulties inherent in organizing diverse groups of people with sometimes divergent interests, but it also had to learn how to continue to influence the shifting regulatory and political environments during those decades.

By the 2000s, Northern Plains had refined an organizing model that combined volunteer citizen activism with professional expertise, and it orchestrated campaigns employing interconnected legal, media, legislative, and direct action components. In 2000, it signed an innovative "Good Neighbor Agreement" with the nation's largest producer of platinum and palladium to protect water quality and the small communities downstream of the Stillwater and East Rosebud mines in south central Montana while ensuring the continued mining of these essential industrial metals.[5] Strip mining of coal remained a core issue for the organization at the beginning of the twenty-first century, but the bulk of NPRC's coal work concerned enforcing existing mine reclamation and water and air quality laws. The group's most daunting challenges in the 2000s came from proposals to build a new strip mine and railroad that would significantly affect the Tongue River Valley in southeastern Montana and from plans to drill tens of thousands of wells in eastern Montana to mine methane gas from the coal seams.[6]

Southwest Environmental Service advanced the ability of citizens to participate in environmental decision-making to protect and improve water and air quality in southern Arizona during the 1980s using different tactics than Northern Plains and Save Our Cumberland Mountains, but it similarly demonstrated the pertinence and potency of grassroots environmental activism. The group dissolved after its victories in 1988, but its legacy remained in Arizona's clean water and cleaner air and the continued activism of its staff and board members.[7]

Priscilla Robinson, who was admittedly never anti-mining, used her expertise and connections from her work on water and air quality issues to work as an environmental consultant to mining companies seeking more environmentally sound mining practices.[7] On July 29, 2013, at the age of eighty-two, Robinson passed away. Tucson journalist Tony Davis, who followed the work of SES and environmental issues in southern Arizona for more than thirty years, said of Robinson that she "virtually invented modern-day environmentalism in Tucson."[8] Longtime Tucson conservationist and chairman of the Arizona Democratic Party Bill Roe said, "When she took over the Southwest Environmental Service the environmental movement was quiet, in contrast to the half-dozen or more groups with paid staffs here today." Former U.S. Representative Jim Kolbe remembered, "She knew what she was doing. . . . She was never an ideologue. She knew how to compromise to get things done."[9] The other women who worked for SES remained active in environmental and other progressive advocacy in southern Arizona into the twenty-first century.[10]

In the first decade of the twenty-first century, Save Our Cumberland Mountains built on the organizational capacity and political power created through its campaign against mega-landfills and on its successful and well-publicized campaign to stop a proposed strip mine near Fall Creek Falls State Park on the Cumberland Plateau to continue and expand its work to address issues of social, economic, and environmental injustice in Tennessee. The group tackled mountain-top removal coal mining and continued its work on clean water. It also began initiatives to support the creation of more environmentally sustainable green jobs and a more equitable tax system in the state that would not unduly burden the poor. In 2013, its mission of "working for social, economic, and environmental justice for all" included SOCM's articulated commitment to "overcoming social and institutional racism, and embracing our diverse cultures."[11] Reflecting its expanded mission and its wider territory of operations, SOCM changed its name to Statewide Organization for Community eMpowerment in 2010 and moved its office from Lake City to neighboring Knoxville.[12]

The history of these organizations offers many valuable lessons for today. First is the importance of citizen participation in environmental decision-making and the ways democratic and environmental reform have been intertwined in late twentieth century. As early as 1987, historian Samuel Hays noticed the relationship between the ability of citizens to participate and the enforcement of environmental laws.[13] That same year, the United Nations World Commission on Environment and Development echoed this lesson in its recommendations for sustainable development.[14] As recently as 2011, Chinese scholar Ying Zhao drew the same lesson from his study of American environmentalism and applied it to his home country: he attributed the poor enforcement of well-intentioned environmental laws in China to inadequate public participation procedures there. Ying's prescription for improvement: "encourage public organizations, such as labor unions, youth leagues, and the women's federation to participate in environmental protection."[15] The examples provided by the stories of NPRC, SES, and SOCM add evidence to support the relationship between public participation in governance and environmental quality. Looking forward, the ability and capacity of citizens to participate in environmental decisions must be considered as an essential component in achieving sustainability.

A version of the black-and-white cartoon in figure 13 used to hang on the wall of the Northern Plains Resource Council when I worked there. It depicts a frog nearly swallowed by a heron. The frog, its head already down the bird's throat, reaches out of the bird's mouth and is choking its captor. The picture is captioned: "Don't *Ever* Give Up." I have seen this cartoon in various forms in the offices of other grassroots groups. It is simple but illuminates what I hope is the most obvious but understated lesson from this study: the power of persistent citizen involvement and oversight to affect positive environmental change.

None of the groups I profile in this study achieved exactly what they wanted when they wanted. In fact, veteran Northern Plains activists Wally McRae and Ellen Pfister told me in 2009 that looking back on their nearly four decades of work, they considered their efforts a failure.[16] In their view, the *North Central Power Study* was becoming a reality piece by piece. They did not recognize that, despite the ambitions of industry and government bureaucrats, only a very small portion of the industrial transformation forecast for the region during the 1970s has occurred. The *North Central Power Study* proposed twenty-one new power plants for Montana. Only one was built. The study proposed dozens of new dams and

FIGURE 13. "Don't *Ever* Give Up," author unknown, n.d. Variations on this cartoon are ubiquitous on the Internet and are used by different organizations across the social reform spectrum.

impoundments, including one on the Yellowstone River, one of the last undammed rivers in the United States.[17] The Yellowstone still runs free. What they saved from strip mining is now at risk, however, from natural gas development. When Priscilla Robinson and SES began their work to force Arizona's copper smelters to reduce their pollution, Robinson thought that the whole campaign would be over in a few years.[18] It took a decade and the outcome was far more complicated than Robinson or her allies ever anticipated. SOCM activists never passed a law preventing waste management companies from dumping garbage from out of state on rural Tennessee communities, yet few of the proposed landfills were ever built. In all three cases, as citizen activists worked to protect their communities, public health, and the environment, they expanded the ability of everyday people to take part in environmental decisions, and they succeeded in winning better outcomes than would have resulted if they had remained passive and submissive.

Persistence was a common thread throughout all of these campaigns. By standing up to industry, citizens added a new element to the calculations of businesses and the government. Although corporations rarely admit it in public, their ability to make a profit often depends on externalizing the costs of doing business. As citizens of the developed world and participants in the consumption-based global economy, we all benefit from this reality. Profitability and low consumer prices often depend on treating the environment as a waste sink, depleting natural resources with impunity, and burdening politically weak communities with the environmental repercussions of resource development. Power companies avoid paying the long-term health costs of air pollution and distribute diluted airborne pollutants widely across the population and landscape. Coal mining and natural gas companies foist the costs of extracting fossil fuels on local communities in the form of degraded ground water quality and a host of other social and environmental consequences. Reclamation and air pollution control laws are two attempts to internalize some of those costs, and neither would be the law of the land without citizen activism.[19]

If companies are forced to account for the real costs of their activities, production costs increase. If they are forced to slow down and study the impacts of their activities, expenses go up. At some point, these costs increase to the point where the activity ceases to make economic sense.

Phelps Dodge's "Old Reliable" only reliably returned a profit when the environment and people living near the smelter physically absorbed the cost of doing business. When the government, prompted by citizens, forced the company to mitigate this inequitable application of environmental burdens, the smelter shut down. Citizen activists make all the difference. Sometimes they help pass new laws that require government and citizen review of a proposed activity to expose and mitigate the externalized expenses of doing business. Or they influence the political agenda, placing pressure on government regulators and industry to adhere to existing laws. Prior the 1970s, these costs were either unknown, ignored, or accepted as the price of progress. After the 1970s, citizens demanded new laws or used existing laws to challenge these kinds of harms and inequities. Corporations weigh costs and benefits and may decide to abandon their plans or agree to mitigations designed to improve human and environmental health and well-being. Persistent citizen involvement and oversight in Montana, Arizona, and Tennessee had this effect. Environmental and democratic wins are, of course, accompanied by losses since compromise is the nature of political process. The need for citizen oversight and engagement never ends.[20]

There is a perverse danger in this kind of cost-benefit calculus. When a corporation confronts citizen opposition to its plans and is forced to account for the environmental and social costs of doing business in a particular community, state, or nation, it will logically look for a place with less opposition where it can more easily externalize those costs. This is the story of environmental racism and injustice in the globalized economy of the twentieth century and today. As middle-class Anglo-Americans began to question the price of progress in the mid-twentieth century, corporations and the government diverted pollution to the poor and disenfranchised and communities and people of color. The civil rights movement gave greater voice to people of color. Grassroots environmental activism influenced the expansion of democracy in American governance in the late twentieth century, allowing citizens to take part in environmental decisions. However, social and economic inequality continues to plague the United States and allows the continued inequitable distribution of environmental hazards and amenities. These inequalities are only magnified in the global economy. As environmental justice scholars, activists, and members of many grassroots environmental groups recognized, social, economic, and environmental inequalities are intertwined. Until these inequalities are addressed, a just and sustainable society will remain elusive. Persistent citizen involvement and engagement with environmental decisions was central in curbing pollution and degradation in the late twentieth century. The same commitment will be needed in the twenty-first century.[21]

This leads us to a final lesson from this study: the need for a more expansive definition of environmentalism. The stories presented here blur the lines between mainstream environmental activism and the environmental justice movement. At the grassroots level, interpretation of environmental threats to one's family and community as unfair and unjust often cross racial, ethnic, class, and geographic divides. Inequalities still insidiously constrain the ability of certain Americans to influence the environmental decisions that affect their lives, but at the local level, the efforts to address threats to communities, public health, and the environment provide a common link between diverse groups.

During the 1980s and 1990s, environmental justice activists and scholars, including Robert Bullard, Dorceta Taylor, Sylvia Washington, and Andrew Hurley, rightly brought attention to the disconnect between certain elements of mainstream environmentalism and the plight of the poor and disenfranchised. Taylor argued that the mainstream movement's focus on protecting nonhuman nature and wild places drew attention away from the health and well-being of people. She asserted the critical importance of considering the social and human dimensions of environmental problems.[22] This necessary critique divided environmentalism into two, sometimes antagonistic, camps.

Although useful in examining the diversity of environmental attitudes and activism, this separation was often more academic than real. For activists on the ground whose work demanded the formation of expedient, and what Priscilla Robinson called "unlikely alliances," it did not exist.[23] The histories presented here demonstrate the diversity of tactics, issues, and values within the environmental movement during the late twentieth century. They provide a point from which to begin reconciling this divide. Their histories speak to the need to reconsider how we have classified various elements of the larger environmental movement and develop a more expansive and inclusive definition of environmentalism.

A new definition should consider environmental and social dimensions of sustainability problems as entwined and interdependent. As such, it would begin to identify common ground to address the inequalities that undercut environmental protection, public health, and well-being. It would echo the definition of sustainability offered by Julian Agyeman and Bob Evans as ensuring "a better quality of life for all, now and in the future, in a just and equitable manner, whilst living within the limits of supporting ecosystems."[24]

I think Helen Waller would see herself and her activism within this definition. So would Priscilla Robinson, Barbara Tellman, J. W. Bradley, Maureen O'Connell, and the thousands of activists involved the hundreds of other citizens' environmental organizations across the country in the late twentieth century. They might even shrug it off as common sense and then go back to work protecting their communities and environment. For the rest of us, it provides a way forward in thinking about how to create resilient communities and a sustainable world.

Working within this new understanding of the connection between citizen participation and environmental protection and this expansive notion of environmentalism that recognizes the interdependency of social, economic, and environmental justice, we might stand shoulder to shoulder with activists around the globe and shout, "this is our land, we have the right to be heard."[25]

NOTES

1. Helen and Gordon Waller, interview by author, Waller ranch near Circle, Montana, 3 August 2010; Helen Waller, phone interview by John Smillie, Western Organization of Resource Councils, Billings, Montana, 21 August 2009.

2. See Samuel P. Hays, *Beauty, Health, and Permanence: Environmental Politics in the United States, 1955–1985* (New York: Cambridge University Press, 1987); Hal K. Rothman, *The Greening of a Nation?: Environmentalism in the United States Since 1945* (Fort Worth, TX: Harcourt Brace, 1998). The tendency of grassroots activists to act initially out of immediate self-interest is observed by historians including Samuel Hays and Hal K. Rothman.

3. Many scholars have written about the cultural upheaval of the 1960s. A few that I draw from here include Peter Braunstein and Michael William Doyle, eds., *Imagine Nation: The American Counterculture of the 1960s and 70s* (New York: Routledge, 2002); Dan T. Carter, *The Politics of Rage: George Wallace, the Origins of the New Conservatism, and the Transformation of American Politics* (New York: Simon and Schuster, 1995); Hays, *Beauty*; Maurice Isserman and Michael Kazin, *America Divided: The Civil War of the 1960s* (New York: Oxford University Press, 2004); Lisa McGirr, *Suburban Warriors: The Origins of the New American Right* (Princeton: Princeton University Press, 2001); Doug Rossinow, *The Politics of Authenticity: Liberalism, Christianity, and the New Left in America* (New York: Columbia University Press, 1998); Adam Rome, "Give Earth a Chance: The Environmental Movement and the Sixties," *Journal of American History* 90 (September 2003): 525–54; Rothman, *Greening*; James Miller, *Democracy in the Streets: From Port Huron to the Siege of Chicago* (New York: Simon and Schuster, 1987).

4. See Sarah T. Thomas, "A Call to Action: Silent Spring, Public Disclosure, and the Rise of Modern Environmentalism," in *Natural Protest: Essays on the History of American Environmentalism*, ed. Michael Egan and Jeff Crane (New York: Routledge, 2009), 185–203.

5. The Johnson administration opposed FOIA as a politically motivated attempt by Republicans to undermine Johnson's power—in hearings on the bill, it was opposed by all twenty-seven federal agencies and departments; Thomas

Blanton, ed., "Freedom of Information at 40: LBJ Refused Ceremony, Undercut Bill with Signing Statement," National Security Archive, George Washington University, http://www2.gwu.edu/~nsarchiv/NSAEBB/NSAEBB194/index.htm, accessed 24 November 2013. Although it does not discuss the use of FOIA by environmental groups, a comprehensive analysis of the act, its precedents, and its implementation is found in Herbert N. Foerstel, *Freedom of Information and the Right to Know: The Origins and Applications of the Freedom of Information Act* (Westport, CT: Greenwood Press, 1999). A simple Google search of the paired phrases "environmental groups" and "use of FOIA" returned over six thousand hits.

6. Daniel R. Mandelker, *NEPA Law and Litigation*, 2nd ed. (New York: Clark Boardman Callaghan, 1992). Samuel P. Hays, *A History of Environmental Politics since 1945* (Pittsburgh: University of Pittsburgh Press, 2000), 131–34.

7. Also see Cody Ferguson, "'You Are Now Entering a National Sacrifice Area': The Energy Boom of the 1970s and the Radicalization of the Northern Plains," *Journal of the West* 53, no. 1 (Winter 2014): 70–78.

8. Riley E. Dunlap and Angela G. Mertig, *American Environmentalism: The U.S. Movement, 1970–1990* (New York: Taylor and Francis, 1992), 28–29. The exact number could be in the thousands but precise numbers are not available. Riley E. Dunlap and Angela G. Mertig ran into the same problem in their study *American Environmentalism: The U.S. Environmental Movement, 1970–1990*. They were able to extrapolate some representative numbers for the late 1980s and early 1990s. They found that the National Toxics Campaign, a Boston-based organization that provides technical assistance to grassroots groups around the country, had a mailing list of 1,300 in 1991 and that the Citizen's Clearinghouse for Hazardous Waste reported that it worked with 7,000 grassroots environmental groups in 1989.

9. Erik W. Johnson and Scott Frickel, "Ecological Threat and the Founding of U.S. National Environmental Movement Organizations, 1962–1998," *Social Problems* 58, no. 3 (August 2011): 305–6, 318.

10. In arguing that the 1970s was a transformative decade, Bruce Schulman cites the Arab oil shock and energy crisis as one of the dramatic events (in addition to the end of the Vietnam War, *Roe v. Wade*, the Watergate scandal, and the Indian occupation of Wounded Knee) that shaped American life during the era. The organization of thousands of citizens' groups to address environmental issues during the 1970s, however, counters his assertion that one of the central transformations of the decade was a replacing of social and political activism as a source of cultural and political change with entrepreneurship. Incorporating the proliferation of grassroots environmental groups into an assessment of political culture in this era adds diversity to Schulman's assessment of the 1970s. Bruce J. Schulman, *The Seventies: The Great Shift in American Culture, Society, and Politics* (New York: Da Capo Press, 2001), xii, 257.

11. See Darren Speece, "From Corporatism to Citizen Oversight: The Legal Fight Over California Redwoods, 1970–1996," *Environmental History* 14 (October 2009):

705–36; Karl Boyd Brooks, *Before Earth Day: The Origins of American Environmental Law, 1945–1970* (Lawrence: University of Kansas Press, 2009). Speece illuminates the interaction between citizens' groups and the courts and how it shaped environmental protection through legal precedents.

12. Robert J. Brulle, *Agency, Democracy, and Nature: The U.S. Environmental Movement from a Critical Theory Perspective* (Cambridge, MA: MIT Press, 2000); Erik W. Johnson, "Social Movement Size, Organizational Diversity, and the Making of Federal Law," *Social Forces* 86, no. 3 (March 2008): 967, 986–87; Erik W. Johnson, Jon Agnone, and John D. McCarthy, "Movement Organizations, Syneristic Tactics, and Environmental Public Policy," *Social Forces* 88, no. 5 (July 2010): 2267–69.

13. See Samuel P. Hays, *Conservation and the Gospel of Efficiency* (Cambridge, MA: Harvard University Press, 1959), and Roderick F. Nash, *Wilderness and the American Mind* (New Haven: Yale University Press, 1967); also, Hays, *Beauty*; Philip Shabecoff, *A Fierce Green Fire: The American Environmental Movement* (Washington, DC: Island Press, 1993); Mark T. Harvey, *A Symbol of Wilderness: Echo Park and the American Conservation Movement* (Albuquerque: University of New Mexico Press, 1994).

14. See Brulle, *Agency, Democracy, and Nature*; Johnson, "Social Movement Size"; Johnson and Frickel, "Ecological Threat"; Johnson, Agnone, and McCarthy, "Movement Organizations."

15. Richard White, "Are You an Environmentalist or Do You Work for a Living?: Work and Nature," in *Uncommon Ground: Rethinking the Human Place in Nature*, ed. William Cronon (New York: W. W. Norton, 1995), 171–85.

16. Robert Bullard, *Dumping in Dixie: Class, Race, and Environmental Quality* (Boulder, CO: Westview Press, 1990); Sylvia Washington, *Packing Them In: An Archaeology of Environmental Racism in Chicago, 1865–1954* (Latham, MD: Lexington Books, 2005); Brulle, *Agency, Democracy and Nature*, 211–12.

17. Dorceta E. Taylor, *The Environment and the People in American Cities, 1600–1900s: Disorder, Inequality, and Social Change* (Durham, NC: Duke University Press, 2009), 11.

18. Andrew Hurley, *Environmental Inequalities: Class, Race, and Industrial Pollution in Gary, Indiana 1945–1980* (Chapel Hill: University of North Carolina Press, 1995), xii–xiv. Dorceta Taylor argues that environmental racism, "the process by which environmental decisions, actions, and policies result in racial discrimination or the creation of racial advantages," has existed in the Unites States since at least the mid-nineteenth century; Taylor, *Environment and the People in American Cities*, 5.

19. Julian Agyeman, Robert D. Bullard, and Bob Evans, *Just Sustainabilities: Development in an Unequal World* (London: Earthscan, 2012), 1.

20. This is a foundational premise of environmental racism and environmental justice studies. For this interpretation, I drew from many works but especially

David Naguib Pello and Robert J. Brulle, eds., *Power, Justice, and the Environment: A Critical Appraisal of the Environmental Justice Movement* (Cambridge, MA: MIT Press, 2005).

21. Taylor, *Environment and the People in American Cities*, 25. For more on resource mobilization theory, see Steven M. Buechler and F. Kurt Cylke Jr., *Social Movements: Perspectives and Issues* (Mountain View, CA: Mayfield, 1997). Economist Partha Dasguta links discounting of the future and well-being of parts of a nation's population and failure to take into account the real costs of economic development to inaccurate measurements of a nation's wealth that undercut attempts to achieve sustainability. He argues that a more accurate measurement of national wealth should take into account human well-being including health, ability to participate in civil society, and poverty, and this should be used to craft successful, sustainable regimes. Partha Dasgupta, *Human Well-Being and the Natural Environment* (Oxford: Oxford University Press, 2001).

22. Brulle, *Agency, Democracy, and Nature*, 173–74, 211–20. Brulle and others have categorized the modern or "new" or "second" environmental movement into a series of discourses. These include "reform environmentalism," what might be considered the mainstream environmental movement that evolved out of the social, economic, and political conditions of the postwar era, and "environmental justice," among others. Although the memberships of the three groups profiled here tended to be white and working and middle class, their institutional characters, history, tactics, and goals meant they do not easily fit within this classification. The Southwest Environmental Service most resembles the reform environmentalism discourse; Save Our Cumberland Mountains could be classified under environmental justice, but its membership precludes it from being categorized within "the people of color environmental movement" and its rural character challenges its categorization as a "citizen-worker movement from the toxics tradition"; the Northern Plains Resource Council's rural character and member concerns challenge its categorization as a "citizen-worker movement" within environmental justice but its tactics and institutional organization also challenge its inclusion within reform environmentalism. To simplify my analysis, I examined these three organizations within the inclusive and expansive category of "grassroots" or "citizens'" organizations based on group size, funding, institutional organization, membership characteristics, goals, and tactics.

23. Hays, *Beauty*, 62, 65; Robert Gottlieb, *Forcing the Spring: The Transformation of the American Environmental Movement*, rev. ed. (Washington, DC: Island Press, 2005), 81.

24. Rome, "Give Earth a Chance," 527, 551, 553.

25. Andrew Szasz, *EcoPopulism: Toxic Waste and the Movement for Environmental Justice* (Minneapolis: University of Minnesota Press, 1994), 81, 82.

26. Taylor, *Environment and the People in American Cities*, 24. According to social movement theory, as recounted by Taylor, the environmental movement is categorized as both a "reformative movement," which seeks limited or

incremental change in the systems in which participants are embedded, and a "transformative movement," which rejects and seeks to change the social structures and ideological foundation of the system. The movement to protect public lands and parks and to regulate industrial activity or pollutants may be considered reformative; environmental justice and elements of the radical environmental movement, transformative. For more on social movement theory, see D. McAdam and D. Snow, "Social Movements: Conceptual and Theoretical Issues," in *Social Movements: Readings on Their Emergence, Mobilization, and Dynamics*, ed. D. McAdam and D. Snow (Los Angeles: Roxbury, 1997), xix–xx.

27. See Joni Adamson, Mei Mei Evans, and Rachel Stein, *The Environmental Justice Reader: Politics, Poetics, and Pedagogy* (Tucson: University of Arizona Press, 2002); Dorceta E. Taylor, "Women of Color, Environmental Justice, and Ecofeminism," in *Ecofeminism: Women, Culture, and Nature*, ed. Karen Warren and Nisvan Erkal (Bloomington: Indiana University Press, 1997), 36–81; Elizabeth D. Blum, *Love Canal Revisited: Race, Class, and Gender in Environmental Activism* (Lawrence: University of Kansas Press, 2008); Glenda Riley, *Women and Nature: Saving the "Wild" West* (Lincoln: University of Nebraska Press, 1999); Vera Norwood, *Made from This Earth: American Women and Nature* (Chapel Hill: University of North Carolina Press, 1993). Environmental justice scholars Joni Adamson, Mei Mei Evans, Rachael Stein, and Dorceta Taylor observe the prominence of female leadership in the environmental justice movement and in local environmental issues as does Elizabeth Blum in her work on Love Canal; historians Glenda Riley and Vera Norwood argue that women understood the environment and their environmental activism as an extension of gender ideology in the twentieth century.

28. Andrew Dobson, *Justice and the Environment: Conceptions of Environmental Sustainability and Dimensions of Social Justice* (Oxford: Oxford University Press, 1998); Julian Agyeman and Bob Evans, "'Just Sustainability': The Emerging Discourse of Environmental Justice in Britain?" *Geographical Journal* 170, no. 2 (June 2004): 159, 157; Daniel Faber, *The Struggle for Ecological Democracy: Environmental Justice Movements in the United States* (New York: Guilford Press, 1998).

29. This definition for the environment was first proffered by Louis Head and Michael Guerrero in 1992 and has been widely adopted by environmental justice scholars. See Louis Head, Michael Guerrero, and Rini Templeton, *Fighting Environmental Racism* (Albuquerque, NM: South West Organizing Project, 1992); see also Patrick Novotny, *Where We Live, Work, and Play: The Environmental Justice Movement and the Struggle for a New Environmentalism* (Westport: CT: Praeger, 2000), 36; and Adamson, Evans, and Stein, *The Environmental Justice Reader*, 4.

30. Dunlap and Mertig, *American Environmentalism*, 28–29.

31. Taylor, *Environment and the People in American Cities*, 25.

32. Brulle, *Agency, Democracy, and Nature*, 173–74; SES was organized along what Brulle defines as the "reform environmentalism discourse."

33. Ibid., 191–92. Brulle notes that reform environmentalism, the dominant discourse we typically associate with the modern environmental movement after

1970, had almost no new major environmental initiatives and limited success after its initial decade partly because its emphasis on scientific analysis limits the social learning capacity of the American social order and its ability to address the social and political structures that perpetuate environmental degradation.

34. Adamson, Evans, and Stein, *The Environmental Justice Reader*, 4.

35. Hays, *Beauty*, 62, 65; Dunlap and Mertig, *American Environmentalism*, 6, 32–33; Douglas Bevington, *The Rebirth of Environmentalism: Grassroots Activism from the Spotted Owl to the Polar Bear* (Washington, DC: Island Press, 2009), 35–37; David del Mar, *Environmentalism* (Harlow, UK: Pearson Education, 2006), 163–64; Hays, *Beauty*, 65; Jacqueline Vaughn Switzer, *Environmental Politics: Domestic and Global Dimensions* (Belmont, CA: Thomson Wadsworth, 2004), 39; Brulle, *Agency, Democracy, and Nature*, 173–74, 196, 222, 228, 207–8, 221, 248–51, 257. Rather than attempting to define what constitutes grassroots groups, Brulle categorizes environmental movement organizations according to discourse: reform environmentalism, deep ecology, environmental justice, ecofeminism, and ecotheology. He correlates institutional organization, funding sources, and tactics with member activity and group effectiveness and success.

36. "Let *your* voice be heard," informational flier, 1989, private collection, Statewide Organizing for Community Empowerment, Lake City, TN.

CHAPTER 2   COAL BOOM ON THE PLAINS

1. Ellen Pfister, interview by author, Billings, Montana, 14 November 2009; in the early 1970s, Ellen Pfister went by her married name, Ellen Pfister Withers, but she dropped Withers from her name after that marriage ended. Anne Goddard Charter, *Cowboys Don't Walk: A Tale of Two* (Billings, MT: Western Organization of Resource Councils, 1999), 136. Portions of this chapter also appear in Cody Ferguson, "'You Are Now Entering a National Sacrifice Area': The Energy Boom of the 1970s and the Radicalization of the Northern Plains," *Journal of the West* 53, no. 1 (Winter 2014): 70–78.

2. Charter, *Cowboys Don't Walk*, 135; K. Ross Toole, *Montana: An Uncommon Land* (Norman: University of Oklahoma Press, 1959), 91–92; Samuel P. Hays, *Conservation and the Gospel of Efficiency: The Progressive Movement, 1890–1920* (Cambridge, MA: Harvard University Press, 1959), 84.

3. Charter, *Cowboys Don't Walk*, 135, 136.

4. Ibid.

5. David Hopper, "STRIPMINE.ORG," http://www.stripmine.org/forms/tripmine1.xls, accessed 6 October 2011; this site includes statistics for all draglines operating in North America between 1941 and 2008.

6. Wallace McRae, interview by author, Billings, Montana, 13 November 2009; Ferguson, "You Are Now Entering a National Sacrifice Area," 71.

7. Ibid.; Michael Parfit, *Last Stand at Rosebud Creek: Coal, Power, and People* (New York: E. P. Dutton, 1980), 36.

8. McRae interview, 13 November 2009.

9. Parfit, *Last Stand at Rosebud Creek*, 18; Sally Jacobsen, "The Great Montana Coal Rush," *Science and Public Affairs: Bulletin of the Atomic Scientists* 29, no. 4 (April 1973): 39; Thomas Bass, "Moving Gary, Indiana, to the Great Plains: The Oil Companies Head for the Prairies," *Mother Jones Magazine* 1, no. 5 (July 1976): 34–35; Ferguson, "You Are Now Entering a National Sacrifice Area," 74.

10. McRae interview, 13 November 2009; Jeanie Alderson, interview by author, Billings, Montana, 13 November 2010; Dave Earley, "$6.4 Million Mail Spur Planned for Coal Haul," *Billings Gazette*, 16 June 1971; U.S. Bureau of Reclamation, *North Central Power Study*, phase 1, vol. 1 (Washington, DC: Government Printing Office, 1971), 37.

11. Adam Rome, *The Bulldozer in the Countryside: Suburban Sprawl and the Rise of American Environmentalism* (New York: Cambridge University Press, 2001), 46, 73; David E. Nye, *Consuming Power: A Social History of American Energies* (Cambridge, MA: MIT Press, 1998), 199.

12. "The Changing Geopolitics of the Worlds' Oil," *U.S. News and World Report*, 14 April 1969, in Karen R. Merrill, *The Oil Crisis of 1973–1974: A Brief History with Documents* (Boston: Bedford/St. Martin's, 2007), 40–41.

13. Nye, *Consuming Power*, 218–19; David Lewis Feldman, ed., *The Energy Crisis: Unresolved Issues and Enduring Legacies* (Baltimore: Johns Hopkins University Press, 1996), 28–29; Martin Melosi, *Coping with Abundance: Energy and Environment in Industrial America* (Philadelphia: Temple University Press, 1985), 279, 287; Ferguson, "You Are Now Entering a National Sacrifice Area," 71.

14. To put this in perspective, consider that only 132 nuclear reactors were ever built and operated in the United States between 1953 and 2008 and only 104 were operating in 2008; Nye, *Consuming Power*, 219–20; Amory B. Lovins, Imran Sheikh, Alex Markevich, "Nuclear Power: Climate Fix or Folly?" (Boulder: Rocky Mountain Institute, 2009), 10; U.S. Energy Information Administration, "Total Energy," http://www.eia.gov/totalenergy/data/annual/index.cfm, accessed 6 October 2011.

15. Nye, *Consuming Power*, 218–19; Feldman, ed., *The Energy Crisis*, 28–29; Melosi, *Coping with Abundance*, 279, 287.

16. Richard H. K Vietor, *Energy Policy in America since 1945: A Study of Business-Government Relations* (New York: Cambridge University Press, 1987), 326.

17. *North Central Power Study*, phase 1, vol. 2, I-2, I-3, I-57; *North Central Power Study*, phase 1, vol. 1, 3, 5, 29.

18. *North Central Power Study*, phase 1, vol. 1, 5.

19. Jacobsen, "The Great Montana Coal Rush," 37; Keith Edgerton, "Bridging Ideology in Rural America: The Northern Plains Resource Council, 1971–1975," Montana State University–Billings, 2002, 1; Edward Darby, "Ecology Brings Money Back to Colstrip," *Billings Gazette*, 21 November 1971.

20. *North Central Power Study*, phase 1, vol. 1, 34, 37, 49, 59; Parfit, *Last Stand at Rosebud Creek*, 48, 50; U.S. Energy Information Administration, "Table 8.4a Consumption

for Electricity Generation by Energy Source: Total (All Sectors), 1949–2000," http://www.eia.gov/totalenergy/data/annual/txt/ptbo804a.html, accessed 6 October 2011; U.S. Energy Information Administration, "U.S. Nuclear Statistics," http://www.eia.gov/cneaf/nuclear/page/operation/statoperation.html, accessed 6 October 2011; U.S. Energy Information Administration, "Existing Generating Units in the United States by State, Company, and Plant, 2003," http://www.eia.gov/cneaf/electricity/page/capacity/capacity.html, accessed 6 October 2011.

21. Richard F. Hirsch, *Power Loss: The Origins of Deregulation and Restructuring in the American Electric Utility System* (Cambridge, MA: MIT Press, 2002), 68–70; Ferguson, "'You Are Now Entering a National Sacrifice Area,'" 71, 72. In reality, the economies of scale for large power generating facilities actually ended after the 1970s. Historian Richard Hirsch demonstrates that as electricity prices outpaced consumers' abilities to pay for them, consumers conserved electricity, undermining the extraordinary predictions of energy forecasters. As demand dropped, so did the ability of power companies to pay for and justify the construction of massive power plants. American electricity consumption grew roughly one and a half times between 1980 and 2000, about half the rate predicted by the study. To provide for this increased demand, only sixty-two new nuclear plants were constructed, little more than a quarter of the two hundred envisioned by the Ford administration. Hundreds of coal-fired power plants were built, but only eleven were the enormous facilities that produced more than a thousand megawatts called for in the study. In 1971, however, energy forecasters could only imagine continued extraordinary growth.

22. Hirsch, *Power Loss*, 68–70; *North Central Power Study*, phase 1, vol. 1, 34, 37, 49, 59; Parfit, *Last Stand at Rosebud Creek*, 48, 50.

23. *North Central Power Study*, phase 1, vol. 1, 38.

24. *North Central Power Study*, 38, 44, 45.

25. U.S. Environmental Protection Agency, "Indoor Water Use in the United States," http://www.epa.gov/WaterSense/pubs/indoor.html, accessed 2 August 2014; the average American family used 400 gallons of water per day in 2014 according to the EPA, or approximately 146,000 gallons of water per year.

26. Ibid.; Montana State Library Natural Resource Information System, "Montana Average Annual Precipitation, 1961–1990," http://nris.mt.gov/gis/gisdatalib/down loads/precip.gif, accessed 3 October 2010; Montana Department of Environmental Quality, "Climate Change and Water," http://deq.mt.gov/ClimateChange/NaturalResources/Water/WaterUses.mcpx, accessed 6 October 2011. These figures are based on calculations included in the *North Central Power Study*, phase 1, vol.1 that estimate water use by coal-fired electricity generating plants in the Gillette-Colstrip region to be 28 cubic feet per second per 1,000 kilowatt-hours produced. Cubic feet were converted to gallons (28 cubic feet = 209.454 gallons) and then multiplied to estimate use of water per 1,000 kilowatts produced per minute and per day. 1.2 million acre-feet (an acre-foot is equivalent to about 326,000 gallons) is based on peak production of roughly 50,000 megawatts and was the

amount of water the study identified as essential, but the plan proposed the production of roughly 180,000 megawatts, which would require a more than three times as much water. Despite the optimism of the study's authors, the availability of water in the region remained a limiting factor. This discrepancy is typical of the confusion surrounding the proposal and the development of coal strip mines and power plants in the 1970s and the decades that followed.

27. Ferguson, "You Are Now Entering a National Sacrifice Area," 72; Jacobsen, "The Great Montana Coal Rush," 39.

28. Charter, *Cowboys Don't Walk*, 137.

29. Ibid.

30. Ibid.; Dave Earley, "Ranchers Fight Strip Mining," *Billings Gazette*, 15 April 1971; Dave Earley, "Environmentalists Arise! Battle's Only Half Done," *Billings Gazette*, 28 May 1971; Dave Earley, "Strip Mining Battle Heading for Helena," *Billings Gazette*, 28 May 1971; Dave Earley, "Bull Mountain Mine to Test Reclamation," *Billings Gazette*, 20 June 1971; Dave Earley, "Strip Mining vs. Landownership," *Billings Gazette*, 13 July 1971.

31. Ibid.

32. Pfister interview, 14 November 2009.

33. Charter, *Cowboys Don't Walk*, 138.

34. Pfister interview, 14 November 2009.

35. Charter, *Cowboys Don't Walk*, 139.

36. Ibid.

37. Ibid.; "Strip Mine Opponents," *Billings Gazette*, 15 March 1971.

38. "Strip Mine Hearing Set," *Billings Gazette*, 30 May 1971.

39. Ibid.; John Kuglin, "Divided Roundup Area Argues Strip Mining," *Great Falls Tribune*, 19 June 1971.

40. Parfit, *Last Stand at Rosebud Creek*, 46; emphasis in original.

41. Jim Schwab, *Raising Less Corn and More Hell: Midwestern Farmers Speak Out* (Urbana: University of Illinois Press, 1988), 18; Ferguson, "You Are Now Entering a National Sacrifice Area," 73.

42. Ferguson, "You Are Now Entering a National Sacrifice Area," 73.

43. McRae interview, 13 November 2009.

44. Parfit, *Last Stand at Rosebud Creek*, 73; McRae interview, 13 November 2009; Ferguson, "You Are Now Entering a National Sacrifice Area," 73, 74.

45. Parfit, *Last Stand at Rosebud Creek*, 119, 121.

46. "Energy Futures: Can You Fight Progress?" *Atlantic Monthly*, April 1978, 57; McRae interview, 13 November 2009.

47. Ibid.

48. Pfister interview, 14 November 2009; Charter, *Cowboys Don't Walk*, 145; Parfit, *Last Stand at Rosebud Creek*, 93; McRae interview, 13 November 2009.

49. Charter, *Cowboys Don't Walk*, 145; Pat Sweeney, interview by author, Billings, Montana, 2 August 1010.

50. Douglas W. Scott, "A Wilderness-Forever Future: A Short History of the National Wilderness Preservation System" (Washington, DC: Pew Wilderness Research, 2001), 18; Charter, *Cowboys Don't Walk*, 145; Pfister interview, 14 November 2009; Sweeney interview, 2 August 2010; Ferguson, "You Are Now Entering a National Sacrifice Area." 74.

51. Charter, *Cowboys Don't Walk*, 145.

52. Ibid.; Pfister interview, 14 November 2009; Sweeney interview, 2 August 2010; Ferguson, "You Are Now Entering a National Sacrifice Area," 74.

53. McRae interview, 13 November 2009; Charter, *Cowboys Don't Walk*, 149; Ferguson, "You Are Now Entering a National Sacrifice Area," 74.

CHAPTER 3　THE NORTHERN PLAINS RESOURCE COUNCIL DURING THE ENVIRONMENTAL DECADE

1. Pat Sweeney, interview by author, Billings, Montana, 2 August 1010; Gary Langley, "Million Acres of Coal Marked," *Billings Gazette*, 9 March 1973.

2. Steve and Jeanne Charter, interview by author, Billings, Montana, 13 November 2010.

3. Michael P. Malone, Richard R. Roeder, and William L. Lang, *Montana: A History of Two Centuries*, rev. ed. (Seattle: University of Washington Press, 1991), 394. Portions of this chapter also appear in Cody Ferguson, "'You Are Now Entering a National Sacrifice Area': The Energy Boom of the 1970s and the Radicalization of the Northern Plains," *Journal of the West* 53, no. 1 (Winter 2014): 70–78.

4. "Environmental Council May Go Without Funds," *Billings Gazette*, 13 March 1971; Jerry Holloron, "Legislature Was Lukewarm on Environmental Issues," *Billings Gazette*, n.d. (1971); John Mundinger and Todd Everts, *A Guide to the Montana Environmental Policy Act*, rev. (Helena, MT: Legislative Environmental Policy Office, 1998), iii.

5. Montana Constitution, art. 2, sec. 3 and art.9, sec. 2.

6. Ibid., art. 2, sec. 9; Harry W. Fritz, "The Origins of Twenty-First-Century Montana," *Montana: The Magazine of Western History* 42 (Winter 1992): 78; Harry W. Fritz and William E. Farr, *Montana: Land of Contrasts* (Sun Valley, CA: American Historical Press, 2001), 114; Malone, Roeder, and Lang, *Montana*, 394; Dan Flores, *The Natural West: Environmental History of the Great Plains and Rocky Mountains* (Norman: University of Oklahoma Press, 2003). 191; Ferguson, "You Are Now Entering a National Sacrifice Area," 76.

7. Sweeney interview, 2 August 1010.

8. Michael Parfit, *Last Stand at Rosebud Creek: Coal, Power, and People* (New York: E. P. Dutton, 1980), 93; Ferguson, "You Are Now Entering a National Sacrifice Area," 75.

9. Sweeney interview, 2 August 2010.

10. K. Ross Toole, *Montana: An Uncommon Land* (Norman: University of Oklahoma Press, 1959), and K. Ross Toole, *The Rape of the Great Plains: Northwest America, Cattle and Coal* (New York: Little, Brown, 1976); Flores, *The Natural West*, 191; Ferguson, "You Are Now Entering a National Sacrifice Area," 75.

11. Sweeney interview, 2 August 2010; Pfister interview, 14 November 2009; Charter interview, 13 November 2010.

12. Sweeney interview, 2 August 2010; Pfister interview, 14 November 2009; Anne Goddard Charter, *Cowboys Don't Walk: A Tale of Two* (Billings, MT: Western Organization of Resource Councils, 1999), 148.

13. Pfister interview, 14 November 2009.

14. Northern Plains Resource Council, *Newsletter*, June–July 1972, private collection, Northern Plains Resource Council, Billings, Montana.

15. Ibid.

16. Ibid.

17. Ibid.

18. Ibid.

19. Ferguson, "You Are Now Entering a National Sacrifice Area," 70; Pfister interview, 14 November 2009; Wallace McRae, interview by author, Billings, Montana, 13 November 2009; Helen and Gordon Waller, interview by author, Waller ranch near Circle, Montana, 3 August 2010; Charter, *Cowboys Don't Walk*, 158; Parfit, *Last Stand at Rosebud Creek*, 163. In research of oral testimony and interviews with activists involved with the Northern Plains Resource Council including Wallace McRae, Ellen Pfister, and Helen Waller, the "code of the West" came up repeatedly. The "code" may be attributable to a code of conduct written by author Zane Grey for Johnson County, Wyoming, in 1934. It imparted a code of conduct that implied mutual respect of individuals, honor, and unwritten rules of propriety; by extension, this meant not intruding or interfering in the affairs of others.

20. Northern Plains Resource Council, *Newsletter*, June–July 1972, private collection, Northern Plains Resource Council, Billings, Montana.

21. Ibid.; Ferguson, "You Are Now Entering a National Sacrifice Area," 74.

22. Northern Plains Resource Council, "From Washington, DC," *Newsletter*, 31 July 1972.

23. Northern Plains Resource Council, *Newsletter*, October–November 1972; "'We Intend to Win': Rancher, Housewife, Young, Old Speak Out to Defend Their Land," *Sheridan Press*, 26 October 1972.

24. Northern Plains Resource Council, *Newsletter*, December–January 1973; Fred Garretson, "Warning Sounded on Strip Mining," *Oakland Tribune*, 1 December 1972.

25. Louise Cross, "Statement for the Natural Resources and Agriculture Hearing," 10 February 1972, Louise Cross Papers, A: 6 2-1, Montana Historical Society

Archives, Helena, Montana; Louise Cross, "Thoughts from a Committee Chair-man—on February 26, 1972," 26 February 1972, Louise Cross Papers.

26. "Political Parties," Northern Plains Resource Council, *Newsletter*, October–November 1972.

27. Ibid.

28. Ibid.

29. *House Journal*, Forty-third Legislative Assembly of the State of Montana, 1 January 1973–10 March 1973, and 12 March 1973–24 March 1973, 395, S-74, Montana Historical Society Research Center, Archives, Helena, Montana; Pfister interview, 14 November 2009.

30. Pfister interview, 14 November 2009; Wallace McRae, interview by author, Billings, Montana, 13 November 2009; "Caudill's Visit," *Plains Truth*, December–January 1972–1973. Comparisons of strip mining in Montana with the devastation experienced in Appalachia was ubiquitous in discussion of the coal boom in Northern Plains and the legislature; in January 1973, Kentucky lawyer, author, and anti-strip-mining activist Harry Caudill visited Montana and met with members of Northern Plains, representatives from the United Mine Workers, and legislators to explain his interpretation of the damage strip mining had caused in Appalachia.

31. "Mansfield Urges Ban," *Billings Gazette*, 19 January 1973.

32. Sweeney interview, 2 August 2010; "Moratorium Still Alive: One Vote Needed to Pass," *Plains Truth* 2, no. 1 (February 1973); "Minutes, Feb. 6–8, 1973, House Natural Resources," Montana Legislature (43rd: 1973) records, 1973–1974, Legislative Records 43, box 2, folder 17, Montana Historical Society Research Center, Archives, Helena, Montana; "Minutes, Feb. 9–24, 1973, House Natural Resources Committee," Legislature (43rd: 1973) records, 1973–1974, Legislative Records 43, box 2, folder 18, Montana Historical Society Research Center, Archives, Helena, Montana; Montana Strip and Underground Mine Reclamation Act, *Montana Code Annotated*, sec. 82-4-201, sec. 82-4-202 (2009); *Senate Journal*, Forty-third Legislative Assembly of the State of Montana, January 1, 1973–March 10, 1973, and March 12, 1973–March 24, 1973, S-71, Montana Historical Society Research Center, Archives, Helena, Montana; Charter, *Cowboys Don't Walk*, 148.

33. "Minutes, Feb. 27–Mar. 10, 1973, Senate Natural Resources Committee," Montana Legislature (43rd: 1973) records, 1973–1974, Legislative Records 43, box 7, folder 18, Montana Historical Society Research Center, Archives, Helena, Montana; Major Facility Siting Act, *Montana Code Annotated*, sec. 75-20-102 (2009); Ferguson, "You Are Now Entering a National Sacrifice Area," 74. During the 1973 Montana legislative session, the Department of Health and Environmental Services was being sued by landowners and the Northern Plains Resource Council for allowing the construction of the Colstrip I and II power plants without permits and adequate environmental analysis as required by the Montana

Environmental Policy Act and state Clean Air Act. Their support partially reflects their desire to create a clear permitting process for power utilities to avoid such litigation in the future.

34. "Minutes, Feb. 6–8, 1973, Senate Natural Resources Committee," Montana Legislature (43rd: 1973) records, 1973–1974, Legislative Records 43, box 2, folder 17, Montana Historical Society Research Center, Archives, Helena, Montana.

35. "Minutes, Feb. 6–8, 1973, House Natural Resources Committee," Montana Legislature (43rd: 1973) records, 1973–1974, Legislative Records 43, box 2, folder 17, Montana Historical Society Research Center, Archives, Helena, Montana.

36. Charter, *Cowboys Don't Walk*, 141–43.

37. Ibid.; Dave T. Earley, "Bull Landowners Talk to Congress," *Billings Gazette*, 29 November 1971.

38. "Resource Study Lauded," *Billings Gazette*, 4 October 1974.

39. "Melcher Denounces Coal Study," *Billings Gazette*, 5 October 1972.

40. "Three Senators Tackle Government on Mining," *Billings Gazette*, 8 December 1972.

41. Sweeney interview, 2 August 2010; "Forsyth Rancher Appeals to Congress for Power to Veto Strip-Mine Operations," *Great Falls Tribune*, 16 May 1973. 17

42. "Strip Mining Expands As Prices Move Up," *Baltimore Sun*, 6 September 1975; Chad Montrie, *To Save the Land and People: A History of Opposition to Surface Coal Mining in Appalachia* (Chapel Hill: University of North Carolina Press, 2003), 128, 138–53, 187; Stephen L. Fisher, ed., *Fighting Back in Appalachia: Traditions of Resistance and Change* (Philadelphia: Temple University Press, 1993), 20. Montrie chronicles the transition in the coal mining industry from underground mining to strip mining from the 1940s to the 1970s; growing opposition to strip mining; the passage of state laws to address the environmental, economic, and social issues associated with strip mining in Ohio, Pennsylvania, and Kentucky; and attempts by the federal government to address these issues. He demonstrates that in these three states, and also in Tennessee, the attempts of state legislatures to regulate strip mining and to enforce regulations was rarely effective and heavily influenced by the coal mining industry, partly prompting opponents to purse federal legislation.

43. Sweeney interview, 2 August 2010.

44. "National Legislation Summary," *Plains Truth* 2, no. 3 (March 1973).

45. "Federal Legislation," *Plains Truth* 2, no. 4 (April–May 1973).

46. Ibid.

47. Ibid.

48. Ibid; "Federal Stripmining Legislation," *Plains Truth* 2, no. 6 (June 1973).

49. Library of Congress, "Search Bill Summary and Status, 93rd Congress" (1973–1974), http://www.thomas.loc.gov/cgi-bin/thomas, accessed 28 March 2011.

50. Ibid.

51. "Council News," *Plains Truth* 2, no. 6 (June 1973); Library of Congress, "Search Bill Summary and Status, 93rd Congress" (1973–1974), http://www.thomas.loc .gov/cgi-bin/thomas, accessed 28 March 2011; "NPRC Testifies at Strip Mining Hearings," *Plains Truth* 2, no. 3 (March 1973); "Council News," *Plains Truth* 2, no. 6 (June 1973); "Federal Legislation," *Plains Truth* 2, no. 8 (August 1973); Laney Hicks, "Who Owns the Big Sky?" *Sierra Club Bulletin*, July–August 1974; "The Conference Committee: Can Surface Owner Protection Survive?" *Plains Truth* 3, no. 8 (August–September 1974); "Federal Legislation," *Plains Truth* 2, no. 10 (October 1973); Martin Melosi, *Coping with Abundance: Energy and Environment in Industrial America* (Philadelphia: Temple University Press, 1985), 302.

52. "Ford's !*$*?!! Energy Message," *Plains Truth* 4, no. 1 (January–February 1975); "Citizen Energy Platform," *Plains Truth* 4, no. 2 (March 1975).

53. "Strip Mine Bill," *Plains Truth* 4, no. 3 (May 1975); Helen Thomas, "Ford to Veto Mining Bill," *St. Joseph News-Press*, 19 May 1975; "Ford Blocks Strip Mine Bill," *Plains Truth* 4, no. 5 (June 1975); "News from Washington   ," *Plains Truth* 4, no. 8 (October 1975); "Strip Mine Bill Alive!" *Plains Truth* 4, no. 10 (December 1975).

54. Library of Congress, "Search Bill Summary and Status, 95th Congress" (1977– 1978), http://www.thomas.loc.gov/cgi-bin/thomas, accessed 28 March 2011; Melosi, *Coping with Abundance*, 302; "Washington, DC, Update: Strip Mining Legislation," *Plains Truth* 6, no. 1 (January–February 1977); "Washington, DC, Update: Strip Mining: Action Needed Now!" *Plains Truth* 6, no. 2 (March 1977); "Strip Mining Law Signed by Carter," *Ellensburg Daily Record*, 3 August 1977; "Federal Strip Mining Bill Signed into Law by President Carter," *Plains Truth* 6, no. 6 (August 1977).

55. "NPRC Affiliates," *Plains Truth* 9, no. 2 (February 1980); "NPRC Staff," *Plains Truth* 9, no. 2 (February 1980).

56. "New Affiliate Organization," *Plains Truth* 4, no. 7 (August–September 1978); Waller interview, 3 August 2010.

57. Robert J. Brulle, *Agency, Democracy, and Nature: The U.S. Environmental Movement from a Critical Theory Perspective* (Cambridge, MA: MIT Press, 2000), 173–74. Brulle's description of the reform environmentalism discourse encapsulates most of what members of NPRC might have considered "traditional environmental issues."

58. "Alternatives: Now!!" *Plains Truth* 3, no. 1 (January 1974).

59. "Nuclear Vote: NPRC Endorses Initiative 80," *Plains Truth* 7, no. 9 (October– November 1978).

60. "Wilderness Bill Gains Support," *Plains Truth* 7, no. 2 (March 1978).

61. "Council News," *Plains Truth* 2, no. 7 (July 1973); "Dakota Resource Council Organizes," *Plains Truth* 7, no. 3 (March 1978); "Dakota, Powder River, Northern Plains: Resource Councils Unite," *Plains Truth* 8, no. 10 (December 1979).

62. "To the Members from W. R. McKay, Jr.," *Plains Truth* 7, no. 8 (September 1978).

63. Parfit, *Last Stand at Rosebud Creek*, 93.

64. Sarah L. Thomas, "A Call to Action: Silent Spring, Public Disclosure, and the Rise of Modern Environmentalism," in *Natural Protest: Essays on the History of American Environmentalism*, ed. Michael Egan and Jeff Crane (New York: Routledge, 2009), 185–203, quote on 186. Recent histories of the environmental movement have emphasized a connection between environmental and democratic reform. In her work on Rachael Carson, Sarah Thomas argues that Carson's pesticide reform work in the early 1960s "contributed to a growing emphasis on access to information and public participation, both of which emerged as key tenets of the new environmentalism."

CHAPTER 4   CITIZEN ENVIRONMENTAL ACTIVISM IN THE SOUTHWEST: TUCSON'S SOUTHWEST ENVIRONMENTAL SERVICE

1. Priscilla Robinson, interview by author, Tucson, Arizona, 1 September 2011.

2. Kevin Moran, "Environmentalist Out of Service," *Tucson Citizen*, 31 March 1988; Joe Burchell, "Group That Helped in Smelter Fight Is Shutting Down," *Arizona Daily Star* (Tucson), 30 March 1988; Robinson interview, 1 September 2011; Priscilla Robinson, "SES Activities—April 1 to April 18," 18 April 1975, Records of the Southwest Environmental Service, MS 269, box 3, folder 9, University of Arizona Special Collections, Tucson, Arizona, hereafter referred to as SES Records.

3. Concern about and resistance to urban growth in Tucson dates back to at least the 1950s. As Michael Logan convincingly demonstrates in *Fighting Sprawl and City Hall: Resistance to Urban Growth in the Southwest*, opposition to urban growth was one of the foundational issues in the emergence of environmentalism in Tucson and the American Southwest in the mid-twentieth century. He describes this environmentalism related to opposition to urban growth as a kind of "preservationism at once conservative and activist," a description that might also be applied to the environmental values of the founders of the Northern Plains Resource Council as they worked to protect their property and way of life. Michael Logan, *Fighting Sprawl and City Hall: Resistance to Urban Growth in the Southwest* (Tucson: University of Arizona Press, 1995), 9.

4. See Samuel Hays, *Beauty, Health, and Permanence: Environmental Politics in the United States, 1955–1985* (New York: Cambridge University Press, 1987); Robert J. Brulle, *Agency, Democracy, and Nature: The U.S. Environmental Movement from a Critical Theory Perspective* (Cambridge, MA: MIT Press, 2000), 173–74.

5. Hays, *Beauty, Health, and Permanence*, 3, 13, 22; Robinson interview, 1 September 2011; Brulle, *Agency, Democracy, and Nature*, 248–49. According to Brulle, organizations like SES, formed within the reform environmentalism discourse, are more likely to be oligarchical in structure, have larger, more professional staffs, and rely more on foundation funding.

6. It should be noted that Priscilla Robinson does not characterize SES as being grassroots. This is despite the fact that the group was a local, community-based advocacy organization that at the time of its closing counted a membership

of roughly 600 from which it derived a significant portion of its revenue in 1987, and that it employed democratic decision-making processes on its board. To explain her reasoning, she cites the tendency of the organization to concentrate decision-making in a few experts, including herself, and the fact that it derived most of its revenue from a single foundation. The author recognizes that the definition of "grassroots" is contested, and that it could apply somewhat to SES because the group sought to encourage citizen participation in environmental decision-making. Instead of using the term grassroots, the author chooses to refer to local, community-based environmental organizations as "citizens groups" that emphasize the kinds of members—mostly nonprofessional volunteers and staff—that made up the organization rather than organizational structure or strategy. For more on what constitutes a grassroots group, see Hays, *Beauty, Health, and Permanence*, 62, 65; David del Mar, *Environmentalism* (Harlow, UK: Pearson Education, 2006), 163–64; Jacqueline Vaughn Switzer, *Environmental Politics: Domestic and Global Dimensions* (Belmont, CA: Thomson Wadsworth, 2004), 39; and Douglas Bevington, *The Rebirth of Environmentalism: Grassroots Activism from the Spotted Owl to the Polar Bear* (Washington, DC: Island Press, 2009), 35–37; Robinson interview, 1 September 2011.

7. Robinson interview, 1 September 2011.

8. In *Rivers of Empire: Water, Aridity, and the Growth of the American West*, Donald Worster argues that it is wrong to view the American West as "a colony of the American Empire, an empire centered on Eastern metropolises" after World War II. "Indeed," he asserts, "since the war it has become a principal seat of the world-circling American Empire." For southern Arizona in the period preceding World War II, the description seems apt. Donald Worster, *Rivers of Empire: Water, Aridity, and the Growth of the American West* (New York: Oxford University Press, 1985), 14–15.

9. Thomas Sheridan, *Arizona: A History* (Tucson: University of Arizona Press, 1997), 146, 165–66; Linda Gordon, *The Great Arizona Orphan Abduction* (Cambridge, MA: Harvard University Press, 1999), 27. Sheridan, *Arizona: A History*, 234–35.

10. Sheridan, *Arizona: A History*, 270–73, 280.

11. Ibid.; Carl Abbott, *The Metropolitan Frontier: Cities in the Modern American West* (Tucson: University of Arizona Press, 1998); Abbott describes the divergent developments of Phoenix into a "network" city and Tucson into a "regional" city.

12. *Arizonans for Water Without Waste Newsletter* (Tucson: Arizonans for Water Without Waste), 15 October 1966; Editions of this newsletter from 1966 to 1982 can be found in the University of Arizona Special Collections, Tucson, Arizona. Arizonans for Water Without Waste changed its name in February 1970 to Arizonans for Quality Environment but retained the acronym "AWWW." (From this point forward, this newsletter will be referred to as *AWWW Newsletter*.) For a more detailed description of the fight over the Grand Canyon dams and the Central Arizona Project, see Marc Reisner, *Cadillac Desert: The American West*

and Its Disappearing Water (New York: Penguin Books, 1986), chap. 8, and Byron Pearson, *Still the Wild River Runs: Congress, the Sierra Club, and the Fight to Save Grand Canyon* (Tucson: University of Arizona Press, 2002); Douglas E. Kupel, *Fuel for Growth: Water and Arizona's Urban Environment* (Tucson: University of Arizona Press, 2006), xv, xx; *AWWW Newsletter,* March 1969; *AWWW Newsletter,* February 1970.

13. *AWWW Newsletter,* October 1976; *AWWW Newsletter,* October 1973; *AWWW Newsletter,* April 1974.

14. *Southern Arizona Environmental Council Bulletin* 9, no. 2 (November 1979), found in the Arizona Collection, Hayden Library, Arizona State University, Tempe, Arizona (hereafter, the *Southern Arizona Environmental Council Bulletin* will be referred to as *SAEC Bulletin*). *SAEC Bulletin* 3, no. 1 (1973–1974); *SAEC Bulletin* 7, no. 1 (September 1977); *SAEC Bulletin* 7, no. 3 (January 1978); *SAEC Bulletin* 6, no. 4 (March 1977). From the 1971 bylaws of the Southern Arizona Environmental Council, included in the *AWWW Newsletter,* October 1971.

15. Ibid.

16. "Catalyst For Action" was the byline SES chose for itself in its first brochure produced in 1977; Southwest Environmental Service, organizational brochure, n.d., SES Records, MS 269, box 1, folder 10.

17. Robinson interview, 1 September 2011; Joe Burchell, "Group That Helped in Smelter Fight Is Shutting Down," *Arizona Daily Star* (Tucson), 30 March 1988.

18. Priscilla Robinson, "SES Activities—April 1 to April 18," 18 April 1975, SES Records, MS 269, box 1, folder 2; Priscilla Robinson, "Proposal for an Experimental Community Education Program in Land Use Planning," 15 May 1975, SES Records, MS 269, box 1, folder 2.

19. Priscilla Robinson, "Proposal for an Experimental Community Education Program in Land Use Planning," 15 May 1975, SES Records, MS 269, box 1, folder 2.

20. Ibid.

21. Priscilla Robinson, "Director's Report," 30 April 1976, SES Records, MS 269, box 1, folder 2; Hays, *Beauty, Health, and Permanence,* 54–55, 60–61; for a more in-depth discussion of this transition in environmental issues and the environmental movement, see Hays, *Beauty, Health, and Permanence.*

22. Priscilla Robinson, "Director's Report," 16 August 1977, SES Records, MS 269, box 1, folder 3; "Southwest Environmental Service, Minutes of Board Meeting, Board of Directors' 26 January 1977," SES Records, MS 269, box 1, folder 3.

23. Victoria Dahl, "Television Public Service Spot on The Water Workshops," n.d., SES Records, box 3, folder 9; Victoria Dahl, Coordinator, Southwest Environmental Service, to Ms. Pat Stevens, News Director, KGUN-TV, 30 November 1976, SES Records, box 3, folder 9; Priscilla Robinson, "Director's Report," 30 March 1977, SES Records, MS 269, box 1, folder 3; Priscilla Robinson, "Director's Report," 25 May 1977, SES Records, MS 269, box 1, folder 3; Priscilla Robinson, "Director's Report," 18 July 1978, SES Records, MS 269, box 1, folder 3.

24. Barbara Tellman, interview by author, 1 September 2011; Claudia Goldin, *Understanding the Gender Gap: An Economic History of American Women* (New York: Oxford University Press, 1990). Tellman's explanation of the rationale behind hiring women makes economic sense and reflects historic patters of hiring in American society observed by historian Claudia Goldin. Goldin demonstrates how women were systematically paid less because of their lack of education relative to men and their tendency to leave the workplace upon getting married or having children, which prevented them from accruing the benefits for graduated pay scales.

25. Glenda Riley, *Women and Nature: Saving the "Wild" West* (Lincoln: University of Nebraska Press, 1999), xiv.

26. Robinson interview, 1 September 2011; Tellman interview, 1 September 2011; Senator John McCain, "Statement for the Introduction of Betsy Rieke before the Senate Energy and Natural Resources Committee, April 27 1993," http://www .mccain.senate.gov/public/index.cfm/speeches?ID=c350188f-5e03-4157-a73a -a4b13d87e221, accessed 14 December 2013; Senator Harry Reid, "Recognizing Elizabeth Ann 'Betsy' Rieke," 28 July 2008, Capitolwords, http://capitolwords .org/date/2008/07/28/S7565-2_recognizing-elizabeth-ann-betsy-rieke/, accessed 14 December 2013; Riley, *Women and Nature*, xiv.

27. Robinson interview, 1 September 2011; Priscilla Robinson to Cody Ferguson, email, Subject: Enjoyed meeting, 2 September 2011, author's private collection, Tempe, Arizona.

28. Priscilla Robinson to Cody Ferguson, email, Subject: Enjoyed meeting, 2 September 2011, author's private collection, Tempe, Arizona.

29. Ibid.

30. Ibid.

31. See Michael Logan, *The Lessening Stream: An Environmental History of the Santa Cruz River* (Tucson: University of Arizona Press, 2002), chaps. 11 and 12.

32. Pima Association of Governments, "Population estimates," http://www.pagnet .org/RegionalData/Population/PopulationEstimates/tabid/582/Default.aspx, accessed 23 August 2011.

33. Bonnie Haynes, "SAEC Statement on Air Quality and Transportation as Presented to the Tucson City Council and Pima County Board of Supervisors, November 20, 1978," *SAEC Bulletin* 8, no. 2 (January 1979), SAEC Bulletin, Tucson: Southern Arizona Environmental Council, Arizona Collection, Arizona State University, Tempe, Arizona (hereafter referred to as *SAEC Bulletin*).

34. Priscilla Robinson, "Director's Report," 19 March, 1976, SES Records, MS 269, box 1, folder 2; Priscilla Robinson, "Director's Report," 30 April 1976, SES Records, MS 269, box 1, folder 2; "Tortolita Area Plan," *SAEC Bulletin* 5, no. 3 (January 1976), SAEC Bulletin; "Canyon Del Oro Interceptor," *SAEC Bulletin* 5, no. 3 (January 1976), SACE Bulletin; Priscilla Robinson, "Director's Report," 10 January 1978, SES Records, MS 269, box 1, folder 3.

35. Priscilla Robinson, "Director's Report," SES Records, MS 269, box 1, folder 3; "Environmentalist Out of Service," *Tucson Citizen*, 31 March 1988, 8C.

36. Priscilla Robinson, "Summary, Meeting with Ben Carter, Colorado Open Land Foundation," 10 June 1977, SES Records, MS 269, box 1, folder 3; Priscilla Robinson, "Director's Report," 16 August 1977, SES Records, MS 269, box 1, folder 3; "Southwest Environmental Service Minutes of the Board of Directors," 6 December 1977, SES Records, MS 269, box 1, folder 3; "Southwest Environmental Service Minutes of the Board of Directors," 14 November 1978, SES Records, MS 269, box 1, folder 3.

37. "Southwest Environmental Service Minutes of the Meeting of the Board of Directors," 10 January 1978, SES Records, MS 269, box 1, folder 3; "Southwest Environmental Service Minutes of the Meeting of the Board of Directors," 14 February 1978, SES Records, MS 269, box 1, folder 3; "Southwest Environmental Service Minutes of the Meeting of the Board of Directors," 18 April 1978, SES Records, MS 269, box 1, folder 3. SES's budget in 1977 was $41,000 of which $34,500 came from the Wilson Foundation, $1,660 from the Arizona Department of Health, Education, and Welfare, and $988 from the Pima Association of Government, the latter two for services it provided organizing public meetings or educational workshops; in 1978, SES received $12,000 from the Wilson Foundation.

38. Robinson interview, 1 September 2011.

CHAPTER 5   REINING IN THE SMELTERS: THE FIGHT FOR CLEAN AIR IN SOUTHERN ARIZONA

1. Jane Kay, "'Old Smoky' Is Not All That's Fuming in Douglas," *Arizona Daily Star* (Tucson), 14 June 1981, E1.

2. Edward Stiles and Richard E. Wilbur, "EPA to Smelters: Eight Is Enough," *Tucson Citizen*, 4 April, 1978; Jane Kay, "Arizona Smelters: Mount St. Helens-Size Issue," *Arizona Daily Star* (Tucson), 21 June 1981, E1; Jane Kay, "Arizona Lets Copper Industry Be Its Own Watchdog," *Arizona Daily Star* (Tucson), 21 June 1981, 12 E.

3. John D. Wirth, *Smelter Smoke in North America: The Politics of Transborder Pollution* (Lawrence: University of Kansas Press, 2000), 135–39. Wirth argues that keeping the Douglas smelter open was never in Phelps Dodge's long-term plan and that it never intended to upgrade the facility. Wirth demonstrates that Phelps Dodge used the threat of closing the smelter and the connected loss of jobs to leverage Arizona's congressional delegation, state regulators, and administrators within the Environmental Protection Agency to support continued exemptions for the smelter from the Clean Air Act, allowing it to stay open for more than fourteen years after the passage of the law.

4. Walter A. Rosenbaum, *Environmental Politics and Policy*, 8th ed. (Washington, DC: Congressional Quarterly, 2010), 58.

5. Ibid.

6. Ibid.

7. Ibid., 58, 192; Environmental Defense Fund, "Clean Air Act Timeline," http://cleartheair.edf.org/page.cfm?tagID=60844, accessed 20 September 2011.

8. Rosenbaum, *Environmental Politics and Policy*, 192; U.S. Environmental Protection Agency, "History of the Clean Air Act," http://www.epa.gov/air/caa/caa_history.html#caa77, accessed 20 September 2011; Samuel P. Hays, *Beauty, Health, and Permanence: Environmental Politics in the United States, 1955–1985* (New York: Cambridge University Press, 1987), 242.

9. Priscilla Robinson, "Director's Report," 6 December 1977, Records of the Southwest Environmental Service, MS 269, box 1, folder 3, University of Arizona Special Collections, Tucson, Arizona.

10. Ibid.

11. Priscilla Robinson, "Director's Report," 14 February 1978, SES Records, MS 269, box 1, folder 3.

12. Ibid.

13. Priscilla Robinson, "Director's Report," 14 March 1978, SES Records, MS 269, box 1, folder 3.

14. Priscilla Robinson, "Director's Report," 20 June 1978, SES Records, MS 269, box 1, folder 3.

15. *Southern Arizona Environmental Council Bulletin* 8, no. 1 (September 1978), found in the Arizona Collection, Hayden Library, Arizona State University, Tempe, Arizona.

16. Priscilla Robinson, "Director's Report," 18 July 1978, SES Records, MS 269, box 1, folder 3; Robinson, "Director's Report," 22 August 1978, SES Records, MS 269, box 1, folder 3; Robinson, "Director's Report," 14 November 1978, SES Records, MS 269, box 1, folder 3; Robinson, "Director's Report," 10 October 1978, SES Records, MS 269, box 1, folder 3; Southwest Environmental Service, "Minutes of the Meeting of the Board of Directors," 12 December 1978, SES Records, MS 269, box 1, folder 3.

17. Wirth, *Smelter Smoke in North America*, 139, 158–65.

18. Priscilla Robinson, "Smelter Chronology: Southwest Environmental Service Monthly Reports—1978 through 1987," 1 November 2008, author's private collection, Tempe, Arizona; Wirth, *Smelter Smoke in North America*, 139, 158–65; Stiles and Wilbur, "EPA to Smelters: Eight Is Enough"; Southwest Environmental Service, "Clean Air Alert," March 1979, SES Records, MS 269, box 3, folder 1; Priscilla Robinson, "Fact Sheet on Non-Ferrous Smelter Orders," 27 February 1979, SES Records, MS 269, box 3, folder 1; Priscilla Robinson, interview by author, Tucson, Arizona, 1 September 2011; Priscilla Robinson, "Director's Report," 13 March 1979, SES Records, MS 269, box 1, folder 4. In his *Smelter Smoke in North America*, John Wirth provides a rough chronicle of SES's air quality work from 1978 through 1987 derived from the "Smelter Chronology: Southwest Environmental Service Monthly Reports—1978–1987" that Priscilla Robinson compiled in June 1988 after the smelter campaign concluded and the group disbanded. Because

Wirth and I both used versions of Robinson's "Smelter Chronology"; some of the quotes from Robinson appear in both works. My citations come directly from the "Smelter Chronology" or primary documents; Wirth is acknowledged where appropriate.

19. Priscilla Robinson, "Director's Report," 13 March 1979, SES Records, MS 269, box 1, folder 4; Robinson, "Director's Report," 21 April 1979, SES Records, MS 269, box 1, folder 4.

20. Robinson, "Smelter Chronology"; Wirth, *Smelter Smoke in North America*, 115; Robinson interview, 1 September 2011.

21. Priscilla Robinson, "Director's Report," 11 September 1979, SES Records, MS 269, box 1, folder 4.

22. Kristi Essick, "Starting Over in Later Life," *Wall Street Journal Online*, 20 March 2011, http://bx.businessweek.com/air-pollution/view?url=http%3A%2F%2Fc.moreover.com%2Fclick%2Fhere.pl%3Fr4341484350%26f%3D9791, accessed 21 September 2011.

23. Ibid.

24. Priscilla Robinson, "Director's Report," 13 November 1979, SES Records, MS 269, box 1, folder 4; Robinson interview, 1 September 2011; Wirth, *Smelter Smoke in North America*, 137.

25. Priscilla Robinson, "Director's Report," 12 February 1980, SES Records, MS 269, box 1, folder 4; Robinson, "Director's Report," 11 March 1980, SES Records, MS 269, box 1, folder 4; Robinson interview, 1 September 2011. The two traveled to Salt Lake City in July to testify on the EPA's proposed visibility regulations. Robinson, "Director's Report," 8 July 1980, SES Records, MS 269, box 1, folder 4; Robinson, "Smelter Chronology."

26. Robinson, "Director's Report," 11 March 1980, SES Records, MS 269, box 1, folder 4.

27. Ibid.; Robinson, "Smelter Chronology."

28. Priscilla Robinson, "Director's Report," 9 December 1980, SES Records, MS 269, box 1, folder 4.

29. Robinson interview, 1 September 2011; Robinson, "Director's Report," 14 April 1981, SES Records, MS 269, box 1, folder 5; Robinson, "Smelter Chronology."

30. Robinson interview, 1 September 2011; Robinson, "Smelter Chronology"; Robinson, "Director's Report," 10 March 1981, SES Records, MS 269, box 1, folder 5; Robinson, "Director's Report," 14 April 1981, SES Records, MS 269, box 1, folder 5.

31. Priscilla Robinson, "Director's Report," 14 July 1981, SES Records, MS 269, box 1, folder 5.

32. Ibid.

33. Robinson, "Smelter Chronology."

34. Kay, "'Old Smoky' Is Not All That's Fuming in Douglas."

35. Kay, "Arizona Smelters."

36. Robinson interview, 1 September 2011; Robinson, "Smelter Chronology"; Tony Davis, "Increased Birth-Defect Study Asked: High Rate Shown by 3 Mining Towns," *Tucson Citizen*, 16 March 1982; "State Birth-Defect Rate Found to Be 33% over U.S. Average," *Arizona Daily Star*, 17 March 1982; Kurt Pfitzer, "Air Pollution Here to Worsen, Official Says," *Tucson Citizen*, 17 March 1982. Kay eventually won the prestigious Edward J. Meeman Award from the Knight Center of Environmental Journalism at Michigan State University for outstanding environmental journalism for her series on the smelters.

37. Robinson interview, 1 September 2011; Priscilla Robinson, "Director's Report," 8 September 1981, SES Records, MS 269, box 1, folder 5.

38. Robinson interview, 1 September 2011.

39. Ibid.; Robinson, "Smelter Chronology"; Robinson, "Director's Report," 8 September 1981, SES Records, MS 269, box 1, folder 5.

40. Robinson, "Director's Report," 8 December 1981, SES Records, box 1, folder 5; Robinson interview, 1 September 2011; Robinson, "Smelter Chronology."

41. Robinson, "Director's Report," 8 December 1981, SES Records, box 1, folder 5.

42. Ibid.; Robinson interview, 1 September 2011; Robinson, "Smelter Chronology."

43. Robinson interview, 1 September 2011.

44. Ibid.; Robinson, "Smelter Chronology"; Kay, "Arizona Smelters"; James Wyckoff, "Protesters Spend Night on Smokestack," *Tucson Daily Citizen*, 10 February 1982.

45. Robinson, "Smelter Chronology."

46. Wyckoff, "Protesters Spend Night on Smokestack."

47. Ibid.

48. Robinson, "Smelter Chronology."

49. Wirth, *Smelter Smoke in North America*, 153; Robinson, "Smelter Chronology"; Priscilla Robinson, "Director's Report," 9 February 1982, SES Records, MS 269, box 1, folder 5; Robinson, "Director's Report," 9 March 1982, SES Records, MS 269, box 1, folder 5; Robert E. Yuhnke, regional counsel, Environmental Defense Fund, to Representative Morris K. Udall, 23 March 1982, Morris K. Udall Library Manuscript Collection, MS 325, box 144, folder 24, University of Arizona Special Collections, Tucson, Arizona (hereafter referred to as MKUP); Robinson interview, 1 September 2011; Priscilla Robinson, "Director's Report," 13 April 1982, SES Records, MS 269, box 1, folder 5.

50. Priscilla Robinson, "Director's Report," 11 May 1982, SES Records, MS 269, box 1, folder 5; Robinson, "Director's Report," 28 August 1982, SES Records, MS 269, box 1, folder 5.

51. Dr. Frank and Udiko Lewis to Honorable Morris K. Udall, 27 March 1982, MKUP, MS 325, box 144, folder 24.

52. T. M. and G. A. Korn to Representative Morris K. Udall, 23 April 1982, MKUP, MS 325, box 144, folder 24. The last two citations are two of at least twelve letters Udall received from constituents in southern Arizona during March and April 1982. Many referenced statistics provided by SES, which can be found in MKUP, MS 325, box 144, folder 24.

53. Robinson, "Director's Report," 13 April 1982, SES Records, MS 269, box 1, folder 5.

54. Ibid.

55. Robinson, "Smelter Chronology"; Priscilla Robinson, "Director's Report," 28 August 1983, SES Records, MS 269, box 1, folder 5; Robinson, "Smelter Chronology"; "Hard Times and Smelters," *Arizona Daily Star* (Tucson), 4 April 1982, C2; Robinson, "Director's Report," 9 November 1983, SES Records, MS 269, box 1, folder 5.

56. Wirth, *Smelter Smoke in North America*, 177.

57. Robinson interview, 1 September 2011; Robinson, "Director's Report," 9 November 1982, SES Records, MS 269, box 1, folder 5; Robinson, "Director's Report," 8 February 1983, SES Records, MS 269, box 1, folder 5; Robinson, "Director's Report," 12 April 1983, SES Records, MS 269, box 1, folder 5; Robinson, "Director's Report," 11 October 1983, SES Records, MS 269, box 1, folder 5; Richard E. Wilbur, "Copper Firms' Profits Plunge in Arizona," *Tucson Citizen*, 5 May 1981; Robinson interview, 1 September 2011; Robinson, "Smelter Chronology"; Wirth, *Smelter Smoke in North America*, 177; Robinson, "Director's Report," 14 June 1983, SES Records, MS 269 box 1, folder 5.

58. Thomas Sheridan, *Arizona: A History* (Tucson: University of Arizona Press, 1997), 324; Wirth, *Smelter Smoke in North America*, 117. See Barbara Kingsolver, *Holding the Line: Women in the Great Arizona Mine Strike of 1983* (Ithaca, NY: Cornell University Press, 1989).

59. Robinson, "Smelter Chronology"; Priscilla Robinson, "Director's Report," 12 June 1984, SES Records, MS 269, box 1, folder 6; Robinson, "Director's Report," 10 July 1984, SES Records, MS 269, box 1, folder 6. In April 1984, the Arizona Department of Health Services denied Phelps Dodge's application for a renewal of its operational permit for the company's Morenci smelter. The department cited Phelps Dodge's seventeen violations of ambient air quality standards in the first six months of 1984 alone. Phelps Dodge appealed the department's decision to the state Air Pollution Control Board. SES, at the advice of EDF and the Arizona Center for Law in the Public Interest, intervened in the appeal in opposition to Phelps Dodge, but the company withdrew its appeal four days before the 18 June 1984 hearing.

60. Robinson, "Smelter Chronology"; Michael Oppenheimer, Charles B. Epstein, and Robert E. Yuhnke, "Acid Rain, Smelter Emissions, and the Linearity Issue in the Western United States," *Science*, 30 August 1985, 859–62.

61. Robinson, "Smelter Chronology."

62. Robinson interview, 1 September 2011; Robinson, "Smelter Chronology."

63. Priscilla Robinson, "Director's Report," 14 August 1984, SES Records, MS 269, box 1, folder 5; Robinson, "Director's Report," 19 September 1984, SES Records, MS 269, box 1, folder 5.

64. Priscilla Robinson, "Director's Report," 13 November 1984, SES Records, MS 269, box 1, folder 5; Robinson, "Director's Report," 11 December 1984, SES Records, MS 269, box 1, folder 5; Robinson, "Smelter Chronology"; Robinson interview, 1 September 2011; Wirth, *Smelter Smoke in North America*, 154; Ellen Ridge, "Environmental Tiff over Copper," *Modesto Bee*, 30 December 1984, F-4.

65. "Environmentalists Seek Smelter Cleanup: Suit Adds to Copper Firms' Woes," *Los Angeles Times*, 7 January 1985.

66. Robinson, "Smelter Chronology."

67. Robinson, "Smelter Chronology"; Robison, "Director's Report," 18 April 1985, SES Records, MS 269, box 1, folder 7.

68. Wirth, *Smelter Smoke in North America*, 128; Tom Shields, "Environmentalists Get OK to Voice Objection at PD Smelter Hearing," *Tucson Citizen*, 16 November 1985; Robinson, "Smelter Chronology"; Joe Burchell, "Lawmakers Hope to Give EPA Power to Close PD," *Arizona Daily Star* (Tucson), 7 December 1985.

69. Robinson, "Smelter Chronology"; Robinson, "Director's Report," 19 December 1985, SES Records, MS 269, box 1, folder 7.

70. Shields, "Environmentalists Get OK to Voice Objection at PD Smelter Hearing."

71. Ibid.

72. Robinson, "Smelter Chronology."

73. Howard Fischer, "Babbitt Wants PD Smelter Restricted If Emissions Are Hurting Asthmatics," *Arizona Daily Star* (Tucson), 13 February 1986.

74. Robinson, "Smelter Chronology"; Robinson interview, 1 September 2011; Robinson, "Director's Report," 20 February 1986, SES Records, MS 269, box 1, folder 8.

75. Wirth, *Smelter Smoke in North America*, 135–39; Robinson, "Smelter Chronology"; Robinson, "Director's Report," 30 July 1986, SES Records, MS 269, box 1, folder 5.

76. Wirth, *Smelter Smoke in North America*, 135–39; Robinson, "Smelter Chronology"; Robinson, "Director's Report," 30 July 1986, SES Records, MS 269, box 1, folder 5.

77. Wirth, *Smelter Smoke in North America*, 135–39; Robinson, "Smelter Chronology"; Robinson, "Director's Report," 30 July 1986, SES Records, MS 269, box 1, folder 5.

78. Robinson, "Smelter Chronology."

79. Robinson interview, 1 September 2011.

80. Ibid.; Robinson, "Smelter Chronology"; "Clean Air Costly for Arizona Town: Closure of Copper Smelter Will Slash Jobs, Tax Revenue," *Los Angeles Times*, 5 January 1987; Wirth, *Smelter Smoke in North America*, 163, 194.

81. Priscilla Robinson, "Director's Report," 19 November 1987, SES Records, MS 269, box 1, folder 9; Brulle, *Agency, Democracy, and Nature*, 251, 257. Brulle notes that environmental organizations' source of funding influences their choices of

strategy and organizational characteristics. Oligarchically structured, reformist environmental organizations like SES also tended to employ a professional staff and tactics that involved members at only a superficial level. In SES's case, this meant that most of the fundraising work fell on the shoulders of Robinson and her few employees.

82. "Phelps Dodge Topples Douglas Smokestacks," *Arizona Daily Star* (Tucson), 19 January 1991.

83. Keith Ray, "Visit Douglas and Get Agua Prieta as a Bonus," *Arizona Daily Star* (Tucson), 1 May 1992.

84. Robinson interview, 1 September 2011.

85. Ibid.

CHAPTER 6 CITIZEN ENVIRONMENTAL ACTIVISM IN APPALACHIA: SAVE OUR CUMBERLAND MOUNTAINS

1. Chad Montrie, *To Save the Land and People: A History of Opposition to Surface Coal Mining in Appalachia* (Chapel Hill: University of North Carolina Press, 2003), 128; U.S. Department of the Interior, Appalachian Regional Commission, "*Study of Strip and Surface Mining in Appalachia: An Interim Report to the Appalachian Regional Commission*" (June 1966), 8.

2. Montrie, *To Save the Land and People*, 128; Department of the Interior, *Study of Strip and Surface Mining in Appalachia*, 8; Maureen O'Connell and Charles "Boomer" Winfrey, interview by author, Lake City, Tennessee, 11 June 2010.

3. Montrie, *To Save the Land and People*, 128; Department of the Interior, *Study of Strip and Surface Mining in Appalachia*, 8; O'Connell and Winfrey interview, 11 June 2010.

4. O'Connell and Winfrey interview, 11 June 2010.

5. Ibid.

6. Kai T. Erikson, *Everything in Its Path: Destruction of Community in the Buffalo Creek Flood* (New York: Simon and Schuster, 1976), 28–32.

7. "Lawsuit of the Month: Beech Groove Tragedy Has Yet to Be Settled in Courts," *S.O.C.M. Sentinel*, 31 October 1973.

8. "Flood Hits Lick Fork," *S.O.C.M. Sentinel*, 28 April 1972.

9. U.S. Department of the Interior, "Study of Strip and Surface Mining in Appalachia," 30 June 1966.

10. Ibid.

11. O'Connell and Winfrey interview, 11 June 2010.

12. Ibid.; Montrie, *To Save the Land and People*, 86, 101; John M. Glen, "Like a Flower Slowly Blooming: Highlander and the Nurturing of an Appalachian Movement," and Bill Allen, "Save Our Cumberland Mountains: Growth and Change Within a Grassroots Organization," both in *Fighting Back in Appalachia: Traditions of*

Resistance and Change, ed. Stephen L. Fisher (Philadelphia: Temple University Press, 1993), 35 and 85; Colman McCarthy, *Disturbers of the Peace: Profiles in Nonadjustment* (Boston: Houghton Mifflin, 1973), 163. The collaboration of antipoverty and anti-strip-mining activism in Appalachia was not unique to eastern Tennessee. Chad Montrie observes similar collaboration in Kentucky during the 1960s, and John M. Glen argues that antipoverty workers associated with the Appalachian Volunteers funded as part of the federal government's War on Poverty were an essential element of organized resistance to strip mining in Appalachia.

13. O'Connell and Winfrey interview, 11 June 2010.

14. Ibid.

15. Montrie, *To Save the Land and People*, 4, 186.

16. O'Connell and Winfrey interview, 11 June 2010; Allen, "Save Our Cumberland Mountains," 87.

17. O'Connell and Winfrey interview, 11 June 2010.

18. Ibid.; Allen, "Save Our Cumberland Mountains," 68.

19. O'Connell and Winfrey interview, 11 June 2010; Allen, "Save Our Cumberland Mountains," 68.

20. O'Connell and Winfrey interview, 11 June 2010.

21. Ibid.

22. Tennessee General Assembly, *Senate Journal of the Eighty-seventh General Assembly of the State of Tennessee*, convened at Nashville, Tennessee, Monday, 7 February 1972; *Biographical Sketches of the Members of the Senate of the Eighty-seventh General Assembly* (Berkley: University of California Press, 1973); Tennessee General Assembly, "Tennessee House of Representatives 87th General Assembly," http://www.capitol.tn.gov/house/archives/87GA/Members/Members.htm, accessed 29 April 2011; Billy Christopher, "'Save Our Cumberland Mountains' to Washington," *S.O.C.M. Sentinel*, 28 April 1972; "Congressional Round-Up," *S.O.C.M. Sentinel*, August 1972; "Washington Trip to Lobby Success," *S.O.C.M. Sentinel*, October 1972; Montrie, *To Save the Land and People*, 140; Library of Congress, "Bill Summary and Status 93rd Congress (1973–1974) H.R. 15860," http://thomas.loc.gov/cgi-bin/bdquery/D?d093:5:./temp/~bd1s4r:@@@L&summ2=m&|/home/LegislativeData.php?n=BSS;c=93|, accessed 12 October 2011.

23. O'Connell and Winfrey interview, 11 June 2010; Save Our Cumberland Mountains, "The Era of the '70's—A Few Highlights," October 2007, unpublished document, private collection, Statewide Organizing for Community Empowerment, Lake City, Tennessee.

24. Drew Von Bergen, "Appalachian People Speak at Strip Mine Hearings," *Middlesboro Daily News* (Kentucky), 18 April 1973.

25. O'Connell and Winfrey interview, 11 June 2010; Save Our Cumberland Mountains, "The Era of the '70's."

26. Save Our Cumberland Mountains, "The Era of the '70's"; "Severance Tax Passed," *S.O.C.M. Sentinel*, 28 April 1972; O'Connell and Winfrey interview, 11 June 2010.

27. "Conservation Groups Sue TVA for Ecology Report," *Kentucky New Era* (Hopkins-ville), 24 October 1972; "TVA Suit Filed," *S.O.C.M. Sentinel*, October 1972.

28. "Another Whitewash for TVA," *S.O.C.M. Sentinel*, August 1973.

29. Allen, "Save Our Cumberland Mountains," 87, 89; "Wanted: Paralegal and Secretary for New Law Office," *S.O.C.M. Sentinel*, July 1973.

30. O'Connell and Winfrey interview, 11 June 2010; Allen, "Save Our Cumberland Mountains," 93; Montrie, *To Save the Land and People*, 191.

31. Save Our Cumberland Mountains, "The Era of the '80's A Few Highlights," unpublished document, private collection, Save Our Cumberland Mountains, Lake City, Tennessee, October 2007; O'Connell and Winfrey interview, 11 June 2010.

32. As previously mentioned, last minute changes to SMCRA caused SOCM to retract its support for the bill. The organization was a key player in its introduction and movement through the legislative process until that point; Allen, "Save Our Cumberland Mountains," 89; O'Connell and Winfrey interview, 11 June 2010.

33. O'Connell and Winfrey interview, 11 June 2010.

34. *National Environmental Policy Act of 1969*, U.S. Code, vol. 42, sec. 4321-47.

35. Montrie, *To Save the Land and People*, 190.

36. "U.S. to Police Coal Strip Mines in 2 States," *Los Angeles Times*, 7 April 1984, A10.

37. *Surface Mine Control and Reclamation Act*, U.S. Code, Vol. 30, sec. 25, 1272; Save Our Cumberland Mountains, "The Era of the '80's"; O'Connell and Winfrey interview, 11 June 2010.

38. Save Our Cumberland Mountains, "The Era of the '80's"; O'Connell and Winfrey interview, 11 June 2010.

39. Allen, "Save Our Cumberland Mountains," 95, 95.

40. Save Our Cumberland Mountains, "The Era of the '80's"; Allen, "Save Our Cumberland Mountains," 85, 94, 95; Montrie, *To Save the Land and People*, 191.

41. Joni Adamson, Mei Mei Evans, and Rachel Stein, eds., *The Environmental Justice Reader: Politics, Poetics, and Pedagogy* (Tucson: University of Arizona Press, 2002), 4. See Robert Bullard, *Dumping in Dixie: Class, Race, and Environmental Quality* (Boulder, CO: Westview Press, 1990); David Naguib Pellow and Robert J. Brulle, *Power, Justice, and the Environment: A Critical Appraisal of the Environmental Justice Movement* (Cambridge, MA: MIT Press, 2005); and Sylvia Washington, *Packing Them In: An Archaeology of Environmental Racism in Chicago, 1865–1954* (Latham, MD: Lexington Books, 2005).

CHAPTER 7   DUMPING IN TENNESSEE

1. "Roane County SOCMs Win Victories in Landfill Fight," *SOCM Sentinel*, May 1990, private collection, Statewide Organizing for Community Empowerment, Lake City, Tennessee.

2. Betsy Kauffman, "Protesters Accuse State of Landfill Laxity," *Knoxville News-Sentinel*, 10 May 1990.

3. Duncan Mansfield, "East Tennessee Residents Picket Over Landfills," *Greenville Sun* (Tennessee), 10 May 1990.

4. Ibid.

5. Kauffman, "Protesters Accuse State of Landfill Laxity."

6. Ibid.

7. "Roane County SOCMs Win Victories in Landfill Fight," *SOCM Sentinel*, May 1990, private collection, Statewide Organizing for Community Empowerment, Lake City, Tennessee; Kauffman, "Protesters Accuse State of Landfill Laxity."

8. From "Table 4, Per Capita Hazardous Waste Generation of Selected Countries," n.d., no author, solid waste research, private collection, Statewide Organizing for Community Empowerment, Lake City, Tennessee, cited as from Harvey Yackowitz, "Harmonization of Specific Descriptors of Special Wastes Subject to National Controls of Eleven OECD Countries," in *Transformation Movements of Hazardous Wastes* (Paris: Organization for Economic Cooperation and Development, 1985), 53.

9. David Naguib Pellow, *Garbage Wars: The Struggle for Environmental Justice in Chicago* (Cambridge, MA: MIT Press, 2002); Robert J. Brulle, *Agency, Democracy, and Nature: The U.S. Environmental Movement from a Critical Theory Perspective* (Cambridge, MA: MIT Press, 2000), 212; Robert Bullard, *Dumping in Dixie: Race, Class, and Environmental Quality*, 3rd ed. (Boulder, CO: Westview Press, 2000). Pellow traces this phenomenon—how people of color, immigrants, and low-income populations came to bear a disproportionate of the burden of wastes—in Chicago dating back to 1880; Brulle recounts a report prepared for the California Waste Management Board in 1987 in which the authors recommended siting municipal waste and toxic-waste incinerators in communities that did not find the developments offensive, characterized as low-income, low-education, high-minority population and desperate for economic development.

10. See Rachel Carson, *Silent Spring* (New York: Houghton Mifflin, 1962).

11. Lois Marie Gibbs, *Love Canal and the Birth of the Environmental Health Movement* (New York: Island Press, 2010); Robert Emmet Hernan, *This Borrowed Earth: Lessons from the Fifteen Worst Environmental Disasters Around the World* (New York: Palgrave Macmillan, 2010).

12. Bullard, *Dumping in Dixie*; David Naguib Pellow and Robert J. Brulle, *Power, Justice, and the Environment: A Critical Appraisal of the Environmental Justice Movement* (Cambridge, MA: MIT Press, 2005); Joni Adamson, Mei Mei Evans, and Rachel

Stein, *The Environmental Justice Reader: Politics, Poetic, and Pedagogy* (Tucson: University of Arizona Press, 2002).

13. Tennessee Association of Businesses, testimony before the Tennessee Department of Health and Environment, Division of Solid Waste Management, Knoxville, Tennessee, 7 September 1989, private collection, Statewide Organizing for Community Empowerment, Lake City, Tennessee; Charles W. Burson, attorney general, "Opinion No. 89-56, Constitutionality and Applicability of T.C.A. 68-46-108," 17 April 1989, Nashville, Tennessee. The Alabama legislature passed a bill that banned the importation of waste from states that banned out-of-state wastes in 1989. The South Carolina legislature considered a similar bill at the same time. *Hazardous Wastes Management and Minimization Act, Code of Alabama* 22, sec. 30, 11 (1989); Gerald E. Ingram, Division of Solid Waste Management, to Recipient, memorandum, Subject: Proposed Regulations and Public Hearings, 11 August 1989, private collection, Statewide Organizing for Community Empowerment, Lake City, Tennessee; *The Jackson Law, Tennessee Code Annotated* 60, sec. 211, 701 (1989).

14. Save Our Cumberland Mountains, "How These Regulation Hearings Came About," internal document, private collection, Statewide Organizing for Community Empowerment, Lake City, Tennessee, n.d.

15. Ingram to Recipient, memorandum, Subject: Proposed Regulations and Public Hearings; Save Our Cumberland Mountains, "How These Regulation Hearings Came About."

16. Dr. Michael Crist, to the editor of the *Tennessean*, 28 August 1989, private collection, Statewide Organizing for Community Empowerment, Lake City, Tennessee.

17. Ibid.

18. Save Our Cumberland Mountains, "We the People Say," informational flier, 1989, private collection, Statewide Organizing for Community Empowerment, Lake City, Tennessee; emphasis in original.

19. Ibid.; "Let *Your* Voice Be Heard," informational flier, 1989, private collection, Statewide Organizing for Community Empowerment, Lake City, Tennessee.

20. Paul and Sylvia Morrill to representatives of the Tennessee Division of Solid Waste Management, 20 September, 1989, private collection, Statewide Organizing for Community Empowerment, Lake City, Tennessee.

21. Ibid.

22. Ibid.

23. Betty Anderson, testimony before the Tennessee Department of Health and Environment, Division of Solid Waste Management, Knoxville, Tennessee, 7 September 1989, private collection, Statewide Organizing for Community Empowerment, Lake City, Tennessee.

24. Carol J. Spiller, PhD, "WRITTEN COMMENTS REGARDING THE PROPOSED HAZARDOUS WASTE FACILITY SITING REGULATIONS, Submitted as part of the public

hearing process held by the Division of Solid Waste Management, Tennessee Department of Health and Environment, September 5, 6, 7," 25 September 1989, private collection, Statewide Organizing for Community Empowerment, Lake City, Tennessee.

25. Ibid.

26. Tennessee Association of Businesses, testimony before the Tennessee Department of Health and Environment, Division of Solid Waste Management, Knoxville, Tennessee, 7 September 1989, private collection, Statewide Organizing for Community Empowerment, Lake City, Tennessee.

27. Ibid.

28. Save Our Cumberland Mountains, "How These Regulation Hearings Came About."

29. Bill Allen, "Save Our Cumberland Mountains: Growth and Change within a Grassroots Organization," in *Fighting Back in Appalachia: Traditions of Resistance and Change*, ed. Stephen I. Fisher (Philadelphia: Temple University Press, 1993), 85; "AN UPDATE ON THE PRIVATE DUMP ISSUE IN HUMPHREYS COUNTY," Citizens Against Pollution, Waverly, Tennessee, n.d., private collection, Statewide Organization for Community Empowerment, Lake City, Tennessee; "Group Fights Landfill Expansion," *Commercial Appeal* (Memphis), 26 August 1993; "Toxics Committee Off and Running," *S.O.C.M. Sentinel*, January 1990. Allen traces the origins of internal discussion about landfills and whether SOCM should work on toxic issues back to a leadership retreat in 1988. By the following year, it was a high priority for the group.

30. Ibid.

31. The "Jackson Law" was incredibly complicated in its legal application. One of the best descriptions of the history of the law as well as an explanation of the state assembly's extension of its expiration date first to 1994 then to 1995 and finally its removal of an expiration date altogether comes from a court case that originated in 1992 when waste management company Profill Development, Inc., applied for a permit to build a new landfill in Fayette County from the Tennessee Department of Environmental Conservation. It took more than three years of back and forth between the company and the department before for the department declared Profill's application complete and began the permitting process. Before it granted the permit, however, the department received a notice that Fayette County had opted in to the Jackson Law in 1995, and it ceased its permit review. Profill then sued the department; part of the suit questioned the constitutionality of the local veto. In 1997, the Davidson County Chancery Court sided with the department and intervener Western Tennesseans for Clean Water and Environment, and upheld the Jackson Law and the ability of local governments to approve or deny landfill proposals. See *Profill Development, Inc., v. Dills*, 95-1748-III (Davidson County Chancery Court, 1997).

32. "Campbell County Chapter Gains Great New Members and Several New Issues in One Community," *SOCM Sentinel*, July 1990, 2.

33. "Campbell County Chapter Victorious with Jackson Law," *SOCM Sentinel*, September 1990, 11.

34. "Oliver Springs Victory: County Holds Firm," *SOCM Sentinel*, December 1990, 1, 2.

35. "Landfill Case Goes to Trial," *SOCM Sentinel*, January 1991, 9, 10; "Yeah . . . We Won!" *SOCM Sentinel*, January 1991, 11; "Oliver Springs Celebrates Victory," *SOCM Sentinel*, February 1991, 1, 7. The Campbell County Commission sued Remote Landfill Services and its partner Chambers Development Corporation on 12 December 1990, for violating the Tennessee Sanitary Landfill Areas Act after Remote bulldozed portions of the Cumberland Trail that ran across the proposed landfill area despite the commission's disapproving of the construction of the landfill under the authority granted it by the Jackson Law.

36. "State Hears from SOCM About Waste," *SOCM Sentinel*, December 1990, 8–9.

37. Ibid.

38. "SOCM's Legislative Efforts End after Roller Coaster Ride," *SOCM Sentinel*, June 1991, 5, 6, 7.

39. Ibid.

40. "SOCM's Legislative Efforts End after Roller Coaster Ride"; *Senate Journal of the Ninety seventh General Assembly of the State of Tennessee*, convened at Nashville, 14 January 1992, Second Regular and First Extraordinary Sessions (Berkley: University of California Press, 1993).

41. Sandy Johnson, Tennessee Association of Businesses, testimony to the Tennessee Senate Energy and Natural Resources Committee, Solid Waste Subcommittee, Tennessee General Assembly, 11 March 1991, 12:35 P.M., Tape 1, Tennessee State Library and Archives, Nashville, Tennessee.

42. Ibid.

43. Ibid.

44. "SOCM Members Discuss Solid Waste Plans at Daylong Workshop Put on by Toxics Committee," *SOCM Sentinel*, February 1992, 11; Save Our Cumberland Mountains, "1991 Annual Report," private collection, Statewide Organizing for Community Empowerment, Lake City, Tennessee, 12–13; "SOCMs Win Legislative Fight," *SOCM Sentinel*, May 1992; Landon Medley, interview by author, Spencer, Tennessee, 23 June 2010.

45. "SOCM Drafts Bill to Stop Out-of-State Waste," *SOCM Sentinel*, November–December 1992, 18; Maureen O'Connell, interview by author, Lake City, Tennessee, 25 June 2010; "1993 Environmental Justice Bill: SOCM Works to Stop Corporate Criminals and Out-of-State Waste," *SOCM Sentinel*, January 1993, 1–2, private collection, Statewide Organizing for Community Empowerment, Lake City, Tennessee.

46. O'Connell interview, 25 June 2010.

47. "SOCM Drafts Bill to Stop Out-of-State Waste"; "1993 Environmental Justice Bill."

48. "1993 Environmental Justice Bill."

49. "Freedom: The Right to Say No," *SOCM Sentinel*, November/December 1991, 4, 5.

50. Ibid.

51. "Comparison of Right to Say 'No' Bills," n.d., private collection, Statewide Organizing for Community Empowerment.

52. "Action Alert," Western Organization of Resource Councils, n.d., private collection, Statewide Organizing for Community Empowerment, Lake City, Tennessee.

53. "Right to Say No Federal Bill Update," 9 September 1994, no author, private collection, Statewide Organizing for Community Empowerment, Lake City, Tennessee.

54. Sara Kendall, Western Organization of Resource Councils, to People interested in Right to Say No, memorandum, 19 June 1995, private collection, Statewide Organizing for Community Empowerment, Lake City, Tennessee.

55. Save Our Cumberland Mountains, "*Landfill Enforcement in Tennessee*, A Study of Enforcement of Regulations Governing Class I Solid Waste Disposal Facilities in Tennessee," Lake City, Tennessee, 1 November 1995.

56. Ibid.

57. Anne Paine, "Landfill Foes Judge State as Lax," *Tennessean* (Nashville), 2 March 1994.

58. Ibid.

59. Ibid.

60. "Solid Waste Study Released! Toxics Committee Set to Meet with D.E.C. Officials," *SOCM Sentinel*, November/December 1995.

61. Save Our Cumberland Mountains "*Landfill Enforcement in Tennessee*, A Study of Enforcement of Regulations Governing Class I Solid Waste Disposal Facilities in Tennessee," Lake City, Tennessee, 1 November 1995.

62. Ibid.

63. "Solid Waste Study Released! Toxics Committee Set to Meet with D.E.C Officials"; "*SOCM Wins Major Improvements in Landfill Enforcement!*: Toxics Committee Meets with D.E.C. Deputy Commissioner Wayne Scharber and Other Officials, Wins Concessions," *SOCM Sentinel*, January/February 1996, 1, 4.

64. Save Our Cumberland Mountains, "Update: SOCM Landfill Enforcement Study and Followup, April 15, 1996," private collection, Statewide Organizing for Community Empowerment, Lake City, Tennessee.

65. "Landfill Enforcement Reform Progressing: Toxics Committee Holds Second Meeting with TDEC," *SOCM Sentinel*, September/October 1996, 8, 9.

66. Ibid.

67. Erik W. Johnson, "Social Movement Size, Organizational Diversity, and the Making of Federal Law," *Social Forces* 86, no. 3 (March 2008): 967–93; Erik W. Johnson, Jon Agnone, and John D. McCarthy, "Movement Organizations, Synergistic Tactics, and Environmental Public Policy," *Social Forces* 88, no. 5 (July 2010): 2267–92. Johnson, Agnone, and McCarthy demonstrate that the record

of environmental movement organizations influencing the passage of laws at the federal level is spotty and contingent on other conditions including federal action and which political party is in power. They argue, however, that where environmental movement organizations are the most effective is influencing political agenda setting, which has benefits beyond simply passing laws. While SOCM never passed a law, they effectively influenced the political agenda regarding the location of waste sites at the state level in Tennessee throughout the 1990s.

68. O'Connell interview, 25 June 2010; Medley interview, 23 June 2010.

CHAPTER 8 CONCLUSION: PARTICIPATION, PERSEVERANCE, AND RETHINKING ENVIRONMENTALISM

1. Helen and Gordon Waller, interview by author, Waller ranch near Circle, Montana, 3 August 2010.

2. Statewide Organizing for Community eMpowerment, "Groups Join in Organizing People's Hearing for Oil and Gas Regulation," http://socm.org/index.cfm/m/11/pageID/95/fuseAction/contentpage.main/detailID/259, accessed 13 December 2013. To retain the recognizable SOCM acronym, the group cleverly emphasizes the "m" in empowerment.

3. Northern Plains Resource Council, "Oil and Gas," https://www.northernplains.org/issues/oil-gas/, accessed 13 December 2013.

4. *Promised Land*, DVD, Gus Van Sant, 2012, USA, Focus Features.

5. Ellen Pfister, interview by author, Billings, Montana, 14 November 2009; Wallace McRae, interview by author, Billings, Montana, 13 November 2009.

6. Ibid.; Northern Plains Resource Council, "Coal Bed Methane," http://www.northernplains.org/the-issues/coal-bed-methane/, accessed 15 November 2011; Jan Falstad, "Protesters Line Up Against Beartooth Front Drilling Plans," *Billings Gazette*, 30 October 2013.

7. Priscilla Robinson, interview by author, Tucson, Arizona, 1 September 2011.

8. Tony Davis, "Priscilla Robinson Dies; Conservationist Fought Pollution, Protected Water," *Arizona Daily Star* (Tucson), 30 July 2013.

9. Ibid.

10. Priscilla Robinson, interview by author, 1 September 2011, Tucson, Arizona; John D. Wirth, *Smelter Smoke in North America: The Politics of Transborder Pollution* (Lawrence: University of Kansas Press, 2000), 158; Barbara Tellman, interview by author, 1 September 2011; Senator John McCain, "Statement for the Introduction of Betsy Rieke before the Senate Energy and Natural Resources Committee, April 27 1993," http://www.mccain.senate.gov/public/index.cfm/speeches?ID=c350188f-5e03-4157-a73a-a4b13d87e221, accessed 14 December 2013; Senator Harry Reid, "Recognizing Elizabeth Ann 'Betsy' Rieke," July 28, 2008, Capitolwords, http://capitolwords.org/date/2008/07/28/S7565-2_recognizing-elizabeth-ann-betsy-rieke/, accessed 14 December 2013. After her work with SES, Elizabeth

Ann "Betsy" Rieke attended law school and then became one of the foremost water administrators in the state of Arizona and the Southwest. In 1993, she was drafted by the Clinton administration as assistant secretary of the interior for water and science in the Department of the Interior. Barbara Tellman remained involved in water quality issues after 1987, including influencing implementation of the Arizona Environmental Quality Act of 1986, which was passed with significant input and lobbying from SES. Tellman also remained active with the League of Women Voters and the Arizona Democratic Party. In 2011, she was actively working with other environmentalists on the Sonoran Desert Conservation Plan.

11. Statewide Organizing for Community eMpowerment, http://www.socm.org, accessed 26 November 2013.

12. Ibid.

13. Samuel Hays, *Beauty, Health and Permanence: Environmental Politics in the United States, 1955–1985* (Cambridge: Cambridge University Press, 1987), 63.

14. United Nations World Commission on Environment and Development. *Our Common Future: Report of the World Commission on Environment and Development.* Oxford: Oxford University Press, 1987, 15.

15. Ying Zhao, "A Survey of Environmental Law and Enforcement Authorities in China," *Proceedings of the Fourth International Conference on Environmental Compliance and Enforcement*, http://www.inece.org/4thvol1/4toc.htm, p. 14.

16. Pfister interview, 14 November 2009; McRae interview, 13 November 2009.

17. Ibid.

18. Robinson interview, 1 September 2011.

19. Julian Agyeman and Bob Evans, "'Just Sustainability': The Emerging Discourse of Environmental Justice in Britain?" *Geographical Journal* 170, no. 2 (June 2004): 157, 159; Daniel Faber, *The Struggle for Ecological Democracy: Environmental Justice Movements in the United States* (New York: Guilford Press, 1998); Tom Sandler, *Global Collective Action* (Cambridge: Cambridge University Press, 2004); Partha Dasgupta, *Human Well-Being and the Natural Environment* (Oxford: Oxford University Press, 2001). Sustainability and environmental justice scholars theorize and demonstrate this process of externalizing the environmental, social, and human costs of economic development.

20. Erik W. Johnson, Jon Agnone, and John D. McCarthy, "Movement Organizations, Synergistic Tactics, and Environmental Policy," *Social Forces* 88, no. 5 (July 2010): 2284; Agyeman and Evans, "'Just Sustainability,'" 157, 159; Faber, *The Struggle for Ecological Democracy*; Tom Sandler, *Global Collective Action* (Cambridge: Cambridge University Press, 2004); Dasgupta, *Human Well-Being and the Natural Environment*.

21. This idea is most thoroughly articulated as "just sustainability" in Julian Agyeman, Robert D. Bullard, and Bob Evans, *Just Sustainabilities: Development in an Unequal World* (London: Earthscan, 2012).

22. Dorceta E. Taylor, *The Environment and the People in American Cities, 1600–1900s: Disorder, Inequality, and Social Change* (Durham, NC: Duke University Press, 2009), 15.

23. Robinson interview, 1 September 2011.

24. Agyeman and Evans, "'Just Sustainability,'" 157, 159.

25. Save Our Cumberland Mountains, "We the People Say," informational flier, 1989, private collection, Statewide Organizing for Community Empowerment, Lake City, Tennessee.

SELECTED BIBLIOGRAPHY

Abbott, Carl. *The Metropolitan Frontier: Cities in the Modern American West.* Tucson: University of Arizona Press, 1998.

Adamson, Joni, Mei Mei Evans, and Rachel Stein, eds. *The Environmental Justice Reader: Politics, Poetics, and Pedagogy.* Tucson. University of Arizona Press, 2002.

Andrews, Richard N. L. *Managing the Environment, Managing Ourselves: A History of American Environmental Policy.* 2nd ed. New Haven: Yale University Press, 2006.

Arizonans for Water Without Waste. *Arizonans for Quality Environment Newsletter.* University of Arizona Library Special Collections, Tucson, AZ.

Bevington, Douglas. *The Rebirth of Environmentalism: Grassroots Activism from the Spotted Owl to the Polar Bear.* Washington, DC: Island Press, 2009.

Blum, Elizabeth D. *Love Canal Revisited: Race, Class, and Gender in Environmental Activism.* Lawrence: University of Kansas Press, 2008.

Brooks, Karl Boyd. *Before Earth Day: The Origins of American Environmental Law, 1945–1970.* Lawrence: University of Kansas Press, 2009.

Brulle, Robert J. *Agency, Democracy, and Nature: The U.S. Environmental Movement from a Critical Theory Perspective.* Cambridge, MA: MIT Press, 2000.

Bullard, Robert D. *Dumping in Dixie: Class, Race, and Environmental Quality.* Boulder, CO: Westview Press, 1990.

Carson, Rachael. *Silent Spring.* New York: Houghton Mifflin, 1962.

Charter, Anne Goddard. *Cowboys Don't Walk: A Tale of Two.* Billings, MT: Western Organization of Resource Councils, 1999.

Cross, Louise, Papers. Montana Historical Society Research Center and Archives, Helena, MT.

Del Mar, David Peterson. *Environmentalism.* Harlow, UK: Pearson Education, 2006.

Dunlap, Riley E., and Angela G. Mertig, eds. *American Environmentalism: The U.S. Environmental Movement, 1970–1990.* New York: Taylor and Francis, 1992.

Edgerton, Keith. "Bridging Ideology in Rural America: The Northern Plains Resource Council, 1971–1975." Billings: University of Montana–Billings, 2002.

Egan, Michael, and Jeff Crane. *Natural Protest: Essays on the History of American Environmentalism.* New York: Routledge, 2009.

Erikson, Kai T. *Everything in Its Path: Destruction of Community in the Buffalo Creek Flood.* New York: Simon and Schuster, 1976.

Feldman, David Lewis, ed. *The Energy Crisis: Unresolved Issues and Enduring Legacies.* Baltimore: Johns Hopkins University Press, 1996.

Ferguson, Cody. "'You Are Now Entering a National Sacrifice Area': The Energy Boom of the 1970s and the Radicalization of the Northern Plains." *Journal of the West* 53 (Winter 2014): 70–78.

Fisher, Stephen L., ed. *Fighting Back in Appalachia: Traditions of Resistance and Change.* Philadelphia: Temple University Press, 1993.

Flores, Dan. *The Natural West: Environmental History of the Great Plains and Rocky Mountains.* Norman: University of Oklahoma Press, 2003.

Fox, Stephen. *The American Conservation Movement: John Muir and His Legacy.* Madison: University of Wisconsin Press, 1985.

Fritz, Harry W. "The Origins of Twenty-first-Century Montana." *Montana: The Magazine of Western History* 42 (Winter 1992): 77–81.

Fritz, Harry W., and William E. Farr. *Montana: Land of Contrasts.* Sun Valley, CA: American Historical Press, 2001.

Frome, Michael. *The Battle for the Wilderness.* New York: Praeger, 1974.

Gibbs, Lois Marie. *Love Canal and the Birth of the Environmental Health Movement.* New York: Island Press, 2010.

Gottlieb, Robert. *Forcing the Spring: The Transformation of the American Environmental Movement.* Rev. ed. Washington, DC: Island Press, 2005.

———. "The Next Environmentalism: How Movements Respond to the Changes That Elections Bring—From Nixon to Obama." *Environmental History* 14 (April 2009): 298–308.

Harvey, Mark T. *A Symbol of Wilderness: Echo Park and the American Conservation Movement.* Albuquerque: University of New Mexico Press, 1994.

———. *Wilderness Forever: Howard Zahniser and the Path to the Wilderness Act.* Seattle: University of Washington Press, 2005.

Hays, Samuel P. *Beauty, Health, and Permanence: Environmental Politics in the United States, 1955–1985.* New York: Cambridge University Press, 1987.

———. *Conservation and the Gospel of Efficiency: The Progressive Conservation Movement, 1890–1920.* Cambridge, MA: Harvard University Press, 1959.

———. *A History of Environmentalism since 1945.* Pittsburgh: University of Pittsburgh Press, 2000.

Hernan, Robert Emmet. *This Borrowed Earth: Lessons from the Fifteen Worst Environmental Disasters Around the World.* New York: Palgrave Macmillan, 2010.

Hirsch, Richard F. *Power Loss: The Origins of Deregulation and Restructuring in the American Electric Utility System.* Cambridge, MA: MIT Press, 2002.

Hirt, Paul W. *Conspiracy of Optimism: Management of the National Forests since World War Two.* Lincoln: University of Nebraska Press, 1994.

Hirt, Paul W., Annie Gustafson, and Kelli Larson. "The Mirage in the Valley of the Sun." *Environmental History* 13 (July 2008): 482–514.

Hurley, Andrew. *Environmental Inequalities: Class, Race, and Industrial Pollution in Gary, Indiana 1945–1980.* Chapel Hill: University of North Carolina Press, 1995.

Johnson, Eric W. "Social Movement Size, Organizational Diversity, and the Making of Federal Law." *Social Forces* 86 (March 2008): 967–93.

Johnson, Eric W., Jon Agnone, and John D. McCarthy. "Movement Organizations, Synergistic Tactics and Environmental Public Policy." *Social Forces* 88 (July 2010): 2267–69.

Johnson, Erik W., and Scott Frickel. "Ecological Threat and the Founding of U.S. National Environmental Movement Organizations, 1962–1998." *Social Problems* 58 (August 2011): 305–29.

Kingsolver, Barbara. *Holding the Line: Women in the Great Arizona Mine Strike of 1983.* Ithaca, NY: Cornell University Press, 1989.

Kraft, Michael E. *Environmental Policy and Politics.* New York: Pearson Longman, 2007.

Lazarus, Richard J. *The Making of Environmental Policy.* Chicago: University of Chicago Press, 2004.

Logan, Michael F. *Fighting Sprawl and City Hall.* Tucson: University of Arizona Press, 1995.

———. *The Lessening Stream: An Environmental History of the Santa Cruz River.* Tucson: University of Arizona Press, 2002.

Malone, Michael P., Richard R. Roeder, and William L. Lang. *Montana: A History of Two Centuries.* Rev. ed. Seattle: University of Washington Press, 1991.

McCarthy, Colman. *Disturbers of the Peace: Profiles in Nonadjustment.* Boston: Houghton Mifflin, 1973.

Melosi, Martin. *Coping with Abundance: Energy and Environment in Industrial America.* Philadelphia: Temple University Press, 1985.

Merrill, Karen R. *The Oil Crisis of 1973–1974: A Brief History with Documents.* Boston: Bedford/St. Martin's, 2007.

Montana Legislature (43rd: 1973–1974) records. Montana Historical Society Research Center and Archives, Helena, MT.

Montrie, Chad. *To Save the Land and People: A History of Opposition to Surface Coal Mining in Appalachia.* Chapel Hill: University of North Carolina Press, 2003.

Morris K. Udall Library Manuscript Collection. University of Arizona Library Special Collections, Tucson, AZ.

Mundinger, John, and Todd Everts. *A Guide to the Montana Environmental Policy Act.* Rev. ed. Helena, MT: Legislative Environmental Policy Office, 1998.

Northern Plains Resource Council Records. Private collection. Northern Plains Resource Council, Billings, MT.

Norwood, Vera. *Made from This Earth: American Women and Nature.* Chapel Hill: University of North Carolina, 1993.

Nye, David E. *Consuming Power: A Social History of American Energies.* Cambridge, MA: MIT Press, 1998.

Obach, Brian K. *Labor and the Environmental Movement: The Quest for Common Ground.* Cambridge, MA: MIT Press, 2004.

Parfit, Michael. *Last Stand at Rosebud Creek: Coal, Power, and People.* New York: E. P. Dutton, 1980.

Pearson, Byron E. *Still the Wild River Runs: Congress, the Sierra Club, and the Fight to Save Grand Canyon.* Tucson: University of Arizona Press, 2002.

Pellow, David Naguib. *Garbage Wars: The Struggle for Environmental Justice in Chicago.* Cambridge, MA: MIT Press, 2002.

Pellow, David N., and Robert J. Brulle. *Power, Justice, and the Environment: A Critical Appraisal of the Environmental Justice Movement.* Cambridge, MA: MIT Press, 2005.

Plains Truth (Newsletter of the Northern Plains Resource Council, Billings, Montana). June 1972–December 1980.

Reisner, Marc. *Cadillac Desert: The American West and Its Disappearing Water.* New York: Penguin Books, 1986.

Riley, Glenda. *Women and Nature: Saving the "Wild" West.* Lincoln: University of Nebraska Press, 1999.

Robinson, Priscilla. "Smelter Chronology: Southwest Environmental Service Monthly Reports—1978–1987," 1 November 2008. Private collection of Priscilla Robinson, Tucson, AZ.

Rome, Adam. *Bulldozer in the Countryside: Suburban Sprawl and the Rise of American Environmentalism.* Cambridge: Cambridge University Press, 2001.

———. "'Give Earth a Chance': The Environmental Movement and the Sixties." *Journal of American History* 90 (September 2003): 525–54.

Rosenbaum, Walter A. *Environmental Politics and Policy.* 8th ed. Washington, DC: Congressional Quarterly, 2010.

Save Our Cumberland Mountains Records. Private collection. Statewide Organizing for Community Empowerment, Knoxville, TN.

Schwab, Jim. *Raising Less Corn and More Hell: Midwestern Farmers Speak Out.* Urbana: University of Illinois Press, 1988.

Scott, Douglas W. "A Wilderness-Forever Future: A Short History of the National Wilderness Preservation System." Washington, DC: Pew Wilderness Research, 2001.

Sheridan, Thomas. *Arizona: A History.* Tucson: University of Arizona Press, 1997.

SOCM Sentinel (Newsletter of Save Our Cumberland Mountains, Lake City, TN). April 1972–July 2000.

Southern Arizona Environmental Council Records. Arizona Collection, Hayden Library, Arizona State University, Tempe, AZ.

Southwest Environmental Service Records. University of Arizona Library Special Collections, Tucson, AZ.

Speece, Darren. "From Corporatism to Citizen Oversight: The Legal Fight Over California Redwoods, 1970–1996." *Environmental History* 14 (October 2009): 705–36.

Stoll, Steven. *U.S. Environmentalism since 1945: A Brief History with Documents.* Boston: Bedford/St. Martin's, 2007.

Switzer, Jacqueline Vaughn. *Environmental Politics: Domestic and Global Dimensions.* Belmont, CA: Thomson Wadsworth, 2004.

Szasz, Andrew. *EcoPopulism: Toxic Waste and the Movement for Environmental Justice.* Minneapolis: University of Minnesota Press, 1994.

Taylor, Dorceta E. *The Environment and the People in American Cities, 1600–1900s.* Durham, NC: Duke University Press, 2009.

Tennessee General Assembly Records, 1796–present. Tennessee State Library and Archives, Nashville, TN.

Toole, K. Ross. *Montana: An Uncommon Land.* Norman: University of Oklahoma Press, 1959.

———. *The Rape of the Great Plains: Northwest America, Cattle and Coal.* New York: Little, Brown, 1976.

Vietor, Richard H. K. *Energy Policy in America since 1945: A Study of Business-Government Relations.* New York: Cambridge University Press, 1987.

Washington, Sylvia H. *Packing Them In: An Archaeology of Environmental Racism in Chicago, 1865–1954.* Latham, MD: Lexington Books, 2005.

Wirth, John D. *Smelter Smoke in North America: The Politics of Transborder Pollution.* Lawrence: University of Kansas Press, 2000.

INDEX